Comrades and Chicken Ranchers

COMRADES AND CHICKEN RANCHERS

The Story of a California Jewish Community

Kenneth L. Kann

Cornell University Press

Ithaca and London

International Standard Book Number 0-8014-2807-6 (cloth)
International Standard Book Number 0-8014-8075-2 (paper)
Library of Congress Catalog Card Number 92-54968
Printed in the United States of America
Librarians: Library of Congress cataloging information appears on the last page of the book.

FOR STEPHANIE

CONTENTS

ACKNOWLEDGMENTS

This book has been eighteen years in the making. I have received assistance from many people during that time.

The book would not have been possible without the collaboration of Henry Mayer. Long ago, Henry conceived the unique form of this book as an oral history collection of voices telling the story of a community in choruslike fashion. He has edited more drafts of the manuscript than I can recall, beginning with my first attempted chapters in 1975, up through the final copy. He has made suggestions about every aspect of the story, from general themes and character development to the details of innumerable vignettes, and I inevitably followed his advice. Henry never lost confidence in the book, he never stopped encouraging me.

Zelda Bronstein, whose grandparents were among the early Petaluma Jewish chicken ranchers, first introduced me to the Petaluma Jewish community. Zelda also began this project with me. She conducted many of the early interviews, she helped formulate the conceptual framework, and she remained a source of advice and ideas long after she moved on to other endeavors. Zelda did everything but become a character in the book.

The California Historical Society adopted this project as its own in the 1970s and supported several years of research and writing. I am deeply grateful to Jim Holliday, who directed the society, for his historical vision, personal support, and confidence in me. Stephen Shapiro obtained financial support for the project while acting as assistant director of the society, and he encouraged my work for many years thereafter. Marilyn Ziebarth, who directed the society's publication program in the 1970s, also provided valuable editorial assistance. I am lucky to have enjoyed the support of such imaginative, capable people.

Through the California Historical Society, I received a grant from the National Endowment for the Humanities to support full-time work on the project for two years. I still marvel that this kind of unorthodox historical inquiry could receive such generous public support and I regard it as a great credit to the broad vision of the National Endowment for the Humanities.

Willa Baum, director of the oral history program at the Bancroft Library of the University of California, Berkeley, gave me invaluable assistance with the techniques of oral history for many years. Rose Glickman has assisted me with critical readings of parts of the book concerning east European history, and she has provided Russian transliterations. Eli Katz prepared the Yiddish translations and transliterations. Sarah Crome has been a source of advice and discussions on Jewish-American history throughout my work.

Joe Rapoport and Sheba Rapoport were my primary sources within the Petaluma Jewish community. Several years into my investigation, I began collaborating with them on *Joe Rapoport: The Life of a Jewish Radical* (Temple University Press, 1981), which tells part of the Petaluma story from their perspective. Joe makes only a small appearance in this book, because we have told his story elsewhere, but many of my views have been shaped by years of discussion with Joe and Sheba about Petaluma politics and history. I regret that Joe did not live to celebrate the publication of this book with me.

For many years my main conversational staple was the Jewish socialist chicken ranchers of Petaluma, and I am thankful to the many friends who enjoyed it, or at least tolerated me. I also thank the many friends who continued to inquire about the progress of the project during the years I stopped discussing it. They helped keep the flame burning.

Cornell University Press has my admiration and gratitude for taking on this unique project. My editor, Peter Agree, and his talented colleagues have applied extraordinary understanding and skill to the transformation of my manuscript into this book.

Stephanie Pass has understood what this book means to me and has made possible its completion in unlikely circumstances. More than that, Stephanie, and our daughter, Julia, have made my life a joy all the while.

K. L. K.

San Francisco, California

Comrades and Chicken Ranchers

INTRODUCTION

The Jewish Cemetery is a small enclave in the town cemetery in Petaluma, California, up on the hill off Magnolia Street. The tombstones outline the history of the community: Sephardic Jews from the mid-nineteenth century, German Jews from the late nineteenth century, east European Jews through the twentieth century. A few pebbles on one of the graves, each left by a visitor, are an Old World precaution that the body of the deceased remain in the ground. But the epitaph on a neighboring tombstone—"He Believed in Justice"—proclaims the modern idealism of the east European settlers. They were a community of Jewish farmers, socialists who raised chickens. "We were a rarity in American Jewish life," one of them told me. "Such a community will not happen again."

The east European Jews arrived in the first three decades of the century, when the sign at the railroad station proudly proclaimed Petaluma, population five thousand, "The Egg Basket of the World." It was a bustling country agricultural town with dirt roads, hitching posts, and a Main Street lined with feed mills and hatcheries. In those days Petaluma eggs went all the way to New York, but the big market was thirty-five miles to the south in San Francisco. To reach San Francisco, the eggs traveled by river boat to San Francisco Bay, or they were hauled along a two-lane country highway winding through miles of rolling hills and farms.

Today, as you continue out Magnolia Street, past the cemetery to the west of Petaluma, you might notice long, low wood-frame structures, too small to be barns and too large to be tool sheds. They are old, dilapidated chicken houses, rendered obsolete by huge modern factories where millions of chickens are raised by machines. These rotting chicken houses dot the countryside in a ten-mile arc extending from Cotati, seven miles north of Petaluma, to Two Rock, seven miles west. East Petaluma, with its sprawling tract-home developments beside the freeway, was empty prairie when those chicken houses were in use.

I

Today, Petaluma and its chicken houses are well within the San Francisco Bay Area megalopolis, and the city is famous for its attempts to limit growth and for its wrist-wrestling championship, not for its chickens and eggs.

Many small businesses from the early part of the century are still in town—Pedroni's Delicatessen, Sorensen's Funeral Home, Thomasini Hardware, McLaughlin's Jewelry, Saunderson Ford, the U.S. Bakery. Several of the old downtown feed mills still stand, but they have been remodeled into upscale malls with smart shops. They attract the young families moving into the new tract homes and restoring the old Victorians on shady side streets near downtown. Today Petaluma, with a population beyond thirty thousand, is a bedroom suburb of San Francisco. Out in the countryside, suburban spread has all but displaced the old family farms and the decaying chicken houses. Now corporations raise chickens, far from Petaluma.

A few old-time Jewish farmers still lived on their little five-acre former chicken ranches when I began my inquiry in 1974. The odor of livestock lingered, but the small, aging wood ranch houses creaked in the wind and the ranches were in disrepair. Many of the Jewish old-timers had already moved into a modern efficiency-apartment complex a short way up Magnolia Street from the cemetery. In the Jewish community they jokingly referred to it as "the ghetto."

Most of these old-timers were "pioneers" who had helped build the Petaluma Jewish Community Center on the edge of downtown in 1925. As you drive down Western Avenue today, you will see the twin spires of St. Vincent's at the beginning; a mile farther, dominating a corner two blocks beyond the Jewish Community Center, you will spot bulky Hermann Sons Hall, where Petaluma's Nazis met in the 1930s. But you will notice the Jewish Community Center only if your eye happens on the modest Star of David above the doorway. The nondescript little stucco building stands in dramatic contrast to the modern wood and glass temple built by the neighboring Jews of Santa Rosa.

A large, dramatic photograph hangs in the entryway of the Petaluma Jewish Community Center. Taken at the banquet celebrating the opening of the building in 1925, it shows the main social hall packed with immigrant chicken ranchers and their children. They are sitting around long banquet tables, dignified and ceremonious in their fine suits and dresses, posing with pride in their new community center.

That main social hall displayed its full fifty years when I first attended a community affair in 1975. The wood floor was scuffed, the ceiling bore leakage stains, paint peeled from the walls, the curtains were threadbare. The sorry state of the room reflected a three-decade community stalemate over whether to remodel or rebuild. Yet the commemorative plaques on the walls, an old piano in the corner, a friendly little stage, wood folding chairs, and a full house of two hundred people gave the hall an air of comfortable familiarity. This was a community living room.

That 1975 affair triggered my first reflections on the larger themes of American community life, ethnic identity, and generational change which are at the center of this book. The gathering was a fifty-year-anniversary celebration of the opening of the Petaluma Jewish Community Center. The community's second generation, the children of the immigrants, staged a show recounting the community's history. Even as I recognized the audience's thorough pleasure with the evening, I was astonished by the show's trivialization of the community's history. Here was a group of rural immigrants who, at enormous effort, had kept themselves connected to currents of international politics and culture, who had fought wrenching community battles over their global perspectives, yet their American-born children could only make jokes about chicken ranching and pretend that their community had been one big happy family.

Unlike this second generation, I believed that the uniqueness of the Petaluma Jewish community, its atypicality as a highly politicized, rural immigrant group, rendered it ideal for reaching an understanding of the conflicts and dislocations of ethnic community life and ethnic identity in twentieth-century America. These people did not follow the customary pattern of east European immigrants migrating to enclaves in the great eastern cities, the children migrating to new suburbs, and the assimilated grandchildren spreading out across the American map. These Jewish immigrants settled on California chicken ranches and established a vibrant political community that combined socialist and Jewish internationalism with the parochialism of an ethnic minority in small-town America. Many of their children remained in Petaluma, working on chicken ranches and participating in their parents' Jewish community until decades later, when the town was engulfed by the suburban spread of the San Francisco Bay Area. Most unusual, many grandchildren remained in the Petaluma area and now are raising a fourth generation there. This remarkable continuity permitted me to tell the story of an immigrant community over close to a century and to dramatize the changes in ethnic identity over three generations in that same community. It allowed me to portray the legacy of the extraordinary immigrant comrades of Petaluma to their children and grandchildren.

The second-generation producers of that fiftieth-anniversary community history show, in presenting a myth of community harmony, obscured the political clashes, the cultural conflicts, and the generational tensions that made the community's history so rich and fascinating to an outsider like myself. The community's long continuity allowed me to examine the challenges to sustaining a community over many decades, the dilemmas of maintaining ethnic identity over generations, the external pressures and internal tensions that threatened the cohesion of the community and the identity of its members.

The Petaluma immigrant Jewish chicken ranchers established a community that bore an unmistakable resemblance to the *shtetl,* the Jewish village of tsarist Russia. Succeeding generations of Petaluma Jews struggled to find meaning in this Old World communal form, to recreate it to serve their changing needs as they assimilated into American life. The children and grandchildren of the Petaluma Jewish immigrants had the unusual opportunity and challenge of adapting a secular, highly politicized, modern Yiddish culture to their lives as American-born offspring of immigrants. They contended with the legacy of a generation with enormous vitality, a generation whose emigration to America was part of the larger emergence of east European Jews into the modern world. Despite the harmonious gloss of the second generation's show, the community's history was clearly marked by internal conflict, by challenges from without, by questions over whether the perpetuation of Jewish community and Jewish identity was possible.

The intensity of Jewish community experience in Petaluma allowed me to grasp the concrete human dimensions of these great themes of ethnic community and ethnic identity over generations. Because the Jewish community experience was so profound in Petaluma, because individual lives were inextricably bound together, when the Petaluma Jews spoke to me about their community they inevitably attempted to give definition to their own personal lives and histories. Thus their discussions of their community were charged with emotion, drama, and probing reflection about the meaning of their social experience.

The relatively small size of the Petaluma Jewish community permitted me to understand the community's history through the respective personal experiences of its members. The community was made up of some one hundred families in 1925, when the Jewish Community center first opened, and perhaps three times that number lived in the area at the fiftieth-anniversary celebration. These small numbers permitted an intensive investigation through personal interviews, and in fact required interviews because there were so few documentary sources for historical research. Several hundred interviews afforded an in-depth view of the panorama of community groups, experiences, and opinions.

I began my inquiry in 1974 when I started tape recording the life stories of the immigrant generation, the generation of my grandparents. From the earliest interviews I was deeply impressed by how that generation regarded themselves as actors on the stage of world history. At my first interview, with Morris Rogin, he quickly realized that I did not know what to ask, so he volunteered what was important. He began with his socialist youth in the Crimea, where he had witnessed the Potemkin revolt, and concluded with his life as a prosperous Petaluma grain merchant, clarifying how he reconciled capitalist success with unyielding socialist principles. Hymie Golden, who was not the least bit surprised that I wanted to record him on tape, half-joked about who would own the movie rights to his big story of war, revolution, emigration, and chicken ranching. Ben Hochman, who had been exiled to Siberia for participation in the 1905 Russian Revolution, recounted how he had been tarred and feathered by a Petaluma vigilante mob as part of the great American labor struggles of the 1930s. Jacob Katz, insisting that Petaluma had been "on the map" in the early decades of the community, reflected on twentieth-century Jewish destiny in Russia, Palestine, and America to explain his 1927 migration to Petaluma with a Zionist collective group. Basha Singerman, who had emigrated to Petaluma from Kiev by way of East Africa, gave me boxes of records from her left-wing Yiddish cultural organizations. She urged me to study the Yiddish language and to perpetuate her beloved Yiddish culture.

At first contact, on the telephone, the immigrants seemed brusque; I later decided that the telephone still was an alien form of communication for them. When I arrived at their homes for interviews, I was ushered right to the place where all serious talk occurred—the kitchen table. The words came fast and thick, whether it was a sensuous remembrance of egg bagels in the Old Country, a tearful recounting of a pogrom, a proud description of starting a chicken ranch, an oration on the Soviet solution to "the Jewish problem," or a table-pounding reenactment of the community's political battles during the McCarthy era.

When the tape recorder was off and the conversation slowed, I would notice the picture of a Yiddish poet on a living-room wall, books and magazines in English, Yiddish, Hebrew, and Russian, photos of children and grandchildren, a large-screen color television. Always there was order, spareness, and spotlessness. After the interviews, sometimes there would be a *schnapps*, a whiskey, but usually I was offered storebought cookies and instant coffee. The women no longer baked because they rarely had company. Their lives were scaling down.

The immigrants immediately placed me in the generation of their grandchildren. They assumed my intentions were good but that I was unfamiliar with their historical landscape. From their Petaluma chicken ranches they had maintained a world political and cultural perspective, but they knew that it was lost on succeeding generations. Thus, one started to explain a phase of Petaluma Jewish history, "In 1949, Stalin . . ." She hesitated. "Stalin—you know Stalin?"

Stalin I knew, but she was right to pause. In the first year of interviews I repeatedly asked questions that betrayed my ignorance or lack of sympathy with their experience and views. Some old-timers refused to talk for tape recordings after a preliminary interview, and some clammed up in the middle of interviews. When I asked one of the immigrant Communists why the community's left wing had not challenged a court injunction obtained by the right wing in a disputed Jewish Community Center election, he replied, "You are naive. Don't you know that the courts always would decide against the left?" That was his last frank statement in the interview. One old-timer designated me a "goyishe Yid," a gentile Jew. If I knew so much, why didn't I speak Yiddish? I had learned a few words from my grandparents, but not enough for the immigrants to speak with me in their native language.

Still, they filled my tapes with a lush Yiddishized English, they invited me to community affairs, and they spread favorable reports on my project, for they all agreed that their history merited special study. After all, Petaluma had been virtually unique as an Jewish-American farming community, an "organized" farming community of one hundred families with a rich Yiddish cultural life "like a little New York," a community "known" in Los Angeles and in New York, in Palestine and in the Soviet Union. Indeed, they had been "on the map" because they had been a distinct thread of twentieth-century world history, and they knew it.

By the time I approached their sons and daughters for interviews in 1976, my project was old news on the grapevine. The second generation also insisted on the community's historical significance, but they associated that significance with the history of the immigrant generation, not with themselves, and not with the destiny of the Jewish people in the twentieth century. For them, "history" was something their parents had made.

Nonetheless, during the years that I interviewed this second generation, I gradually was surprised and moved to discover the intensity of their lifelong struggles with the historical legacy of their immigrant parents. During my interviews with the old-timers I had been swept up by their epic tales, their untranslatable expressions from Yiddish, Hebrew, and Russian, their embroidered myths, their wry humor, their political and cultural passions, their wisdom and their foolishness from the perspective of seventy, eighty, and ninety years. But later, as I pored over all the transcribed interviews to write this book, the dilemmas of the American-born second generation emerged as pivotal to my attempt to grasp the transformation of Jewish community and Jewish identity over decades and generations.

I had to look beyond the appearance of comfortable middle-class assimilation of the second generation, my parents' generation, to appreciate the tensions in their historical experience. They frequently invited me for dinner before an interview, and I found myself on familiar terrain. Their homes, often on their old chicken ranches, had been remodeled into modern California suburban ranch-style houses with big picture windows overlooking their five acres. The interviews usually took place in family recreation rooms, which showed the same prosperity as the kitchens packed with appliances and the living rooms with furniture that always appeared new and unused. There was the order and cleanliness of their parents' homes, but rarely a book, a magazine, or a picture that reflected serious interest in history, politics, or literature. Inevitably there would be some *tshatshkes,* knickknacks, testifying to travel in Israel.

The second generation had not forgotten their Old World roots in the immigrant community that their parents had created in Petaluma. They recalled countless community gatherings at the Community Center in the 1920s and 1930s, when their parents staged Yiddish plays and concerts, did public readings of the classical Yiddish writers, fought out Jewish political battles of global proportions, and celebrated all manner of Jewish holidays with tables groaning under the weight of Old World Jewish foods. The second generation evoked nightly communal gatherings at home on the ranches and Saturday-morning discussions in front of the feed mill, with the endless talk of Jewish culture, Jewish politics, and, of course, the chickens. This second generation, too, knew the Yiddish language. They had the feeling of *yidishkeit,* Jewishness, from the homes and community of their immigrant parents.

I discovered that the second generation also were acutely conscious of themselves as Jewish Americans, but because of their discomfort with who they were. They told stories of the excruciating embarrassment they had felt as children when their immigrant parents, with thick accents and strange ideas, met with American schoolteachers or spoke Yiddish when gentile friends visited at home. They recalled gentile children who called them "Christ killer" in grammar school and then, decades later, barred them from membership in the Petaluma Golf and Country Club. Like their immigrant parents, the second generation vehemently insisted that anti-Semitism had never been far below the surface in Petaluma, and I believed them. But every time one of them assured me that he did not want to join the country club because he did not play golf anyhow, I was reminded that in contrast to their parents, this American-born generation had a life-long impulse to seek acceptance in the gentile world around them.

The dilemma of the second generation, pulled between the Jewish immigrant world of their parents and the gentile world around them, was particularly sharp in Petaluma. Growing up in a remarkably cohesive Jewish community that was situated in a small town, the second generation maintained unusual continuity as they came of age, seeking to perpetuate the community of their parents. Many remained in Petaluma, began their own families, used their parents' chicken ranches to launch ambitious farming enterprises, and established their own organizations and activities at the Community Center. By the 1940s and 1950s, they were raising a third generation in the community. Yet the longer they remained within the community of their parents, the stronger were the attractions from without.

Most interesting to me, the second generation attempted to adapt their parents' Jewish community to their own needs and desires. Where their parents recalled the famed Yiddish tenor Yossele Rosenblatt's appearance at the Center before the war, this generation remembered bringing Johnny Mathis for a dance concert. Where the old-timers described Golda Meir passing through Petaluma in the 1930s, raising money for the Labor Zionist movement in Palestine, the second generation recalled Governor Pat Brown coming to speak at an Israeli fund-raising dinner in the 1950s. Where the immigrants had celebrated escape from Old World religious orthodoxy and the marginal role of religion in their Petaluma community, the second generation recounted a decades-long struggle to find a rabbi and to establish a congregation to help them raise their children, the third generation, as Jews. Some had wanted to go further yet and to build a large new synagogue to replace their little community center.

By the time I became acquainted with the second generation, in the 1970s, when they were in their fifties and sixties, they had largely dissociated themselves from the community and the values of their immigrant parents. They criticized their parents for having given more attention to community cultural and political activities than to them as children. They dismissed the community's great political split during the McCarthy era, when the left-wing organizations had been kicked out of the Jewish Community Center, as an example of the immigrant generation's political fanaticism rather than as a clash of political principles. Whereas their immigrant parents had described the chicken farm as the base for a good family life and a unique Jewish community, the American-born second generation made bittersweet jokes about suffocating three-generation families on little farms, about diseased chickens and backbreaking labor, about the disastrous collapse of family chicken ranching in the 1950s and the trauma of finding new work. They were at a loss to explain how and why they had drifted away from the community they had inherited from their parents, except to insist that the community had little to offer after their own children had grown up.

As I worked my way through interviews with the second generation in the late 1970s, I became ever more curious about their legacy to the third generation, the grandchildren of the immigrants, my generation. The second generation clearly identified themselves as Jews, but that identity was precariously balanced between the Old World Jewish community of their parents and a surrounding American society that had both beckoned and rejected them. The second generation had attempted to adapt the immigrant world of their parents, the families and farms and communities, to reflect their own aspirations and uneasy entry into American life. They had tried to make a new place for their children, and I had an opportunity to examine the results of their efforts.

A surprising number of the third generation still lived in the Petaluma area, and many more were in the San Francisco Bay area. During this round of interviews I found myself in modest and grandiose suburban homes, in transient city apartments, and in dilapidated country shacks. Following those interviews I was variously offered coffee, marijuana, and nothing.

Petaluma's immigrant Jewish generation continually had astonished me by their lifelong devotion to family, comrades, and community, to political principles and cultural forms. When I interviewed the grandchildren in the late 1970s and early 1980s, I found many entering their thirties still struggling over whether to create families at all and over what work to pursue. Most were without political commitments or cultural preoccupations. When one of them described a Holocaust refugee as a person who was not "self-actualized," I wondered if the third generation even had the vocabulary for historical reflection.

These informants knew little about the Petaluma Jewish community's history. They had a relatively small emotional investment in it, and thus they were willing to speak frankly about what they did know. They were less guarded about revealing community secrets to an outsider than about revealing too much of their personal lives to a stranger. Assimilation had left them without a strong community and living cultural tradition that could mediate their personal lives and merit their protection.

In interviews the third generation repeatedly identified themselves as Jewish because they "felt" Jewish. I would ask what they meant. After all, they did not speak Yiddish or Hebrew, they did not know the Bible or Jewish history or Jewish literature, they had not experienced anti-Semitism, they were not activist supporters of Israel, they were not religious, they usually were not members of congregations or Jewish community centers. They responded to my question with sentimental memories of a grandmother's Jewish cooking or a grandfather's Jewish humor, and they insisted again that they somehow "felt" Jewish.

Many were looking for ways to give expression to their Jewish feelings. One took Yiddish lessons, some read Jewish history, others found programs at Jewish community centers. One of the grandchildren from a highly cultured Zionist family astonished me by pulling out a copy of *The Jewish Catalogue: A Do-It-Yourself Kit,* as if he could learn to be Jewish just as he could learn to repair a Volkswagen. A handful were active in the Petaluma Jewish community and were sending their children, the fourth generation, to Hebrew school at the Community Center.

The great majority of the third generation were not to be found in the Petaluma Jewish community. The grandchildren have "gone the way of fall flowers," according to one old-timer. Today it is "newcomers" who continue the Petaluma Jewish community. They are young families who have moved into Petaluma over the past twenty years, as it has become a bedroom suburb of San Francisco. These newcomers have legally designated the once secular Jewish Community Center as Congregation B'nai Israel. They are remodeling the old building, but many want to replace it with a new synagogue. Jewish community life in Petaluma now centers on the congregation, the rabbi, and the Hebrew school. Many from the old Jewish community are alienated. One grandson from a pioneer family, referring to himself as "pumpernickel and mustard," calls the newcomers "white bread and mayonnaise." An old-timer says that "now Petaluma is like everywhere else." There is glaring discontinuity with the old community, yet newcomer after newcomer spoke to me of their adopted community as "like one big family," just as the immigrant generation sometimes described their community. It was a puzzle to me.

Now, in 1992, ten years have passed since I taped my last interview in Petaluma. Through recent visits with several community members, I have caught up with the current Jewish community. Most of the immigrants I interviewed have died, as have some in the second generation and even a few in the third generation. Some community members have left Petaluma, more newcomers have arrived, including Russian, Israeli, Iranian Jews, and some of the old "newcomers" have now lived in Petaluma for over twenty years. Several rabbis, too, have come and gone.

I have learned interesting, sometimes surprising things about the lives of the Petaluma Jews during the past ten years. In my mind, the intervening collapse of the Soviet Union has made Petaluma's immigrant generation, particularly the left-wingers, who came of age with the Russian Revolution, seem more susceptible to historical understanding; however, my perspectives on the community's history and on the nature of the current community remain constant, although my views of the third generation, my own generation, have changed.

From the perspective of a decade's distance, I now understand that I interviewed many people from the third generation toward the conclusion of their intense, protracted personal struggles to grow up and to establish families, careers, communities, and cultural identities. In retrospect, I regard the timing of those interviews as fortunate, because the third generation's crises of coming to age illuminated the tensions between the original immigrant community, the second-generation community, and the current assimilated "newcomers" community. Nonetheless, since those interviews over ten years ago, virtually all those third-generation people have established families and careers, have become *"gesettled,"* as the old community might have described it.

In fact, many of the third generation have settled in near proximity to Petaluma and have become active in Jewish community life, but not in Petaluma. They join other Jewish congregations and send their children to other Jewish programs. Their refusal to join the Petaluma Jewish Community Center is, I believe, a last remnant of resistance from the old Yiddish chicken ranching community to the new suburban congregation.

Over the course of eight years, I conducted some two hundred tape-recorded interviews with members of the Petaluma Jewish community and a few gentile observers, I accumulated an enormous mass of spoken words, all of which I transcribed verbatim. Those transcribed interviews are the basis for the story that follows.

From the beginning of the work on this book I decided to tell the community's history entirely in the words of the people I interviewed. Like many other oral historians, I was enchanted by the people I interviewed and intoxicated by the stories they told me. I quickly decided that I would not tell their story as an omniscient historical narrator or participant-observer sociologist; rather, the Petaluma Jewish chicken ranchers should tell their own community history through their own recollections in their own language. I thought that they could best evoke the experiences of a pogrom, of a chicken-house flood, of a community political clash, or of one generation's attempt to understand another. I believed that they could best reveal their shrewdness and their blindness about their own personal experience, their insights, and myths about their own history.

At the same time I wanted to highlight certain historical and sociological patterns I saw in the lives of the community's individuals and families and groups and generations. I sought to avoid the great trap of oral history, wherein historians become so seduced by narrators and interviews that they merely provide an anthology of verbatim conversations without conveying any larger meaning to the reader. I regarded the Petaluma Jewish community as more than a collection of fascinating people who told good stories. In this unique little Jewish chicken-ranching community I saw a microcosm of the great patterns of immigration and assimilation, ethnic community life, and ethnic identity in twentieth-century America. I wanted to convey that epic tale through the color and passion of the Petaluma Jewish experience. I could not do it simply by transcribing interviews.

I thereby encountered the central problem of oral history: How does the oral historian give perspective to someone else's experience without violating that person's view of his or her own experience? How does the oral historian provide historical and sociological perspective on the personal experience of narrators, particularly where the narrators are unaware of those perspectives or disagree with those perspectives? Resolving this methodological and ethical problem became fundamental to my construction of this book.

To turn those spoken narratives of the Petaluma Jews into a written narrative, I selected and arranged their words so as to convey my own perspectives on their community history. I chose which narrators to include and which to exclude, which interviews to emphasize and which to ignore, which interview passages to use and which to omit. Beyond that, I have placed one narrator's story alongside another's for contrast, for agreement, for illumination of truths and lies and insights and myths—for any number of reasons that were mine rather than theirs. These decisions and selections are typical of all historical writing insofar as the historian must always decide which sources to rely on in support of his or her themes and interpretations. Other historians employing the same source materials could make countless other decisions about selection and placement, depending on their own perspectives. In this case they are able and welcome to do so, because all my source materials are being deposited with the research library of the Judah L. Magnes Museum in Berkeley, California.

This book also follows conventional historical scholarship in the editing of each narrator's story to render it clear, lively, and purposeful reading. Like any historian editing primary source documents, I have edited these interviews to focus on the themes and perspectives I consider important, to capture the language rhythms of the narrators, to highlight personality traits, to render spoken words coherent on paper by avoiding repetition, digression, and unintelligibility.

I have pushed against the boundaries of historical scholarship in several instances by combining multiple accounts of a single event into the voice of a single representative character; that is, I have supplemented the stories of a few narrators with information about the same events provided not only by newspaper accounts but also by other people I interviewed. In so doing I could develop a small number of distinct characters whose stories could be shaped into narratives with dramatic tension and thematic coherence. These constructs are the creative editing required by the demands of oral history rather than those of fiction.

For example, one narrator in the book is Ben Hochman, a Communist chicken rancher who was tarred and feathered by a local vigilante mob in the 1930s. For many reasons Ben became a central character in this book and a voice for the story of the immigrant left wing. I also interviewed over a dozen of his comrades, some of whom appear in the book by way of contrast and some of whom do not. Because my interviews with Ben Hochman could not fully cover every event, I interpolated a small amount of material from other interviews into Ben's narrative to fill out his political culture and historical experience. Thus, instead of creating a new character to express the immigrant left-wing view of the Soviet invasion of Finland in 1939, I inserted interview material from one of Ben's comrades into Ben's narration. To have done otherwise would have required an unwieldy number of undeveloped characters and a fragmented history. Thus, Ben Hochman is in a way a character I have constructed to render more clearly the historical truths I have found in the corpus of interviews, although most of his story reflects his own life.

In a very few instances, I have buttressed a narration with factual and explanatory material of my own. I have done this by including my own or others' comments that explain some large, complex events that so profoundly affected the community that its members and observers had great difficulty understanding what happened and why.

For example, the narrative of Rabbi Solomon Platt, who provides a summary explanation at the end of Chapter 11 for the community's great McCarthyite split in the 1950s, is based on a real person and a real interview, but I have augmented his outsider's view with my own understanding and words written in his idiom. I have employed a similar method to help another narrator explain the transformation of the poultry industry from family farm to agribusiness, a wrenching change that dislocated the Petaluma community for many years.

Finally, it is important to remember that the historical sources on which this book is constructed, the interviews of narrators, are atypical. In contrast to the historian's relationship to conventional written source material, I have participated in creating the language and data in the sources. That is, I helped to create my primary source material through my own statements, conduct, and strategy in the interviews, through my own dialogue with the narrators.

For all these reasons, this book is not an anthology of verbatim interviews. Through the process of conducting interviews and writing this book, I have come to regard oral history as distinct from verbatim interviews and as distinct from conventional historical or sociological narratives. Good oral history is the product of a singular collaboration between oral historian and narrator, who join together to create the language, the facts, and the perspectives that constitute the work. What follows is a collection of voices, the voices of the Jews of Petaluma, placed in my own choral arrangement. Through extensive editing and rewriting, through my selection and arrangement of the words of the narrators, I have interpreted their experiences.

I have used aliases for everyone mentioned in this book, except for such public figures as Yehudi Menuhin, Pauline Kael, and Harry Bridges. I did so to provide a thin layer of protection for the privacy of the people

I interviewed. Nonetheless, I am confident that the characters, the events, and the perspectives will be familiar and recognizable to the Petaluma Jews. The interpretation I have given them is my own. Thus the responsibility for the words in this book is mine alone.

I thank the Jewish people of Petaluma for showing me a vital community with a living historical legacy. I hope that they will find my account of their community to be as compelling as I found theirs.

1 Two *Khaverot,* Two Comrades

BASHA SINGERMAN [b. 1894; Minsk, White Russia]

When we came to Petaluma I couldn't speak any English at all. Hardly any . . . in Africa I learned a few words. When we came here I wanted to learn the English language, so I went to night school. My teacher said, "Being that you were in East Africa, I would like you to write an essay on how you got there." And I did. This is the essay: "On a picturesque night I passed through the Suez Canal. Its beauty was beyond description. All the passengers on the boat . . ."

Africa? You want to know why I went to Africa? That is a story!

I was born in Minsk in 1894. Minsk was one of the ghetto cities where Jews were allowed to live in the Russian Empire. I was born with a craving for education. Under the tsarist system, they only admitted a 4-percent quota of Jewish children in the Russian schools. But I was ambitious. With the help of Jewish students—idealists who wanted the Jewish people should get more education—I went all the way from *kheyder*—you know *kheyder?*—the Jewish grammar school, all the way through bookkeeping college.

Then I went to work at one of the biggest stores in Minsk. The owner was a Jewish millionaire. And boy was he a despot! When the Revolution came, the Bolsheviks took everything from him. Later the Nazis killed him off. At the time I worked for him, if I had five rubles a week I was a rich girl. I went through hunger, plenty of it. I joined the bookkeepers' union to make improvements. I was seventeen—an adult already.

I joined other organizations, people's organizations. I was a progressive. I belonged to Lenin's party, which was called Iskra at that time. *Iskra* is "spark." The police were terrible against us. Just before I left Minsk, my friends gave me a farewell party, and the police broke in. They searched for literature and they took away two young men. This was 1913. They were afraid of the educated young people, that we would become revolutionaries and overthrow the tsar.

This was a terrible time for me! A terrible time! I was leaving Minsk to go to Africa. I had a friend whose brother was settled in Africa, in Kenya. This friend went to Kenya with his wife and children. When he came to Nairobi he found there were no Jewish girls for his brother. So he said, "I have a wonderful girl for you!" He wrote me a letter that I should come to Africa and if I didn't like the brother I'll go back to Minsk. I showed the letter to my father. He said, "Go, my daughter, because I cannot do a thing for you." Two weeks later he died. He was forty-nine years old.

I had a young man in Minsk. We were in love, but he did something to me which I didn't like and we quarreled. We parted, and I decided to go to Africa, just in spite of the one I loved. When I left Minsk, my sweetheart came to the railroad station to say goodby. He gave me a package, a present. When I took apart my luggage in Africa, I found two books in his package. These books I still have. [Goes to get them.]

Here is one, *Writers and Poets,* a book of Russian literature. And in this book I found these two little cards. He wrote to me, "Basha . . . *Prosti za vsyo*—forgive me for everything. *Vernis*—come back. *Napishi, yesli u tebya okhota*—write, if you have a desire. Boris." No, I did not write to him. I made up my mind. I was married already. My husband was a wonderful man.

When I came to Africa, Shimon met me at the boat in Mombasa. He was twenty years older than me. I was eighteen and he was thirty-eight, but he looked like a young man of twenty-four. He was highly educated, highly cultured. He knew many languages, and besides he was a Talmudist. At the same time he was an ordinary man who didn't blow about his knowledge. So, at last I fell in love with him.

Shimon came to East Africa in 1906, eight years before me. He came when England offered the Kenya colony to the Jewish people as a homeland. The Zionist leaders refused to accept this place because they wanted Palestine. But Jewish people who came, the British government gave thousands of acres. For a couple of years there was a big sign when you entered Nairobi: "Jewish Reserve."

My husband came with a group of student idealists. They wanted the Jewish people should settle on the land and become productive citizens— not middlemen like in Russia. By profession Shimon was a building engineer, but his heart and soul was with the land.

As soon as a white man came the natives looked at you and named you in their language, the Kikuyu language. My husband they named Margoo. *Margoo* is a judge. When the natives had family quarrels, with all their wives, they came to Shimon for help. He solved their problems in a human way. He was heart and soul for the natives. He thought it was unjust on the part of England to colonize the natives' land and drive them into the woods.

When I came to Africa I was tall and thin. I was a pretty good-looking girl. So they named me Matasia. *Matasia* is a young straight tree, a beautiful tree that grows tall and straight.

A white woman in Kenya was looked at as superior, a godsend. If you went out for a loaf of bread, you had to have a little Negro boy to carry your bundle. You were supposed to ride in a rickshaw, but I considered it below human dignity that a native should carry me. The white women did nothing in Kenya! In the beginning I thought I'll go insane!

I was happy with my husband, but I was so lonely! Kenya was a wilderness actually. Shimon had a dairy ranch miles and miles from Nairobi—just Shimon and I—and Shimon was always milking. There were twenty Jewish families near Nairobi, but all they did was play cards when they met. None of them were progressives. I was lonely for my friends and family. Over two hundred people came to the railroad station when I left Minsk. Minsk was a big city. I had there a cultural life.

I was in Africa for eleven months. Shimon knew I was very unhappy there. When terrible disease broke out among the cattle, one day he says to me, "I will sell the ranch and let's go." We went to California. In Africa my husband got a Jewish newspaper from New York that said to go to California for farming. I didn't know about that. I was very unhappy because I was so lonesome for my friends and family in Minsk. But whatever Shimon said, it was so. We went to California.

In San Francisco we found a real estate agent to take us out—to Ukiah, to Eureka, up north. One day the agent brought us to Willits, about 150 miles north of San Francisco. At that time Willits was such a dirty town, dirty and unpaved. It was raining and it was just miserable. It was the most horrible town I ever saw.

The agent took us to see a cattle ranch. What do I know about a cattle ranch? But it was ten miles from Willits! If you were looking for another house, you wouldn't see it for miles! I didn't say a word, but the deal did not materialize.

When we returned from Willits the train stopped in Petaluma. Just thirty-five miles from San Francisco. Shimon wanted me to see the dairy ranches outside Petaluma. We went out of the train and it was so beautiful! It was a sunny day and everything was so white. A great big hen was sitting in a great big basket of eggs on a sign, and it said, "The Egg Basket of the World." In comparison with Willits, oh my God, it was paradise! I said to my husband, "Shimon, right here we will remain!"

This was in 1915. We rented an apartment and we looked for a ranch. Shimon wanted a dairy ranch. He said, "You have to bend to every chicken and keep on bending." But the chicken ranches were close to town. Before I didn't say anything, but here I was determined. We bought a chicken ranch in Petaluma.

When we first moved onto our ranch, a neighbor went to the newspaper and she wrote an article called "The Invasion of the Jews in Petaluma." I'm telling you, this article, it was terrible! But many other neighbors, non-Jews, they came to our ranch after she wrote this anti-Semitic article. They showed us what you have to do on a chicken ranch.

There were just a few Jewish families when we arrived, but within ten years we had a population of about one hundred Jewish families. Shimon brought them here. He wrote to *landslayt* in the East and told them to leave the sweatshops of the big cities. My husband saw that in Petaluma the Jewish people could do productive work on the land. Here our people could make a respectable living and lead a healthy, dignified life. Shimon possessed vision and ideals.

My Shimon and I welcomed all the new Jewish people who came. The manager at the Bank of Italy, Augie Lepore, he would send us the new Jewish people looking for help. Sometimes they stayed with us for weeks, people we didn't know. We took them out to look for a ranch. Shimon signed notes for them at the bank and the feed company so they should get credit. We showed them how to grow the chickens.

Working with live chickens was new and hard. Most of the Jewish people didn't know from farming. Early in the morning you would hitch up the horse to the wagon and pick kale. We had thousands of kale plants because this was the green stuff you mixed into the feed. After you mixed up the feed you gave it to the chickens. At noon we would collect the first crop of eggs. We cleaned the eggs, we packed the eggs, then we had lunch and rest. Until four o'clock we rested. Then we would do the whole thing again, from the kale to the eggs. It was very hard work, but still it was better than the sweatshops.

My husband I, both of us, we loved the life on the ranch! We loved the work! He would plow up a big piece of land and with my bare hands I would dig and plant vegetables. We made a big beautiful vegetable garden. And then we told all our friends, "Please come and help yourself."

In the early days the whole Jewish community was like one big family. We had wonderful times. In the summers we went every Sunday, all of us, to the Russian River for a picnic. Whoever had a car filled it up with people. We brought our lunches and spread long tables. Did we have food!

In the evenings we came to one another for a visit. Every Friday evening there would be a cultural gathering, mostly at our house. We discussed books and current events. Naturally, it was well-read people—everyone was cultured here. Such wonderful discussions we had. I used to bake cakes and pies for after the discussion—did I have spreads! They called our house "Singerman's Hotel."

My husband, being that he was a building engineer, designed a gorgeous house for us. We built it in 1922. We had a big twenty-by-twenty-foot dining room, a sixteen-by-sixteen-foot living room, two bedrooms, a big kitchen, and a pantry. It was an immense house, the most beautiful house in Petaluma. It was open to all our friends from the day it was built.

In 1925 the Jewish people built the Petaluma Jewish Community Center. We did not have enough money to do it ourselves, so we got a loan from Mrs. Haas of the Levi Strauss Company in San Francisco. She had a fund to help the Jewish farmers. Every one of us wanted a Jewish center where all the Jewish people could come.

We lived like one family, regardless of ideological differences, and there were plenty of ideological differences. Each and every one had his own ideology. I was in with the progressive people. Our group met at the Jewish Community Center like the others, the nonprogressive people—I don't want to call them reactionaries [laughing]—the more conservative people. We were all together in the Center.

What does it mean to be a progressive? Well, progressive means we should have a good life for all mankind, for all peoples. There should be no discrimination, no hatred, no exploitation. That's our main point—justice and a good life for all the people.

You know Ben and Miriam Hochman from our progressive group? In 1935 the fascists in Petaluma beat up Hochman because he is a progressive man. He helped a strike of apple pickers near here. The fascists came to his house in the middle of the night and dragged him out. They tarred and feathered him! Oh, it was something awful! What Ben and Miriam went through!

Yes, there were fascists in this area! Nazis! Some of them were my neighbors. German people. Terrible, terrible people! They were in Nazi demonstrations right here in Petaluma in 1936 and 1937. One of my neighbors was a big *makher* [bigshot] with the Nazis. He led these parades on a white horse. I still see this man in town.

It was bad times in the 1930s. This was the Depression. They were going to take away our chicken ranch, being that we couldn't make a cent on the eggs and we couldn't pay the mortgage. First we sold four and a half acres, then another four and a half acres, and finally we were left with nine acres. The bank didn't foreclose on us, but we had to work very hard. That's why my Shimon died. He became sick from aggravation in the Depression. Then he died from a heart attack. He died on the first of September, 1942.

When Shimon died, I didn't have money for the funeral. Yossele Gardner arranged it with the funeral chapel to wait three months until I sold some birds. Yossele was a wonderful friend. He spoke at the funeral. I remember a few of his words: "The tradition of Shimon Singerman I hope will continue in Petaluma . . . that we should help each other like the example of Shimon Singerman."

It wasn't easy after Shimon died. I owed a big mortgage on our ranch. I owed for rebuilding our chicken houses from laying hens to meat birds. I owed medical bills. I was penniless, and again they were going to take our place away. I had to sell more land and I had to work very hard. Fortunately, at that time I was just fifty years old and strong like a horse. So I did it all. I paid the debts and I came out all right.

I kept the ranch until 1966. It was in my heart—not only the house, but the whole place. We built it ourselves, my Shimon and I. I paid off the mortgage and I lived very moderately. I never thought I would sell our place. But I lost all my money and I had to sell.

It happened like this. All my savings were in the bank of the Poultry Producers co-operative. I had so much confidence in them—we bought feed and sold eggs with them since we came to Petaluma in 1915. However, in 1964 the Poultry Producers co-operative went bankrupt. This was when the chicken corporations were taking all the little chicken ranches. The whole thing was crooked!

I was left penniless! I couldn't pay for anything. A whole year I was on welfare! It nearly killed me! Because I always was so independent! This was begging—actually charity. It was so humiliating!

One day I got the tax bill for my ranch. I went to my social worker. In the city hall I used to go. Oooh, I just shiver when I think about it!!! I didn't like the welfare business! However, I came and I said I have no money to pay my tax bill this year. The welfare worker was a nice person, but what could he do? He said if I do not pay my taxes, the government will take my ranch. I nearly fainted when he said it! It occurred to me that I must sell my place! I don't want them to take it.

After I sold my ranch my friends said, "What will we do without Basha's house?" Because all the progressive meetings and all the progressive parties—whatever you can think of—were in my house. It was open to everyone from the first day. So they said, "What will we do without Basha's house?"

So? Okay! We are getting along without Basha's house. That's all. That's the end of it! The whole story of my ranch! *Farshteyst?* This is our wonderful system. Most of my land I had to sell in the 1930s. Then they came and took everything else in the 1960s. But who cares?

Even after I lost my place I continued to be active with the progressive Jewish people in our progressive organizations. Here in Petaluma we had the Jewish People's Folk Chorus, the Jewish Women's Reading Circle, the Jewish Drama Group, the International Workers Order, and the Jewish Cultural Club. All of this was in Yiddish, a beautiful Yiddish.

I saved all the sheet music from our Jewish People's Folk Chorus. [Brings out boxes.] Here is a song by Maurice Rauch, who conducted the Jewish Folk Chorus in New York: "*Yidish iz mayn loshn*—Yiddish Is My Language." [Sings a few lines.] A beautiful song. This one is "*Bin ikh mir a shnayder*—"I Am a Tailor." This one, in English, "Ode to Democracy," is from the poem by Walt Whitman. Here is one you know— "Solidarity Forever." This one is by Shostakovitch, in Russian; it means "For All People." "Neger Vig Lid—Negro Lullaby." We sang Negro spirituals, in Yiddish, of course. "Go Down Moses" we sang too, with Paul Robeson we sang it at a concert in Santa Rosa, to raise money in defense of the Rosenbergs.

Our Jewish People's Folk Chorus sang all over Northern California. One time we sang at the Civic Auditorium in San Francisco. This was during the war, on the fourth year of the attack on the Soviet Union. Representatives of all the nationalities were on the stage, including us. Everyone was singing and dancing, like in the Soviet Union all the nationalities lived together peacefully and beautifully. And all of a sudden it became very dark on the stage—you could hear the bombs blowing. This was very dramatic.

I can't sing like I used to sing. I feel that my strength is failing me. But I keep all the sheet music. I have here all the records from our progressive Yiddish cultural organizations. Because all this is very dear to me, very deep in my heart.

I am a *yidishe tokhter*. You know what that means? A Jewish daughter. I am a *yidishe tokhter* from top to bottom.

Until 1949 all our progressive organizations met at the Jewish Community Center. But there were reactionaries in the Jewish community who couldn't stand the progressive movement. During the time of McCarthy and the Cold War, they threw us out. They called us Communists and they threw us out! Some of them were fascists actually. Some of them were afraid the government will persecute all the Jewish people if the progressives met at the Jewish Community Center. It's a terrible thing that a small Jewish community in a small town should be divided. But they told us to go, so we went. The progressive children went too. We rented halls from the gentiles for our organizations. Since then, I, for one, would not go into the Jewish Community Center for many years.

Since then many of our progressive children have returned to the Jewish Community Center. Here in Petaluma there was nothing for them. Now the whole bunch of them are members of the congregation at the Center. They are not progressive like they used to be. It's because of the American atmosphere, the sentiment. It's the whole combination of life, not just in Petaluma, but all over the United States. They want everyone to be conservative. Today the grandchildren know nothing of our progressive Jewish movement.

Well, the young people have their own lives to live. Now the Petaluma Jewish community is a conservative community. They have their rabbi and their congregation at the Center, and we progressives don't bother them. They have services and services and more services with this rabbi.

When we built the Center in 1925 we built a little *shul* in it. You know what *shul* means? Synagogue. We built a big social hall and a little *shul*, because just a few people went to services. To tell you the truth, I never went into that *shul*. I don't know how it looks. I wasn't interested.

Now, when you read the *Jewish Community Bulletin,* it is full of religion. They put the rabbi's message on the first page, and the rabbi's message is a very long message. Most of this bulletin is filled with religion. Well, okay, this is their pleasure. Fine. I am interested in this *Bulletin* because I still know quite a few people at the Center. But many of the names are strange to me. Their activities are strange—to me and to our progressive people. We continue to work for our progressive movement.

We had to give up most of our progressive organizations. Many of our people left Petaluma to find more life in the cities. Many died. Two weeks ago Haber had a stroke. It's aggravating, it's painful—we are losing our people. But what can we do? This is the process of life.

But we don't give up yet! We still have our Jewish Cultural Club and we are doing wonderful work. We used to have over one hundred people at the meetings, but it's getting lesser and lesser. Last week we were eleven people at the meeting. But still we had an interesting discussion on the Jewish problem in the Soviet Union, and we took up a collection for the NAACP.

I am getting old now. I am over eighty already. Well, time flies for everybody. The only thing different is that one gets born earlier and another later. Literally speaking I am alone, but I manage. Several years ago they raised the rent at my little house on Western Avenue. I moved to Magnolia Street, and a lot of my old *khaverim* live in the building now.

You know what *khaverim* is? Comrades—friends—very good friends. In this building are the Hochmans and the Salzes and the Habers and the Braunsteins. Here we are close. We go to one another. Sometimes in the night we come together in one apartment.

KHAYA FEINSTEIN [b. 1905; Kozhets, Ukraine]

I was born in a small town in the Ukraine. We were real Jewish people in those days. We went to a Jewish school, to *kheyder*. We went to pray in *shul*. We followed all the rules for a kosher Jewish life. This was real Jewish life in a *shtetl*.

In my days people already went out, so they said it, out into the world. They went to countries like England and America where the Jewish people were not in ghettos. They were emancipated.

What do I mean by emancipation? I'm gonna give you the history of the whole thing!

We lived in the Pale of Settlement. It was like a great ghetto in the Russian empire where the Jewish people had to live.

When I was eight years old I started in a Russian school. On Friday the teacher told us to bring pens and paper the next day. But my mother says, "No, my child. If you must write on the Sabbath, you cannot go to school." That was the end of my school until 1918. I had lessons at home with tutors—Jewish students—until the Revolution in 1917. Then the Bolsheviks opened up a junior high school in a building they took from the landlord. I passed an examination and went in with the other children.

I had an ambition to go to *gymnasium* after I graduated from the junior high school in 1919. But that was when the big pogrom took place. It was the end of our schools. It was the end of our *shtetl*. Everything was all burned up.

In our *shtetl* it was the Ukrainian army that made the pogrom. The Ukrainians was trying to set up their own country during the Revolution. When the Bolsheviks came, the Ukrainian armies were running all over. They robbed, they raped, they killed. They did all these things. The Jewish people were the first target.

I remember the pogrom—I remember it even now. It began on a Thursday night. We heard a Ukrainian army is coming and they leave destruction. My father told me to take my younger sister to the school. He said my mother and my older sisters should hide in the fields. My father took the three youngest children to the gentile's place on the edge of town.

The Ukrainian army came, but they didn't go into the school because the teachers were very conscientious. One teacher, he had a pistol in his hand and he said they'll have to go through his dead body to touch any of the children. He protected fifty Jewish kids. That was Thursday night. There was shooting all night. On Friday afternoon we saw flames. Our *shtetl* was burning up. I had to leave my sister and look for my parents.

This is another chapter . . . I don't want to talk about it. It is terrible. I went through town and I see they are killing the Jewish people. Right in the streets the soldiers are shooting people. All the houses were open and everything was thrown out. Feathers were flying from the pillows. And the people . . . [Tears.]

I got to my father. We ran home to see what we could salvage. It was evening and the people that were alive were sitting around the river with whatever was left. All the people were groaning. Two of my girlfriends, gentile girls, they found me and said they will stay with me [crying]—I can't talk about it. You see, that's why I don't want to talk about it. I have to live through it again. Let's forget the pogrom.

That was in 1919. We had a bad winter with the Polish invasion into the Ukraine. We were the inbetweens. Sometimes the Poles would shell the Russians, so we ran to this side. Then the Russians shelled the Poles, so we ran to the other side. They made peace in 1920. That was the time when terrible epidemics broke out. My father got sick with typhus and died. He was forty-seven years old.

How we survived is another story! We went around to the peasants in the villages. We bartered whatever we had for food. We begged! We lived on practically nothing. When the Bolsheviks took over they started to help. All those who could write, like myself, they went to work in an office. The Bolsheviks wanted some organization. I got a food ration, like a pound of grain or a few potatoes. That's how my family survived.

In 1921 I crossed the border into Poland. All the youngsters that could stand on their feet were leaving. There was nothing to eat in the Ukraine! We tried to reach the open world, to get together with family in America. I wanted to get help for my mother and the other children.

In Warsaw the Hebrew Immigrant Aid Society helped us refugees. Before long I found a cutting in the *Forward,* the Jewish newspaper that came from America. It was an announcement from my brother looking for our family: "If anybody sees . . ." [tears]. That's all . . . I can't talk about it now.

[After a break.]

I stayed in Poland for two years. I wanted to go to Palestine to build a Jewish country, but that's another story. They told me, "If you go to Palestine all you can do is crack rocks to build roads. You are too young." They said I must go to America.

I landed with my brother in Philadelphia. This was a beautiful chapter in my life. I went to work in a shirt factory and I became independent. I got acquainted with a Zionist group, *Hashomer Hatsair,* which means Young Zionists. We had meetings and picnics. We went to lectures, we discussed books, we sang and danced. We did as young people do.

Philadelphia was a fine place, but still I wanted to go to Palestine. I wanted to build *our own homeland.* I saw what the people of the world did to our Jewish people. I thought we should not live among strangers. We should have our own corner.

In Philadelphia we organized a group with the ideal to work on the land in Palestine—start a *kibbutz.* We were eight people, all teachers and factory workers, so we had to learn agriculture. From the Jewish Agricultural Society in Philadelphia we heard, "California is the place to learn the poultry business. In Petaluma there are Jewish farmers who will teach you how to raise chickens. Then you can go to Palestine and get land from the Jewish National Fund for your kibbutz."

That's why we came to Petaluma—in 1927, in January. It was a happy time in my life. Because I was among a group of close friends with similar ideas about Palestine, agriculture, and socialism. We were *khaverim*, comrades, three girls and five boys. We lived together in a house in town. The boys worked on the chicken ranches and the girls worked for an egg-packing company in town. We shared everything.

The Petaluma Jews was *so* happy to see us! They was carrying us on their hands! Because we were a group of young idealistic Zionists. Most of the Petaluma people were Zionist inclined. I'm not talking about the other half—the progressives, the left wing. But most of the people were happy to come dance the hora with us.

At that time it was a tremendous Jewish life in Petaluma. The people were from Europe, from a cultural way of life. The chicken farmers got together in the Jewish Community Center for lectures and discussions. Every Petaluma Jew knew how to be a reader of Yiddish literature. The Center was a *lebedike* place—full of life.

I came to Petaluma in January and I got married in October. My husband was born in Palestine. Zev came to the United States in 1922 to study agriculture at the university in Davis, California. During the summers he worked on the chicken ranches in Petaluma. Zev wanted to start a dairy farm in Palestine. After he finished his studies, he figured he'll work in America until he can make some money to start his farm at home. Petaluma chickens was easy money then . . . 1925, 1926, 1927. He rented a chicken ranch.

When I came to Petaluma, I seemed like a godsend to him: together we'll work, we'll save money, and we'll go to Palestine. At first I didn't want these plans. I thought I'll go to Palestine with my group. But then my Petaluma kibbutz started to disappear. This one went by himself, that one went . . .

Before we were married Zev suggested, "Instead of working in egg packing, you can work on my ranch. You have to learn this work and I need help."

Yes [laughing]—my help was very important! I said, "I'm not working for you unless we decide what we're doing!" So we decided we'll get married. We went to a justice of the peace. No rabbi. We both came from religious homes, but we weren't religious anymore. We didn't care about those things.

Boy, was I green in the beginning. Zev had to do the cooking because I didn't know what to do in the kitchen. He didn't want to be the cook, so one day I said, "I'm gonna cook a soup!" I remembered my mother used to make a pearl barley—a very good soup. I put all the ingredients in a pot and let it cook. Cook, cook, cook! Until I start to smell a fire! My soup burned! I said, "Oh, this doesn't look like my mother's pearl barley soup!" We took it out and cut it into pieces. This was my first soup.

We lived in rented chicken ranches for ten years. I was out there feeding the chickens and collecting the eggs with Zev, and I became an expert in preserving, and I was raising our son. It was hard work, but it wasn't bad until the Depression came. Then it was real suffering.

All those years we wanted to settle in Palestine. In 1936 we were sitting on the suitcases ready to go. But they had terrible pogroms then, and Zev's family told us to wait until it is not so dangerous. So we waited. We waited and waited. We had a second son. We bought a ranch. Then we decided to wait until we were a little prosperous on the ranch. So? So! We are still waiting! We should have gone in 1936.

Instead we put a down payment on this ranch in 1937. We got a lot of help from Mr. Lepore at the Bank of Italy. Then business picked up when the war came. We were very busy in those years.

In 1948, when Israel came into existence, Zev decided it's time to go home and see what Israel looks like. We sold all the chickens and went for six months. It was a tremendous experience for me—I felt like I am coming home. But by 1949 it wasn't a country for us. We were settled in Petaluma with two boys and a big ranch. We returned with the idea that later we would settle in Israel. But we should have done it in 1949, because it never worked out later.

Still we had a good life in Petaluma. We had wonderful friends and a good cultural life. When new people came to settle on a chicken ranch, they came to us for help. Zev was an expert farmer, and besides he would cosign so that people should get credit. We had an open house with lots of people and food. There was life around this house.

We were active at the Jewish Community Center with our Zionist movement. For a small town, did we have Zionist organizations: Poale-Zion, Farband, Pioneer Women, Hadassah. After the war the socialists in the Arbeiter Ring and the assimilated Jews in the B'nai B'rith also became supporters of Israel. Only the progressives, the left-wingers—the Communists—they were against Zionism. They did not belong anywheres as far as Israel and Jewish life is concerned.

All the factions in the Jewish community got along very well until the left-wingers became very aggressive after World War II. They brought the Russian flag into the Jewish Center; they had speakers on communism. This was the time of McCarthy. The gentile people in Petaluma warned they would not tolerate Communist activities. You know, they already tarred and feathered Hochman in the 1930s. We had to tell the left-wingers to leave the Jewish Community Center. This was a very bad time for our Petaluma Jewish people. That's all I'm gonna say about it. No more details about the politics from me. You get it from someone else.

At that time Petaluma wasn't the best place to give children a Jewish education. Our sons learned Yiddish in our home, but the Yiddish language is *zhargon*—a collection of different languages. Hebrew is the cultural language. Hebrew is the language of Israel. We tried to teach our sons Hebrew, but they couldn't practice enough. As far as the education goes, the children got a lot in the worldly line of education, but not much in Jewish education.

The children went the way of fall flowers. My own children disappeared from Petaluma. Many of the children stayed, but then the grandchildren disappeared. Those who remain do not participate in our Jewish community life. It happened in our own good Zionist families—the grandchildren married gentiles and went over to the *goyim*.

It is a paradox. For two thousand years our people were scattered all over, but we kept up a Jewish life. We were ready to sacrifice anything for Judaism, even our lives. Here in America the gentiles are good to the minorities—no ghettos, no restrictions, no oppression, no fear. Here the Jewish people can do what they want. So what do we do? We get mixed up and disappear! We are being swallowed up in America!

Today we have a nice Jewish community in Petaluma, but it's not my crowd. The majority of the active people are young professionals who don't know much about Judaism or Zionism. They try to keep up a Jewish life with a rabbi and a congregation. All the years I was here there were hardly enough religious people for a *minyan* [a quorum for a religious service] on Saturday morning, but now everything is religion.

I am glad to see these young people continuing Jewish life here. But there isn't practically anything for me to do in Petaluma now. Zev is gone last year. Most of my Zionist *khaverim* are gone. I don't know where my old bones will rest. It's terrible to be alone. I might go to Los Angeles to be with the children. I don't know if there is happiness for me anywheres. I can't see it. But as long as a person is alive, you have to make the best of it.

It would be wonderful to live in Israel. I feel at home with the people there. I like the warm climate in Israel. The wind always blows out here on the ranch. This house is so cold now. Look how many sweaters I wear. I keep the furnace turned up all day, but still I am cold.

2 "I Found a *Shtetl* in California"

MORRY FINKLESTEIN [b. 1902; Warsaw, Poland]

The *khasidic shul* in Warsaw was a dirty stinky place! That's what it was, except for where they kept the Torah. It was a miserable depressing place. When my father took me among those people, and they were praying and shaking, I imagined I was in an Arab country. I read a lot of books already, and they really seemed like Arabs. You know, they wore the *taleysim* [prayer shawls] over their heads and they prayed like wild men. I didn't like it.

My father let my sisters go to the Polish school, but not me. I went to that medieval *kheyder*. It was in the home of a man who was such a *shlemiel* that the only thing he could do was teach kids. How we were treated there! He'd make you put your hands on the table and he'd smash your fingers. And—I'm not exaggerating—his wife kept a *sheytl* [wig worn by orthodox women] on the window sill, and there were a million lice crawling around it! That's where my father sent me for education! You see? Do you understand why I hate religion so much?

The first time I got a pair of western shoes, I was so proud of them. But the *khasidic* tradition was that you wore boots. When I came into *kheyder* with those nice new modern shoes, the little sons-of-bitches stepped all over them! Because I was wearing worldly shoes!

The clothing I had to wear! For five hundred years they stuck to the same God-damned thing—the boots, the long jacket, and the cloth cap with the visor. I was dressed in those medieval *shmates* [rags]. I was a bashful, sensitive kid. When I walked down the street and little girls saw me, I wanted to bury myself alive. My sisters were dressed nicely, but I looked like a beast. My mother never saw that I suffered. Of course, a boy belongs to his father, but my father wore modern western clothing for his store. Only I was dressed so the Christians knew I was a Jew.

And the Christians tortured you plenty. They knocked the shit out of you. It was a daily persecution. It never stopped. I would compare the life of Jews in Poland to the life of blacks in the South. Of course, the Polish people were miserable too. It's the old story. When you're miserable, it's pleasant to have somebody under you who is more miserable.

I left when they were drafting young men for the First World War. When I snuck across the border into Germany I said, "I'll never go back!"

HYMIE GOLDEN [b. 1894; Ukraine]

I quit going in *shul* when I was a kid. See, five years old, I lost my mother. Every year I go say *kaddish* for her. *Kaddish* is the prayer to remember the dead. When I go in *shul* to say *kaddish* I gotta bring bagels for the men. Them bagels hung on a string—egg bagels. I was so hungry I could eat all them bagels myself; even the string I could eat it up. But I bring them bagels in *shul* to men who just sit there praying, men that never worked in their life. They say *kaddish* and eat up them bagels.

Kaddish didn't make no sense to me either. It says God's judgment is right. I figure, what kind of judgment is it? Took my mother—she was only thirty-five years old. See? And I stopped going. I stop going in *kheyder* too. In *kheyder* they teach one thing: pray, pray, pray. When you come out, you can't do nothing.

We had a right to go in the Russian school two hours every day. There we learn something. So what happened? The rabbi comes in to inspect the Russian school. He sees the tsar's picture . . . sees the Rasputin's picture with the crosses, sees us sitting without a *yarmelke* [skull cap]. He goes like the dog runs away with the tail between the legs. Next day, we can't go to the Russian school. The rabbi says it will make us for *goyim*.

I was mad. Next day in *kheyder* the rabbi says I don't know my *khumesh* [the five books of Moses]. To scare everyone the rabbi slaps me in the face—hard! I thought to myself quick, "He teaches me *ayin takhes ayin*—an eye for an eye." So I gave him right back a slap! He went over the table at me . . . I crawl under the table. He got under the table. I jumped over him and ran home. No more *kheyder*. My father says, "What's gonna be from you?"

My father didn't take good care of me. You know what they say: "When the mother dies, the father gets blind." My father was remarried, and the stepmother didn't like me. I didn't get nothing to eat—no clothes—I was going barefooted. Wasn't like here where the law steps in when the parents discriminates against the children. I could starve to death in my *shtetl* and nobody does nothing.

When I'm thirteen years, my father gives me away to a furrier to learn a trade. You know, that I should go to America . . . you gotta have a trade for America. But he sells me to be a slave for two years! I was working all hunched over a sewing machine until late at night. My eyes was so red I couldn't hardly see them. From this furrier I never got enough food. For two years I was hungry. I was always thinking, "When I grow up, I'm goin' to my brother in America and gettin' something to eat."

I'm fifteen I come home, but I can't live with my father no more. I went in the big city Nikolaevo, and I got me a job there. I'm a furrier. Scared? I was never scared by nothing! If I should have a speedometer like a car has it, and hook it up how many miles I made it through my life, I made more miles than my car.

Comes 1914, the tsar took me in the war. One year I was in the World War. Then I was in a big fight and the Germans took me prisoner. Until 1919 I was a prisoner-of-war in Germany. I was lucky—I was never hurt in the war—but still I was always hungry.

When the war ended I could have gone to my brother in America, but I don't know my brother from Adams. I had a father in Russia, he never took care of me, he never showed me love. Till I got married I was just like in the desert you see a little tree all alone. I didn't have nobody. I figured, "Still he is my father. I'll go home."

ANNA ROSENFIELD GOLDEN [b. 1900; Ukraine]: He never smiled until he came to me. We were a whole year married until I saw a smile. Sad. Sad.

HYMIE: It was February 1919, I go back to Russia. On the train I seen some Jewish people with *peyes* [side curls]—soldiers came in and pulled that hair right off them people! Pogrom! My God, I know I made a mistake coming back.

I came to my town. There was Jewish boys on patrol, because the pogroms was killing people. I came home, the stepmother opens the door wearing my shirt. I told her, "You gave me up for killed." My father comes to the door, says, "You came to make trouble."

ANNA: This is a father!

HYMIE: Coming back to Russia was the biggest mistake I make in my life. There was war. There was pogroms. I had no home, nobody to go around with. I didn't even know how to approach a girl.

ANNA: I felt sorry for you, so I said, "Come over to us sometime." [Much laughter.]

HYMIE: I came to her family. They give me food. I thought to myself, "That's my brothers, that's my sisters, that's my parents." And I got married.

I speculated to make a living then. Some city that didn't have no sugar, they have salt, I took there the sugar and buy salt. I traveled on boxcars at the top. It was cold. And if they catch you, I wouldn't be here to tell the story.

It was big trouble then. They had a civil war—Ukrainians, White Russians, Bolsheviks—every day it's a different army, a different government. They break into the homes and clean up the Jewish people. They take everything. They rape. They kill.

In 1921 I say it's time to leave. Anna was pregnant, but we gotta leave. First we going with her family, but her older sister Molly had a husband Isaac in America. Molly gets a letter and she wants to go right away. Right away! We had an argument and I said, "Go! I don't want to go with you!"

We went a few months later, with Anna's younger brother, a soldier for the Bolsheviks. We hopped freight trains to the border with Latvia. At the last station before the border they caught him and sent him back into the army.

ANNA: *Oy,* such a wonderful boy. It was tragic. He was left behind.

HYMIE: We got to the border town and found farmers to take us across in nighttime. She was six months' pregnant. They brought us over the border, then they left us on our own. What you going to do? We walked, miles and miles we walked. Tired . . . wet . . . don't know where we are going. And two soldiers, Latvians, they catch us.

It's a story! It's a whole book! They take us to the border patrol. Well, there anybody takes a bribe. Just a few dollars—not like the big bribes in America. The sergeant took five rubles gold and left us off at the border again. We walk again. Walked and walked and walked.

ANNA: I was pregnant. Oh boy, was he scared I would die! He was watching me all the time so I shouldn't fall asleep in the snow.

HYMIE: Two soldiers find us again, in a barn. They say we go back to the border. I was always figuring how to get out of it. I told them we are exhausted—let us spend the night here. In the morning I gave them ten rubles gold. You know the *goyim*—they have to celebrate. One went into town and bought vodka. They got so drunk they could hardly move their tongues. Then we sneak away.

Finally we came to Riga. We met up with her family. The HIAS [Hebrew Immigrant Aid Society] helped me get money from my brother in America. We buy false passports and wait for the visa to America. While we was waiting, one night the police put me in jail. That night she had the baby.

ANNA: It was plenty plenty plenty trouble.

HYMIE: When we saw the American consul, they ask why I want to go to America. You know, maybe I am a Communist. So I told them I was a prisoner-of-war, I was in pogroms, I was hungry . . . I want food and I want freedom.

When I get off the ship in New York, I feel like to lean down and kiss the sidewalk. I was free!

We go to California because her family was here. Anna's sister Molly—her husband started a farm in Petaluma. They got chickens! When we came to San Francisco I worked one year in the Crystal Palace Market for one of her brothers. It was rough working at his food stand. See, you sell strawberries you say, "Lady, I'll make you a nice bundle." Then you take them strawberries in the back, leave the good ones and make a bundle with the moldy ones. Was dog-eat-dog.

There was another fruit stand—it was like a border between Russia and Poland. Sometimes the customers was there and none on our side. Her brother tells me to sneak in there, sell them, and take the money on our side. One time he comes in, looks into the register for money, says, "Whatsa matter boy? Shake 'em up, shake 'em up!" I says, "Listen, gimme a half-hour off; I'll go down and take from the bank."

I couldn't take it no more. One day I come home and I says to my wife, "I'm gonna quit!"

She said, "What you gonna do?" You know, I'm making forty dollars a week.

I says, "We'll go to Petaluma like Molly and Isaac. If you want I should stay on this job, I'll be sick with ulcers!"

ANNA: I liked San Francisco, but he said, *"Vest blaybn an almone"*—"So stay here and be a widow. I'm going to Petaluma!" What can I do? I had to go with him.

HYMIE: Can I say something? When you work wages for somebody and you have to cheat to make a living—sell your soul for a bare living—I couldn't take it.

ANNA: He's very honest.

HYMIE: I saw Petaluma when we visited her sister Molly on Sundays. Seemed peaceful. I said, "I'm going to be a chicken rancher."

I told Molly's husband Isaac and he says, "What do you mean, you're coming to Petaluma? You think you can raise chickens?" He didn't want me.

There was another Jewish fellow with him; he says to me, "Do you like to work?"

"Yeah."

"If you like to work, you're going to make a living here."

MOLLY ROSENFIELD LIPSKY [b. 1892; Ukraine. Anna Rosenfield Golden's sister]

I got married when I was twenty years old. My father went to do the shopping and he met a friend in town. They went for lunch together. He comes home, he says to my mother, "Bashiva, I made a *shidekh* [match]!"

"What kind of *shidekh* did you make?"

"I met with Shmiroh. He said, 'I have a boy and you have a girl.' And we made a *shidekh*."

I says, "Pa, did you ask me?" This boy Isaac came around every week and he never says hello to me. "He's a nice boy," I say, "but maybe we don't care for each other. If he likes me he can say so himself."

"It's a *shidekh!* It's a *shidekh!*"

I say, "Pa, I am not for sale."

Went by two weeks and I said, "Pa, did you tell him?"

"No."

I says, "You better tell him, because this *shidekh* is not a *shidekh*."

Went by another month. One Saturday, Isaac came with his mother. They came in kind of friendly, but he was very shy. It was already after *Pesach* and the weather was nice. We all have tea outside. All right, they stay a few hours.

Next Saturday came again the parents and Isaac. At that time he was not even a boyfriend! They figure it out he should take me for a walk. So he took me for a walk. It was 1911 already. On August 30, 1911, we got engaged.

I was married in 1912—a big wedding. Years ago, they liked to have *yikhes* [pedigree] and *koved* [honors]. We tried to do the best. You know, musicians, whiskey, cakes, everything. We started at two o'clock to meet the groom and his family on the road to our house. After the rabbi married us was dinner. Then champagne and dancing. The next morning the wedding was over and the guests went home.

We made a grocery store in my village. Isaac played a recorder; I played the guitar. We were singing. We were happy.

Then comes trouble, lotsa trouble. Isaac goes away to the World War. There were epidemics and my son, Reuben, took sick. Then I got a very high fever. The nurse says, "She's gonna die." But I didn't die! All of a sudden the fever dropped and I got cold. And I'm still alive! [Laughing.]

My husband ran away from the army to America. Across Siberia he went. I got a telegram in 1915, in October, says he is safe in San Francisco. Then I didn't have any letters from him till 1921. Nothing got through. It was the war, the Revolution.

The pogroms was very bad in those years. They killed my father's youngest brother, they killed his wife's parents and two boys. In one room they killed seven from my family. They left one boy, ten years old. He said to them, "You killed my parents; kill me too." They shot him in the arm. In the morning my brothers took him to the hospital and they took off his arm.

In the same house where I stayed with my parents they killed five people. We were in another room. I heard them come in and I started to pray to God: "If they are going to come in here, they should kill me and my boy Reuben together—they shouldn't separate us." They were shooting in the next room. I lay on the floor along the wall and I heard the baby crying—a baby five weeks old. And I heard, "It makes me nervous. Shoot that baby." And I heard them shoot.

In May 1921 I got a letter from Isaac. He says to me, "If you want to be with me, get to a port and come to America." I write to him right away that I am coming. In June we went—Isaac's parents, Isaac's sisters, me with my boy Reuben, and my parents with my brother and two sisters. My sister Anna and her husband, Hymie, they came later.

It took us three months to reach a port. Crossing the border into Latvia is the hardest. Nighttime. We take a little boat on a lake. The boat filled up with water. My sisters cried, "*Oy veh! Oy veh!* God help us!"

I said, "What are you crying to God? God is going to help you if you do something. Take out the water!"

We sneaked across the border; there was more trouble. No passports. Arrests. There was trouble, trouble. We argued about money they sent us from the United States. More trouble. But if you have to be alive, you have to be alive. I makes it. Finally we gets to New York and we go by train to California. By then I weigh a hundred pounds. A hundred pounds! And my four front teeth, they fell out. I was a mess, but I was in America.

In 1922, May the 11, I came with Reuben to my husband's ranch in Petaluma. He bought it with his brother. They knew about the chicken business like I can be a priest! They heard about it while they was working in San Francisco in the business fruit and vegetables. They didn't care for the chickens, but they heard you can shovel the gold on a Petaluma chicken ranch.

When I came, Isaac was taking care the chickens and his brother was the cook. Right away I sent the brother back to San Francisco. I told him, "I am the *baleboste* now!"

SARAH SISKIN WEINSTEIN [b. 1892; Brest, White Russia]

I was born a thousand years too soon. I never had the opportunities for my ambition.

When I was eight years old I told my mother, "I want to work." She said I was too young. But I said, "I can do it. I want to have money to spend the way I want."

I hired myself out to a dressmaker because it pays good and I figured I always will have to work. But my father was unhappy that I live at home. He was complaining he's too old to make a living and feed me. He wanted I should live with a well-fixed family as a servant girl. A maid! I said, "Never!" Because when you keep a house for someone else, then you're never independent.

I was in my first strike when I was fourteen. I convinced the other girls to stop working until the boss gives us more money. We won, but he wouldn't hire me back. I found another job and started another strike. I had the guts to do it.

At that time I was an idealist. I went to political meetings to "better the world." We had to do everything in secret, because the tsar would send you to Siberia if he caught you. We wanted a working-class revolution that should make a free world where you don't need money and everything will be wonderful.

It bothers me to this day that I had no education when I was young. They would not take Jewish children in the Russian schools. If I had the opportunity I would have studied business. Not a little shop, but a high business where I would be president and have a lot of people working for me. I think I would be a success, but this was not for a Jewish girl when I was born.

I came to America to find my opportunity. What could I do on $1.20 a week in Russia? My parents were old and wanted me to stay for them. My younger sister stayed, but I said, "No, I don't see any prospects for my future here."

I was ambitious to find my prospects in America. I came to my brother in San Francisco in 1911. He came here to find work rebuilding after the 1906 earthquake. In San Francisco, he wrote, you can get gold on the streets. That's where my trouble began.

I was a young girl with no one to help me. I thought my brother will wine me and dine me. Turns out he's got no job and he sleeps on the floor. Three days after I came, I had to find a job. I went out to work as a dressmaker—a ladies' tailor, they called it. I was a finisher of garments in a shop. After five months the forelady quit. I said to the boss, "Mr. Greenberg, give me a chance to do it." He said, "You are a greenhorn. You are too young." I said, "I can do it!" I kept on talking and I got the job. I made good wages. I was moving up. The boss always complained that as soon as he trains a good forelady, she gets married. *Oy,* he was disappointed when I got married. Me, I was disappointed too!

I went out with a lot of boys. Bernie acted right to me, treated me nice. I thought, "Well, I better not take a chance he should try someone else. I might miss out." I wasn't even twenty when we married. Turns out Bernie wasn't an easy man to live with. He wanted to do everything his way. He wanted to open his own tailor business. I told him, " You haven't got enough capital. Before you know it, we'll be kaput." So he opens a fancy shop with high-class customers who don't pay. After a year he went kaput.

At that time we heard from friends that Petaluma is a good place to start a chicken ranch. You don't work for anybody. You don't collect bills from customers. Everything is wonderful. There's a war in Europe and the chicken prices is good. In five years you can retire.

We went up there to look around. We stayed overnight at the Singermans' ranch. I wasn't so sure. Singerman was sitting on the front porch telling us it is wonderful to rock in the chair a full day and breathe the fresh air. And Basha was working in the back field like a horse.

Well, Bernie was out of a job, and he didn't like to look for another one. I wouldn't mind finding a job, but I already had two babies. In those days there wasn't such a thing that women go out to work after they are married. I was before my time.

When I came to America to find my opportunity, I never expected to be on a chicken ranch. But I thought, "Well, we better try Petaluma. At least here I can help with the work."

MORRIS ROGIN [b. 1890; Feodoisiya, Crimea]

Yes, I was a successful businessman selling grain to the chicken ranchers in Petaluma. But my sympathies always were with the workingman. I was with the socialist idea all the way since I was a boy in the Crimea. I got my introduction to socialism when I was thirteen. My sister gave me a novel by the American author Edward Bellamy. In Russia it was titled *A Hundred Years from Now.* Here in America we call it *Looking Backward.*

I joined the Social Democratic Workers party—Sotsial Democrat-icheśkaya Robachaya Partiya, we called it. At the age of fifteen I organized a trade union of juvenile hatmakers—Soyuz Maloletnykh Truzhennikov. Because of my abilities, the party sent me all around the province organizing juvenile unions.

This was during the 1905 Revolution. I saw the *Potemkin* when it came to my town Feodoisiya. This was the famous cruiser that revolted against the tsar. In our town they sent sailors in a motorboat to address the people. I was with the people when we broke through the cordon of police to greet the rebels. The tsar's government was not so popular.

Around that time was my first arrest. I was distributing leaflets calling for a meeting of the Russian parliament, the Duma. I went from house to house with the leaflets, until I came to a house where a police captain lived! [Much laughter.] Three months in jail!

No, that did not scare me. Things like that do not interfere with a man that is seriously in a movement. So he is arrested, he is sentenced, he is jailed. Comes out, he is more revolutionary. In the young days a person does not discontinue being a revolutionary through fear. I was arrested more times before I left Russia.

Why did I leave? Well . . . it happens that—it's hard for me to explain. I was organizing hatmakers, I was working to make a revolution against the tsar. But in 1912 my sister in New York sent me a ship's *karty,* a ticket. She was bringing the family, first one, then another. Well, it's a big opportunity to go to go to a foreign country. You know what I mean? It's an enterprise to go to America. That explains it. I went. I am a socialist, but it just so happens that I am an enterpriser too.

I was with socialism all the way, since I saw the *Potemkin* in the 1905 Revolution. It was natural for me, a workingman, a capmaker, to come to unionism and socialism. The more progressive workers, the more developed workers who understood capitalist exploitation, we were all leaning toward socialism.

After I left the Crimea, I became part of the leadership of the capmakers' union in New York. That's where I met my wife—singing in a Jewish workers' chorus. When we moved to Los Angeles in 1922, again I was elected into the leadership of the local union. In 1925 I was put on the payroll of the International as an organizer of capmakers in San Francisco. I was elated that they recognized my abilities as an organizer.

While I was doing union work in San Francisco, I was active with the Arbeiter Ring, the Workmen's Circle. This was a fraternal organization of Jewish socialist workers. The Northern California District Committee sent me as a representative to a meeting of the Petaluma branch. That is how I first came in 1927.

I liked what I saw in Petaluma. Most of the Jewish people were garment workers like me, but now they raised chickens. I was attracted by the independence of the small farm. I liked the cultural life of the Jewish farmers. Within a matter of weeks we moved onto a Petaluma chicken ranch. For me this was a new enterprise.

BEN HOCHMAN [b. 1888; Byalystock, Ukraine]

My father wanted me to be a *rov,* a rabbi, like him and his father and his father's father. It's not like a rabbi here. They were Talmudic scholars. And they were not just teachers, but judges too. The Jews had their own separate life in Russia, so any trouble they had they came to the *rov.* He was the arbitrator.

Nine and a half years I studied at *yeshiva* [rabbinical academy]. My father had everything prepared for me, even a bride. But I went straight away from it. I was more interested in what was going on in the world. See, there was a strike by the textile workers in our city. A strike was criminal in Russia under the tsar. The Cossacks were sent out to disperse the workers and killed some. I saw this and I was enraged! It went against the tradition of justice of the Prophets.

At that time I found small movements of people who talked about oppression. I dropped out of *yeshiva* and studied Russian so I could learn more. I studied mathematics too. Mathematics I learned so fast that I could earn a living off it. I gave mathematics lessons to *gymnasium* students and Talmud lessons to *yeshiva* students.

That's the way it started. Then I discovered Marxism! That was it! [Laughter.] I was fascinated by the philosophy of historical materialism. I cherished the traditions of social justice of the Prophets, but I became a scientist of society. Marx had ethics and morality, but as a product of material conditions. I took it as the real truth. I joined the Russian Social Revolutionary party. It was populist, not Marxist. It wanted to do away with the tsarist dictatorship through the peasantry, not the working class. I read the literature and then I spread it among the people when the 1905 Revolution started.

I didn't see anything like the 1905 Revolution again. A general strike! Not like what I saw in San Francisco in 1934. This was a political general strike. Everything was closed immediately. The goal was to end the tsarist dictatorship. The entire population was on the streets in towns all over Russia. The tsar got scared and issued a manifesto to the people. What did he call them? "My beloved subjects." Beloved! He said, "I give you a constitution."

But the moment he did it, he organized pogroms. He blamed the Jews for all the problems. In our city the pogrom was instigated by the church and the army. There was a religious parade—thousands of peasants from the villages marching with ikons—and an explosion. The tsar's agents said, "The Jews are attacking the Christians." They went to the Jewish section of town, robbing stores. But the revolutionary movement had a strong self-defense organization. Entire sections of the city the police and the peasants would never dare to show up. When they saw our groups in the streets, they stopped the pogrom and ran away.

The pogrom was unsuccessful the first day. So you know what they did? They called in army regiments. Suddenly Cossacks were riding through the streets. They took the main streets; we took the side streets, which were narrow and we knew them well. We were well armed with Brownings smuggled in from Germany. They shot at us, but they were afraid to come after us. For three days we held off three thousand soldiers. Most of the people were killed at the railroad station. They stopped all the trains that came through, took out the Jews, and shot them on the spot. But they never got to the Jews in the city. We fought them off for three days and then it was stopped.

After, they wanted to put me on trial. One of our group was tortured and he gave them my name. They arrested me for shooting at soldiers. I escaped from jail. I was hidden in another town, with new papers, but somehow the police found me. They questioned me with a gun on the table, but they never touched me. They were afraid that my friends will come after them. For shooting at soldiers they could have hanged me, but they had no evidence, no witnesses. So there was no trial. They just sent me to Siberia by order of the tsar's minister.

I spent my three years in Siberia. It was the northern part, hundreds of miles away from a railroad. They took us by sled. No escape. The government paid the political prisoners six and a half rubles a month to work for the farmers there. I didn't care so much for the money, but I wanted to work. I had an urge to show them that Jews can do it. We were forbidden from farming in Russia, and then they turned the peasants against us: "The Jews live off you." But I was raised on the Bible— we were an agricultural people in ancient times. I always wanted to do agricultural work. In Siberia I plowed the ground, I cut hay with a scythe, I chopped wood. I was a political prisoner, but there you could be a free man. The land was free, the forests were free. You could build, you could hunt, you could fish. Everything was free.

After three years I was freed, so I went home. First thing, my comrades told me the police came to my father's home looking for me. In other words, maybe they found some evidence. I stayed home just a couple of hours. While I'm there the police came again. They asked my father, "Is your son Benjamin here?" My father couldn't speak Russian so he didn't tell them anything. They didn't dare to break in. He's not a worker. He's a rabbi. So they didn't find me.

My parents gave me two hundred rubles my brother sent from the United States. It was ready for me all the time I was in Siberia. The revolutionaries smuggled me out of Russia and across Germany to Rotterdam. I had enough money to buy a second-class ticket instead of steerage, so I could get through customs without questions. I wanted them to know that I am a decent person when I came to the United States.

When I came to New York, I couldn't work for my brother's wig-manufacture business. I was fighting for socialism in the 1905 Revolution. I was a free man living on the land in Siberia for three years. I hated business! I went to school at Cooper Union. I passed the mathematics test and they took me for engineering. Five years I studied. That's where I got my degree in electrical engineering in 1917.

When I graduated I enlisted in the American army. It was a capitalist war for markets, but I had one thing in mind—the danger to the Revolution in Russia. This was the time of Kerensky. It was not yet a socialist revolution, but I was afraid Germany would suppress it and the other revolution I hoped for. I knew well the Bolsheviks will do something if they can. But we *got to stop Germany.*

After the war I worked for General Electric as a troubleshooter with the generators and transformers. I marveled at the technical knowledge of the American workers at General Electric. But they were so backward politically! In Russia, when five hundred workers struck the tsar had to send in soldiers because he was afraid. In America, with thousands of workers in a single plant, I thought they should know they could make a revolution.

You see, the Bolshevik Revolution brought out great hopes from those of us in the left-wing Jewish movement in New York. We thought that with the abolition of private property and organized religion in the Soviet Union, there will be an end to exploitation and there will be equality for all nationalities, including the Jewish people. I read *Ten Days That Shook the World* and I saw how the Bolsheviks turned Russia upside down. When the revolutions came in Germany and Hungary, we thought it was the beginning of world revolution. I often thought, "How will we organize it here in America?" But the workers told me I am a greenhorn to expect a revolution.

In 1924 there was still no sign of revolution, so I thought it was time to learn more about America. With a friend I walked across the country. We walked—over three thousand miles we walked. We were offered rides, but we preferred to walk and meet the people. We stopped wherever we saw workers. We asked them about conditions and we discussed the political situation. We were talking with people across the Middle West, up in Yellowstone Park, down through the Rockies, across the desert in Nevada and California. We went to Los Angeles. In New York they called it *"geneydn hatakhtn"*—"the paradise of the earth."

I couldn't find work in Los Angeles. Nothing. It was then a village. The climate was wonderful and the orange trees were beautiful, but there was no industry. I went up to San Francisco and got a job in the electrical works. Then I met a *landsman* who lived in Petaluma. I saw Petaluma in the spring of 1925.

I always had the desire to be in agriculture. In Siberia I had a chance to work the land, to go with a scythe. I liked the open air and the natural things. They always charged Jews were parasites. This was another reason—I wanted to show them that Jews can produce on the land. And besides, I found out that chickens is a paying business.

I figured, "On a chicken ranch in Petaluma you can be a free man."

MENDEL RUBINSTEIN [b. 1891; Kuhamova, Ukraine]

I was supposed to become a rabbi, but I had a change of heart. In 1904, 1905, started a lot of trouble all over Russia. At that time was war and revolution and pogroms. When something big is going on, you don't feel like being in your own little corner. You want to participate. So I quit *yeshiva*.

The Jewish young people in my *shtetl* were sympathetic to the Revolution. The older people thought the tsar ruled with the will of God and that the Revolution was a sin. They had faith that God will protect us against a pogrom. But the young people formed a Self-Preservation Committee. We patrolled the *shtetl* with guns so the peasants shouldn't attack.

During the 1905 Revolution I became acquainted with modern-thinking people who believed that a Jewish state in Palestine is our Jewish destiny. I joined the Histadrut, the Labor Zionists. We wanted that the Jewish people should move to Palestine, settle on the land in kibbutzim, and build socialism. This was a mixture of ideas from modern nationalism and modern socialism, with the biblical ideal that the Jewish people were an agricultural people.

In 1914 I was ready to leave Russia and be a *khulutz,* a pioneer on a kibbutz in Palestine. But when the First World War broke out, they started drafting young men. You could not get away through the war zone in Europe. I had to go through the Far East toward America. I crossed Siberia by train in seven days. I got off at Station Manchuria in May 1915. I thought the war might end by fall, so I stayed there six months teaching Hebrew. At Station Manchuria and all over the Far East were a lot of Jewish people who were sent to Siberia as political prisoners and remained after they were freed. It was a good field for business there.

The war did not end, so I proceeded on to Harbin. I bought a forged passport for twenty-five rubles and I crossed over the Korean border to Changchun. By train I went to Pusan. Then I took a steamer to Shimonoseki—that is already Japan—and by train to Yokohama.

From there I took the boat for San Francisco. We had on that boat a couple of hundred like me—how do you say it?—"draft dodgers."

A month after I arrived in San Francisco, the Revolution started in Russia. In the beginning the Kerensky rule appealed to a lot of people and nobody expected a Communist revolution. Some of my friends returned to Russia in the next months, but I don't decide so fast. When the Bolsheviks dispersed the Constitutional Assembly and proclaimed the dictatorship of the proletariat, I decided absolutely I will not go back to Russia. I thought, "The Communist terror will not be good for the Jewish people." I remained in San Francisco and became active with the Labor Zionist movement. When the Balfour Declaration came out on November 7, 1917, and the British promised us a Jewish state in Palestine, we were busy raising money, spreading literature, giving talks. At that time nobody thought there will be a Jewish state. We were just talking about Jewish colonization in Palestine.

Did I want to go? Well, I'll tell you what happened. Five months after I came I met my wife. My cousin came home from night school and told me he met there a Palestinke! She came to her brother in San Francisco because life was very hard in Palestine during the war. The next time I delivered a lecture on Zionism, she came with my cousin and we met. She liked my delivery! [Much laughter.] She was an active Zionist like me. We went around for several years and married after the war. We lived in the Fillmore District and had our meals at the *stolovaia*, a collective restaurant our group organized.

It happened that during the war the poultry industry prospered in Petaluma. We knew about it because the Jewish farmers in Petaluma had a close relationship with the Labor Zionist movement. Many thought they would move to Palestine one day.

We just had a baby and I couldn't make enough money in San Francisco. I didn't want to wind up in a vegetable stand or a sweat shop. So we moved onto a chicken ranch in Petaluma. I had been thinking about agriculture for a long time. That was the life style in Palestine. The *khalutzim*, the pioneers, they settled on the land. I thought, "I'll learn how to raise chickens in Petaluma and then maybe we'll go on a kibbutz in Palestine."

YOSSELE GARDNER [b. 1899; Kishinev, Bessarabia]

The bug hit me my first year in America. I became a proletarian, a socialist. All the fellows who worked in the store with me, their hope was to become businessmen. I wanted to work in a factory. I became an embroiderer.

That was 1913. A few years later it was different. Then I wanted to settle in Palestine as a farmer. I was Poale Tsion, Labor Zionist—a Zionist and a socialist. You know, Zionism at that time meant a kibbutz. I was eighteen and I was starting to solve the problems of the world.

That was during the Revolution in Russia. I was a sympathizer when the Bolsheviks promised the Jewish people national self-determination within the Soviet system. But I believed that salvation for the Jewish people is to have our own socialist country.

I joined up with the British army to fight in Palestine. I enlisted with the Jewish Legion, the Jabotinsky Battalion, to force the British to let us build a Jewish nation. I was shipped to Canada for training with a group that happened to include Ben-Gurion, Ben Zvi, and many future leaders of Israel. We fought the Turks in the Jordan Valley.

Palestine was very primitive—a few small towns and barren desert. The only bright spot was a Jewish colony. You could go up on a hill and look around, and if there was a green spot this was a Jewish colony. But the kibbutzim were just established and very poor and very weak. We stole British weapons to help the Jewish settlers defend against the Arabs. The British were not sympathetic to Jewish settlement in Palestine. They organized the Jewish Legion only because they needed political and military support during the war. The British promised Palestine to both the Jews and the Arabs if they would fight the Turks. That was British colonial policy: divide and rule. That was the beginning of the whole mess.

I wanted to settle on a kibbutz, but the British didn't want the Jewish soldiers to stay. The only members of the Jewish Legion who could remain were those like Ben Gurion and Ben Zvi, who were there before the war. Otherwise you had to leave.

I returned to New York and started up work in embroidery again. Did I like the work? Who asked such questions then? I had to make a living. I needed money to bring over the rest of my family from Europe. I had to smuggle some of them in after America closed off immigration in 1924. There was a lot of trouble for me.

In 1928, after I got my family into New York, I got married. I met Emma at a Labor Zionist summer camp. She was a waitress at my table. When you leave you are supposed to give the girl a tip, but I said, "Emma, you're not going to get no tip from me."

"Why?"

"Because I intend to take you out in New York."

After we married we decided to go to California. The boss put in automatic embroidery machines and there was no future for me. Then Emma got pregnant—there was no pill at that time—so what you going to do? But she was a sport. She said, "I want to see California."

In Los Angeles we heard about Petaluma from Labor Zionist *khaverim.* Los Angeles was a scab town—no unions, low wages—so we went up to Petaluma and tried a chicken ranch. I still had it in my mind to be a farmer in Palestine. I thought Petaluma was in that direction.

For years and years my dream was to live in Palestine. But you get involved in taking over the family from Europe, then you meet a girl, you get married, and before you look around she's pregnant. You actually never give up the dream, but you delay it. You say "when the children get older we will go," and when the children get older you say "I cannot take these American kids to live in Palestine."

That's the way it goes. I never made it to a kibbutz. Instead, I found a *shtetl* in California.

3 "Here the Kelleys Live in Town and the Cohens Live on the Farm"

HYMIE GOLDEN

I got the deeds to the Petaluma Jewish Cemetery. Go up there, you can see our whole history in them tombstones. Petaluma was like everywheres else. First it was Sephardic Jews—Spanish—we got a Díaz family from the 1860s. We got lotsa German Jews in there. They was in businesses here in the nineteenth century. Then its my people who came from Russia to raise chickens.

I got the Jewish Cemetery from one of them German Jews. Berger was his name. He didn't know nothing Jewish, he just gave out the plot when someone needs a plot. One day Berger don't wanna do it no more. Says to me, "Listen Golden, you take the cemetery deeds cause I know you gonna take good care." Since then I'm running the cemetery all these years. I figure, "Somebody gotta do things like that." This Berger gave me all the records from the German Jews. [Brings out a box.] It was maybe fifteen, twenty families in here. They had a Society B'nai Israel. For thirty years they made minutes of all the meetings. [Turning pages from a minutebook:] collect dues, rent halls, send money for starving Jews in Russia, find a cantor for the High Holidays, take care the cemetery.

Why did I save it? I figure, "This is our Petaluma history. We gotta keep things like this."

But I'm gonna tell you, the German Jews, they're no good. I know them from World War I, when I was a Russian prisoner of war in Germany. One time the prison camp lets me go to the *shul* for Pesach. I come in my prison uniform, stand by the door for maybe half an hour. They see I am a Jewish prisoner, but nobody comes over. Nobody! They want to show they are good Germans. Actually, them German Jews is Jew haters.

Same thing with the ones I found in Petaluma. Don't wanna have nothing to do with us. The Allens, the Martains, the Bergers . . . more

45

American than the Americans. They had big stores, nice homes in town. Married gentiles. They're mixing in and they don't like the Russian-Jewish people coming here on the chicken ranches.

I figures, "To hell with them. They're gonna disappear. To hell with them."

"DOC BILL" RUTHERFORD [b. 1894; Petaluma]

They had a big influx of Russian Jews come here after World War I. The German Jews that were here already, they called them low class and kikes. That was the first time I heard the word *kike*.

The older Jewish families were upper crust—the backbone of Petaluma in those days. The Steins had the grocery store downtown and that beautiful home up on Liberty Street; they had a Chinese cook and the finest dishes in town. The Bergers had the big yardage store; their son Art sold it and worked for the Petaluma *Argus*. Art married a Christian, like all those kids. We accepted them as part of the upper strata. They were people just like you and I. We never thought of nationalities in those days. There was none of that kind of trouble in this town. We didn't know what a Jew was. People were people.

The German Jews wouldn't have anything to do with the new ones, the ones who settled on the chicken ranches. The Russian Jews were different. They talked with their hands—you know [waving his arms]—excited.

They'd bargain with you . . . tried to beat you down on the price. That's how they paid in the Old Country, because they lived hand-to-mouth back there. Every bill, they'd come in and try to Jew you down. They'd start right in with the . . . [waving his arms]. The German Jews didn't like it. I didn't like it either. I never overcharged, so there was nothing to argue about. I'd let the nurse handle it. And if they did it again, next time she wouldn't give them an appointment. That's what I did. I stopped taking them.

HYMIE GOLDEN

It's a strange thing—very rich German Jews, they always wanted the Russian Jews should be farmers. Baron Rothschild and Baron Hirsch, they gave millions of dollars for it. They wanted to prove that Jewish people are not all merchants and bankers like them.

We had such a thing in Petaluma. There was a High German family in San Francisco, the Haas family from the Levi Strauss Company—they gave money for the Jewish farmers here. They liked it that we raise chickens in Petaluma.

Daniel Koshland, Chairman, Abraham Haas Memorial Fund, remarks from *Second Annual Report,* 1924.

The Abraham Haas Memorial Fund was established by Mrs. Fannie K. Haas and her children with a gift of $50,000.00 "to stimulate Jewish interest in agricultural enterprises." Conditions are such that the Jews may not hope or desire to become an agricultural people. But we feel safe in asserting that there are among the Jews of California many who have a love for the soil.

Since the Fund has come into being, the bulk of our loans were made to the Jewish agricultural settlement in and around Petaluma. We cannot express too strongly the co-operative spirit of the Jewish residents of Petaluma. They have elected a local committee, which gives all our applications the most careful investigation and the most stringent recommendation. Though we have from the beginning felt that the loans which we are making will be repaid, we are more than agreeably surprised at the promptness and regularity of payment thus far.

We believe that this Jewish settlement is making a contribution to the development of agriculture in the life of the Nation, even as the Jewish immigrant has made to the growth of industrial and commercial phases of American life. They may require guidance and help; they surely do not ask for or need "charity." Our work is that of guiding and helping.

HYMIE GOLDEN

I rent this place what I now own on March the nine, 1927, for fifty dollars a month. Start in business with a thousand-dollar loan from the Avram Haas Fund. I got chicks on credit from the hatchery and I got more credit from the Golden Eagle feed company for the food. I raised up six thousand chicks—them little white leghorns.

In twelve weeks I sell the pullets for someone to raise to be laying hens. The cockerels, the roosters, I sell them for meat birds—for the slaughterhouses in San Francisco. Was little birds—in them days, if you raised it to a pound and a half you had a big bird! Made twelve hundred in my first raise! Was a fortune in them days! I take in new chicks and I make more money. With the feed company I establish credit. I work hard and I made pretty good.

Petaluma was a real chicken town in them days. Was called "the Eggbasket of the World." It had that good weather for the chickens— not too hot and not too cold. The land didn't cost much and you gotta lot of people to feed in San Francisco. You walk on Main Street in Petaluma and you seen feed mills and hatcheries. Everything was for the chicken farmer.

Was four, maybe five thousand people around Petaluma then. You had Italian and Portuguese and German and Scandinavian and American.

They was on chicken ranches, dairy ranches, dirt farms. You had a lot of people growing apples and pears and cherries—none of them farmers is in the Jewish cemetery. The most part in here was chicken ranchers and all the Jewish farmers, they was on little chicken ranches. You could raise a whole family on ten acres and a couple thousand hens.

We had maybe one hundred Jewish families when I came in 1927. It was nice—no jealousy between the Jewish people. Some didn't have nothing, some got a little bit, some had more. Nobody's concerned about it. Anybody that came in, they had help from the Jewish chicken ranchers that was here. You need credit from the feed company, somebody's gonna sign to back you. You need an extra fifty dollars for the gas bill, someone just sold the chickens, he's gonna borrow you the money.

When I came in, everybody thought I get help from my brother-in-law Isaac Lipsky. But he thought I was not fit. See, I used to dress nice. He says, "Gigolo! You gonna be a farmer? You never chased a nail in with a hammer. You never had nothing to do with a chicken before. How you gonna do this?" When he comes over to see how much I make a mess, he sees I make a better job than him. I says, "What is it? I give the chickens feed and water. Common sense! You gotta go to college to grow chickens?"

But pheeuuuw, its lotsa hard work! I was growing my own greens for the feed, thousands of plants of kale . . . five in the morning I'm hitching my horse to the wagon cause I'm goin' to pick kale. That kale, I'm cuttin' it up and mixin' with grain . . . carrying them hundred-pound sacks of grain on my shoulder. That's the mash I'm making for my chickens. Sixty buckets of that mash I'm carrying in the morning, eighty pounds in this hand, eighty pounds in that hand. Then I'm doing the whole thing again in the afternoon—seven days a week.

Pretty soon I built me some brooder houses and I'm keeping some of them pullets to be laying hens. You got two thousand of them hens you're like a *kulak* [wealthy peasant] in the 1920s, but them hens make you work. You got hens, then you got eggs. You gotta collect the eggs and you gotta clean the eggs. With a brush on a motor you're cleaning eggs—I'm a good shoeshiner with the eggs! Then you pack 'em. Twice a day, every day, you're collecting and cleaning and packing eggs. I was handling 120, 130 cases a week . . . till twelve, one o'clock at night we were packing eggs. We got the kids sleeping out in the chicken house while we're doing it.

I'm doing everything myself—plumbing, carpenter, I'm doing it all. My chickens need vaccinating, I'm doing it. The chickens get sick from coccytiosis, I'm washing them chicken houses every day. It's hard work, but hard work never killed nobody. You know what kills you? Worries!

Worries will kill you like rust goes in the pipes. You work hard, you eat, you sleep . . . then you gonna be fine.

ANNA ROSENFEILD GOLDEN: I missed the city. When you go outside in the city there's people, there's stores, there's parks. When you live in the city you've got plumbing inside, you can clean the inside, you don't got dirt and bugs all the time. But he said his ulcers will kill him in the city.

And I will tell you, he didn't like the chicken life very much when the chickens got sick with their eyes. You gotta go in there three times a day to wash their eyes. So he says, "I don't want the chickens! I don't like the chickens! You wanna do it, you go wash the chickens in the eyes." So he gets some cows to milk and I take care the chickens.

And nobody's chickens were like my chickens. When I cooked a chicken you could smell it across the hills. You could smell my chicken soup across them hills. How did I make a chicken soup? You take a chicken, you salt it, you cut it up . . . everything, the feet too, you gotta have the feet. You put it in the cold water, oh maybe three quarts, and you cover it and boil it. For an hour you cook it slow and you take off the foam. Then you throw in the vegetables—a carrot you slice, a couple stalks celery, an onion. Salt and pepper too. Then you cook it slow for a couple more hours. When its done you can put it in the refrigerator and take off the fat later. Then you heat it up with the matzo balls or the *kreplakh*. This is chicken soup.

Yeah, the chickens he liked when I'm cooking them. It's when they was alive he hated the chickens.

HYMIE: Anything you do, you gotta have a feeling you like it. Then you succeed. The most Jewish people in Petaluma, they didn't come here to get rich. You can't get rich from the chickens cause you're always gonna hit a bum market one day.

The Jewish people in here, they came to have a better life. In the city, you gotta punch the clock, you gotta smile for the customer even if you feel like to cry. On the chicken ranch I holler any time I want. I like the chickens. I like the birds singing in the morning, I like a garden. On a chicken ranch you can enjoy nature. I love the nature—that's why I was a good rancher. This is the good life for me.

BEN HOCHMAN

I started my ranch with almost no money. I bought four thousand chicks at the hatchery, I said, "What do I have to pay?"

"Two hundred dollars now, if you've got it, two hundred dollars after you sell the chicks."

Then I go to the Golden Eagle feed mill. You need a couple thousand dollars' feed by the time you sell the birds. The credit manager asks me, "How much money do you have?"

"Three hundred dollars."

He says, "All right, give a hundred dollars down and we'll give you credit."

Now mind you, just like that I go into Thomasini Hardware and buy tools. You know, you need shovels and a hammer. He makes out the bill and says, "Shall I charge it?"

I said, "What do you mean 'charge?' " I didn't understand. I lived in New York thirteen years and nobody would trust me anything. I come in there a stranger and he asks me if I want to charge it! I say, "Charge it!"

That's what made Petaluma. The feed companies controlled the land, the banks, the businesses, everything. They gave credit to people so there would be business. They made millions from selling the land and the feed. That's my idea of the picture. And people made a nice living in here with the chickens. The first raise of chickens I made three hundred dollars. I found out quick how to do it.

My second raise, when the feed bill reached two thousand dollars, I needed more credit for feed. The credit manager says, "As a Jew you can get a loan from the Haas Fund."

I applied to the committee of farmers here for a loan of seven hundred dollars, until I sold my chickens. The secretary of the committee, a fellow by the name of Brinkman, says, "We'll recommend you for the Haas Fund committee in San Francisco.

Abraham Haas Loan Fund, *Minute Book,* San Francisco Committee, Meeting of May 10, 1926

New application no. 122, Ben Hochman, Petaluma, applicant for loan of $700. Petaluma committee reporting adversely. Loan declined.

BEN: I waited to hear for some time, but no reply. Brinkman said he doesn't know. So I went to San Francisco to the secretary of the Haas Fund. He said, "We hold it up because the amount is too much for one cosigner. We want two more cosigners."

I told my *landsman* in San Francisco who was my cosigner. He was so mad they refused his signature alone! He said, "To hell with them! I will speak to a friend in Petaluma, Mordecai Haller." So Haller signed for me at the feed company and I made a good profit from this raise.

Later I found out why I did not get a loan from the Haas Fund. These people here, they knew I was exiled to Siberia after the 1905 Revolution, they knew I was a Communist. Mordecai Haller, he was orthodox religious, he didn't care—a Jew is a Jew. But Brinkman, the secretary of the Haas Fund committee here, he was active in the B'nai B'rith. They didn't want any more Communists here. They tried to get rid of me, but they couldn't.

I stayed and I raised chickens. It was a nice life. I had twenty acres of land on the ranch I rented. Not only was I raising chickens, but with a fourteen-inch plow I broke the ground. I grew kale, carrots, potatoes, everything. A Russian friend once told me, "You are a real peasant."

I worked harder on my ranch than I would in a shop, but I felt easier. It made me think of Siberia. On my ranch I had freedom.

MIRIAM HOCHMAN [b. 1895; Tarnapot, Ukraine]: Oooh, it was hard work. Five in the morning we got to do the planting. But I liked it. I came from Montreal with my boys after my first husband died. I had an uncle here. I liked the ranching life. I liked it for the children. It was a nice group of people in here. So I stayed.

BEN: And you liked me too I suppose.

MIRIAM: The machine is recording. Do you have to tell this too?

BEN: Why not?

MIRIAM: The proof is in the pudding. The proof is in the pudding.

SARAH SISKIN WEINSTEIN

If one of my granddaughters asked my advice about going to live on a farm? I would say, "Would you like to take care of chicks, take care of vegetables, take care of the house, wash clothes, iron and sew, and take care of children? And then, when you cook dinner, you have to go outside and pick your own vegetables! Too much work!"

I came to America that I should find my fortune, but all I found was a lot of hard work in Petaluma. Oh, I used to get so disgusted. I'd clean the house in the morning, already in the afternoon you could write your name on the table. And earwigs—you know earwigs?—we got them by the thousands! Bugs and dirt everywhere.

We put $1,200 down payment on a ranch for $5,500. What could you expect for $5,500? It was indoor plumbing, but the house didn't have no gas or electric. No telephone came out there. Old used furniture we had. We didn't even have enough chicken houses. Bernie said, "If you will raise the chicks, I'll build another brooder house." I was green when I made that arrangement. You have to watch chicks all the time, like little babies. When they were five weeks old, they got a sickness like diarrhea and they died like flies. Oh, it was terrible! Then I wished I would be doing my dressmaking in San Francisco better than these things with chickens. I thought about leaving the ranch. Bernie said, "Well, if you want to go back to the city I can start another tailor shop." I thought, to myself, "We'd better stay on the ranch. At least we'll come to something in Petaluma."

That's when I decided I *must* learn to drive. Because the ranch was my life, and I was very isolated on the ranch. Whenever Bernie was ready to go, he couldn't wait ten minutes for me. But when *I* was ready, I had to wait a long time for him. It's not good to depend upon your husband for a ride when you live in the country. So one day I got up the courage and said, "I'm driving to town!" My son Irving wanted to come along. I said, "No! If I have to get killed, I'll get killed by myself!"

I'll never forget it. When I took that car out, it wouldn't stay straight on the road. It went zig zag, zig zag. I thought the whole world was watching me drive crazy. But I made it! I went to town, I turned around, and I came back. And from that time, I drove!

FEYGELE ZEPKIN [b. 1903; Nodvornaya, Ukraine]

I was condemned in Petaluma because I left. They said, "She deserted her husband to become a nurse. She'd rather clean bedpans than be with her husband on the ranch."

I met my second husband, Gus Zepkin, while I was in San Francisco divorcing my first husband. I had a friend—Etta Jacobs—who lived on a Petaluma chicken ranch. We had been together in a vegetarian group back in the New York garment shops. Gus was a bachelor with a big ranch in Petaluma, and when Etta told him about me, he decided he'd like to meet this creature. He came to San Francisco and propositioned me to come work for him as a housekeeper. He lured me up to the country and ended up marrying me. He insisted.

I stayed with Gus on the ranch from 1924 to 1927. I couldn't stand that rural life. All they ever talked about was chickens and chicken feed. Even someone with a fine mind like Hochman. I was suffocating on those chickens and I had to leave. No divorce. I visited Gus from San Francisco, but I could not live on that ranch. I think a number of the Petaluma women wished they had the nerve to do what I did. But most of the Petaluma Jews were jealous because I left the chickens and became a professional. They were all bogged down with "how many eggs did you get today?"

MORRY FINKLESTEIN

What Jewish radical wasn't a vegetarian in the 1920s? We were immigrants from small towns in Europe. The New York life made us sick. That rush—the speed-up in the shops—we couldn't even go to the toilet on time. Our whole generation had stomach troubles. So we became vegetarians.

Evelyn Zepkin and Etta Jacobs—I knew them from New York when they were in a group called the Hygeologists. They were going to save the world if everyone ate raw vegetables only. I once visited their camp near Peekskill. While I was there they said they are going to have supper. I looked for the tables—no tables! Everyone walked around, one with a raw potato, one with a raw carrot, one with raw cabbage.

There were a bunch of them in Petaluma in the 1920s—vegetarian anarchists. Some lived here and others visited for a few months at a time during the slack season in the New York needle trades. These working girls would hitchhike across the country and take a vacation on a Petaluma chicken ranch.

Etta Jacobs' home was their headquarters. Yisroelke couldn't stand them—said they were parasites. For a few months they'd do nothing but eat vegetables and flirt. Some moved in with men here and it turned into permanent living arrangements. For years they didn't marry, because these women didn't believe in any man-made laws.

I first met Petaluma, Petaluma met me, in 1928, ten years before I settled here. I came out to see California like every other Jewish radical in the 1920s. At the Young Communist League in San Francisco I heard about the Jewish chicken ranchers in Petaluma. I came up here and stayed with the Sokolovs. He was very much ahead of his time—a beard, long hair, an anarchist and a vegetarian. He had been a workingman and said, "The hell with the city. I'm going to raise chickens."

In those days, it was a miserable existence here. They worked *so hard* and they were *so poor.* [Laughing.]

Raising chickens was backbreaking work—hauling sacks of feed, picking kale for making feed, taking care of sick chickens. All hours, seven days a week, no vacations, in all kinds of weather. You got that chicken-killing heat in the summers when the chickens would drop like flies, and then the freezing rains in the winter . . . the chicken house floods—can you imagine thousands of chicks swimming for their lives? [Laughing.] Just cleaning those chicken houses between raises . . . a lot of prominent people in this community began by hiring themselves to shovel chicken shit out at chicken houses.

And it was the poverty of the *shtetl.* Outhouses, egg crates for chairs, ragged old clothes. In fact, the Jewish ranches even looked like the ugly muddy homes of the *shtetl*. No flowers. No landscaping. The Jewish ranches were deserts.

But still, I liked it. [Laughing.] There was nature. There was leisure. There was freedom. And there were people—all kinds of interesting people. This was an interesting place.

BASHA SINGERMAN

Such idealists we had in Petaluma! Louis Menuhin—Yehudi's uncle— he was a man, I am telling you! He came to Petaluma before the war. From Palestine he came first to study agriculture at the university in Davis. He wanted to work on a chicken ranch in the summers. So who did he come to? To the Singermans, naturally. We became very dear friends.

At the time of the First World War, in 1917, Louis Menuhin wanted to fight against Germany. He said that any human being with dignity and consideration for mankind must fight against Germany. So what did he do? He joined the Jabotinsky Battalion and he was a soldier in Palestine to help build a Jewish country while he is fighting Germany. While he was there he married a Palestinke and they came to Petaluma after the war. Batya and Louis Menuhin. Shimon helped them start on a ranch. After that, every Zionist who came in here was like the family of the Menuhins.

We also were friends with the brother—Moses Menuhin. They would come from San Francisco to stay on the chicken ranch with the Petaluma Menuhins. In their limousine was a little *teppel* [potty] for Yehudi. He was four years old.

Yehudi! Yes! Yehudi Menuhin! With his violin. Did Yehudi play here in Petaluma? Oh ho ho! He would play a lot. Little Yehudi Menuhin with his little violin.

KHAYA FEINSTEIN

Yehudi's first concert was in San Francisco at the Civic Auditorium. He was nine years old, but they dressed him up in red pants to look younger. Everyone in Petaluma came to see it. Yehudi was from us.

Then the San Francisco Menuhins became very high people. With their limousine they stayed in San Francisco. The father, Moses, he didn't want anything to do with us. Yehudi too . . . his autobiography I read from cover to cover, and not a word about Petaluma. He doesn't want to be associated with chicken farmers.

JACOB FELDMAN [b. 1894; Chelm, Poland]

The Jewish farmers, they didn't want no association with a Jewish businessman in here. The most part of them was radicals. Not all Communists but socialists of one kind or another, the Zionists too. I'll tell you, it was a very wonderful community, but I didn't have no Jewish trade at all. And a couple of times they tore me down that I am a capitalist . . . [Laughing.] They said I am living off the sweat of the poor farmer! I worked eighteen hours a day in my store!

MILLIE FELDMAN [b. 1898; Lodz, Poland]: He didn't want a store when I met him in New York. He made good money cutting ladies' coats, but they were getting consumption. I said, "What's money? Money isn't everything. Let's go to my brother in Fresno."

JACOB: A secondhand store we opened in Turlock. Its near Fresno. I was making money, but in Turlock there was only one other Jew—from Turkey.

MILLIE: Aaach! Jewish! He couldn't talk Jewish! I told Jacob, "We got to live among some Jewish people!"

JACOB: When you give up a business, then you look for another business. I heard there is a nice secondhand store for sale in Petaluma. I didn't even heard of the town, but I packed in the children with the wife and we went to Petaluma. We looked around and in a store window we saw a sign: "Selling out."
  I started in. I said, "My name is Feldman. What you trying to do, sell the stock?" I was just asking.
  "Yeah, I'll sell the stock and the lease."
  He told me $3,000. I said $2,500. We set a deal at $2,700. We went right to the lawyer. I said, "Millie, stay in the store while we make the deal. See if you can sell anything."

MILLIE: We was always working together to help ourselves in the store. Oooh, I got mad at him sometimes. But I didn't show my temper. Never! I never had no temper! Not even with the Jewish people. And the Jewish farmers was very hard customers.

JACOB: I wouldn't say hard and I don't say hard. They was radicals, but they still shopped around where they could buy for a nickel cheaper. No, I don't blame them. They was like all the other customers.

KHAYA FEINSTEIN

We weren't just people who said, "Petaluma looks like a good place for a secondhand store." We weren't just Jewish peasants raising chickens. This was intelligent people who wanted a different kind of life. It was socially active people—cultured people. This was a community of choice people.

We was famous in them days. Yiddish newspaper reporters came to Petaluma from the centers of Jewish culture in New York and Chicago. Every year they wrote about us. Everybody wanted to read about the Jewish life in the *provints*. One reporter who stayed on our ranch, he said it exact. The first day he comes back from a look in town, he says, "It's the strangest thing I have seen in this country. Here the Kelleys live in town and the Cohens live on the farms."

ARTHUR LaSALLE [b. 1901; Petaluma]

The Jewish poultry farmers were accepted by the non-Jewish community. Here in Petaluma no one charged that the Jewish people were rich unproductive merchants who lived off gentile farmers. They were respected as hard-working people who made a decent living in our poultry industry.

In the days of my youth there was a German-Jewish community that was widely known and highly accepted. This was a small, merchant community prior to World War I. They were very successful and mixed in very well. There was great respect shown them by the non-Jewish community.

After World War I we had Jewish people of Polish and Russian citizenship move onto our poultry ranches. These people were well received in the main. They were law-abiding citizens. They were kind and charitable and compassionate. Their children went to our schools without friction. There was no refusal to have them in our lodges and clubs. Of course, like most of our immigrant groups, they were somewhat clannish. In those days they did not mix in civic life, but they were accepted.

Oh, from time to time you'd hear a remark about the Communists in their community. They had some ideological differences which became a problem later. But it didn't result in any real change in the attitude of respect to the Jewish people.

As an attorney, I tried to cement a unity between these fine people and the non-Jewish community. I volunteered my assistance for their community legal business. I attended many of their social functions and made donations to their charities. When they came to me with problems, I offered counsel. I worked closely with Joe Holtzman, the leader of the

Jewish community. He was American-born, from German-Jewish background. He owned our largest department store. Joe was a sparkplug type of man—very energetic, very articulate—a nice-appearing man. He became president of the Chamber of Commerce, a member of our city council, a leader in the Elks and the Lions. He was too busy to be really active in the Jewish community, but he represented their interests to the rest of Petaluma. He was very well thought of, a credit to his people in Petaluma. We worked together for the acceptance of the Jewish people.

DR. MEYER FRIEDMAN [b. 1906; Pruszkow, Poland]

Joe Holtzman was a real *gantser makher* [bigshot] in Petaluma. Of course, they don't like it when a Jew is that successful. The gentiles who praised Joe Holtzman, deep in their hearts they didn't like to see him as the town's outstanding citizen. I know, because I socialized with the prominent people of Petaluma in the twenties and thirties. I was the only Jewish professional man in town.

You see, my grandfather Ben Zion Friedman was the first Jewish chicken rancher in Petaluma. He was an adventurer who left Poland, farmed in Palestine and Argentina, and then made his way to California. In San Francisco he heard it was easy to start a chicken ranch in Petaluma, and that's what he did in 1900. Later he brought four of his children and their families to Petaluma. We were the pioneers.

My father hated Petaluma from the moment we arrived in 1919. He had been a high administrator in Poland. . . . We were the kind of Jews who didn't speak Yiddish—but we lost everything in the war. My father never adjusted to chicken ranching, and he didn't want me to adjust. "You'll not be like these other Jewish children," he'd tell me. "You'll do better than shoveling chicken manure."

I went through college and dental school with help from Joe Holtzman and Augie Lepore, the town banker. Then I established a nice little practice in Petaluma, except that I had no Jewish patients. I never figured out why, but it was all gentiles. They'd say, "We come to you because we know Jewish doctors are good."

I left Petaluma for greater opportunities in San Francisco, but it was a good little town in the twenties and thirties. I had a congenial life there. I'd go to formal-dress dinner parties with town leaders like Arthur La-Salle and Augie Lepore. Joe Holtzman and Art Berger and I were the only Jewish members of the Petaluma Golf and Country Club. My wife was the only Jewish member of the Petaluma Women's Club. Our associations were almost entirely with gentiles.

My only Jewish contact was through B'nai B'rith, which was mostly Jewish businessmen from Santa Rosa and the elite of the Petaluma Jews.

B'nai B'rith was American-oriented, while most of the Jewish chicken ranchers kept to their Yiddish-oriented organizations and affairs. We had to speak for them to the rest of Petaluma. It's a funny thing, I was recognized by the gentiles as a leader of the Jewish community, but I had almost no contact with the Jews.

LOUIS KAEL [b. 1907; Pruszkow, Poland]

One time a committee of *makhers* [big shots] from the B'nai B'rith came to our yard. They wanted Pop to join, but he wouldn't do it. He said, "These High Germans look down on the plain Litvak from Poland. I'll never join."

My pop, Ike Kael, was the real leader of the Petaluma Jewish community. He was the one who built the Petaluma Jewish Community Center. Ike Kael was one of the big men in town. He bought a ranch out by Two Rock, near my grandfather Ben Zion Friedman. That was during World War I, when people in the cities were begging for chicken and eggs. Pop built that place up to a capacity of twenty-five thousand birds.

Pop was a real dealer. He made big money speculating in grain during the war. He always won big in those terrific card games of the Petaluma Jews. He'd bet on anything, outfigure anybody. The wheels were always turning with Pop.

He was respected by the gentiles in Petaluma. Augie Lepore at the Bank of Italy gave loans to dozens of Jewish people on Pop's say-so: "If Ike Kael will cosign, it's good enough for me." One time, after Pop gave a speech at the founding meeting of the Poultry Producers co-operative in Petaluma, everybody gathered around him, and I heard one guy says, "Ike Kael is the one white Jew in Petaluma."

Ike Kael is the man who built the Petaluma Jewish Community Center. Before then the Jewish people rented meeting rooms at Redman's Hall or Danish Hall or the Moose Hall. But with one hundred Jewish families, they needed their own place.

For a couple of years they raised money for a Jewish Center by holding affairs and selling shares for the building. There still wasn't enough, so Ike Kael went down to San Francisco and raised the rest from the Haas family. He convinced them all to come up to Petaluma for the cornerstone ceremony: Mrs. Haas, Walter Haas, Dan Koshland, a couple of rabbis and professors.

That was on March 22, 1925, one of the greatest days in the history of the Petaluma Jewish community. Pop spent the morning taking the Haas family around to see the Jewish chicken ranches. Everyone came back to our ranch for a big lunch of roast chicken. We had apple strudel for desert—no one could make apple strudel like my mom. Ike Kael presided over the ceremony that afternoon. The entire Jewish community was there. All the Petaluma business and political and religious leaders were there. The Haas family was there. Mrs. Haas layed the cornerstone.

There was a banquet at Danish Hall that evening. Joe Holtzman was the emcee. It was a big feast, lots of speeches, and the Haas family gave more money. Then there was singing and dancing late into the night. You should have seen Pop dancing with Mrs. Haas.

KHAYA FEINSTEIN

We was afraid to tell the Haas Fund about all the fighting over building the Jewish Community Center. They want to think all the Jewish chicken ranchers is together, but there was lotsa fighting. See, there was a few orthodox people—the *shul yidn*—they wanted a *shul* [synagogue] where they can *davn* [pray]. Was some Communists, they didn't want no *shul*—you know, religion is the opiate of the people. They just want a community center. The most people here was secular Jews, but the majority felt there should be a *shul* for *yidishe mentshn* who want it. So the compromise was to build a big social hall and a little *shul* in the Jewish Community Center.

Then the *farbrente* Communists—the red hots—they want the *shul* should have a separate entrance. [Laughing.] They said they don't want to walk in the same door with people who are going to pray. We built the Center with one door for all the Jewish people. Some of these Communists was such fanatics they wouldn't buy any shares in the Center because it has a *shul* and one door. [Laughing.] That's why we had more votes than them when the big fights come later.

JACOB FELDMAN

It wasn't just the Communists against the *shul*. It was the Communists, the socialists, the Labor Zionists, the anarchists. They was all radicals in here. They said the *shul yidn* are parasites who do nothing but *davn* [pray] and study, like in the Old Country. You know, *benkl kvetchers*—people who just sit and squeeze whoever will feed them. They said the *shul yidn* are religious fanatics like in the Old Country. But these radicals was the fanatics. They think they gonna get some disease if there's a *shul* in the Center.

You want to know why all these radicals were persuaded to have a *shul*? They gave a little room in the Center for a *shul* so they get free taxes for the building. These radicals didn't want to pay no three hundred dollars a year tax. That's the end of the fight over the *shul*.

HYMIE GOLDEN

When we came it was everyone together in the Jewish Community Center. The women brought food, you could feed a whole Salvation Army. We made masquerade balls at Purim. We had *latke* parties at Channukah. For Pesach it was a big *seder*. Not much religion, but always it is a traditional celebration. Why not? This is our history.

Every night something's doing at the Center. All the political organizations was meeting there. In them days everybody's in the Arbeiter Ring [the Workmen's Circle], even the religious people. Comes a meeting, first it's business—minutes, social affairs, money we are raising. Then there's a talk . . . maybe Jacob Katz talks about what's happening in Palestine or Ben Hochman talks about what's going on in the Soviet Union. We had the Rosen brothers, Rafoelke and Yisroelke—they did readings from the classical Yiddish writers.

Each meeting, another person brought the corned beef. Until two o'clock in the morning we stayed in the Center talking and eating and singing. In them days there was no janitor, so we washed the dishes too.

Lotsa times we had in the Center professional entertainers from the stage in New York. Yiddish entertainers who came to San Francisco—singers, comedians, drama troups—they came to perform for us. We filled the Center for every performance. The Center was packed in them days. Oh yeah! Everybody looked up to the Center. Was like a second home.

SARAH SISKIN WEINSTEIN

There wasn't much doing in Petaluma. The life was boring, kind of lonely—even after I was driving. Where can you drive to in Petaluma?

Yes, we were at the Center. One year Bernie was the president of the Center; another year I was president of the Jewish Women's League. There was dances, holidays, poker games. There was lots of things going on, but the life at the Center didn't thrill me. See, in Petaluma you didn't have no privacy with the Jewish people. They knew what you're feeding the chickens, what you are eating for dinner, how much money you owe the feed company, everything. It was a gossiping community. During the day you would see Jewish men at the feed company talking about such things! In the evening they would just drop in at your ranch and see for themselves. I didn't like it.

JACOB FELDMAN

Was like one family in here. Everybody cares about what's going on with everybody. Everybody comes in the Center. Anytime you feel like it, you take a ride and drop in on somebody. You didn't have to ask in them days. You were welcome. What happened when you drop in? Talk. You talk about the chickens, you talk about the politics, you talk about the other people. You talk and you eat. If you want to do something else, you had a card party. All the time we got together for cards. You show me a Jewish home in Petaluma where they didn't play cards! Show me one house!

I liked to play poker. I liked to play a pinochle. I liked a gin rummy. I wouldn't risk my store. I wouldn't put cards above everything, but I wouldn't make myself for a *tsadik* [holy man] either. We was very big cards players in Petaluma.

BASHA SINGERMAN

Oh, did they play cards in here! Even some of the progressive *khaverim* played cards. Shimon and I never played cards! I was not interested! I would rather read a newspaper and know what is going on. I would rather have a cultural meeting. Such wonderful evenings we had talking about books in Petlauma. Yiddish books—the classical writers, history, politics. Books were our life in Petaluma.

FRAN RUBINSTEIN GINSBERG [b. 1919; Petaluma]

My father always said, "Petaluma is like a little New York." We had maybe one hundred families of Yiddish-speaking people on little chicken ranches, but it could have been the Lower East Side of New York. Our parents belonged to political organizations from New York, they subscribed to all the Yiddish newspapers from New York, they talked about Zionism and communism and socialism and Yiddish culture as if we were in New York. Petaluma had a national and international reputation in those days. "We are *on the map*," my father would say, "because we are an *organized* Jewish farming community. We are something rare in American life."

Many great political leaders who played a part in the formation of Israel visited here. Golda Meir came. Ben Zvi, the second president of Israel, was here. The third president, Zalman Shazar, he came. All the top Zionist leaders, when they came to California to raise money they made three big stops: Los Angeles, San Francisco, and Petaluma.

All the great Jewish intellectuals and artists came to see how the Jewish farmers lived in Petaluma. Our parents came out to hear them lecture. Chaim Ginsberg, a world Zionist leader, he spoke here on Spinoza and Job and the *khasidic* movement. Dr. Zhitlowsky, a great left-wing Yiddishist, he spoke on culture and politics many times. There was a great Hebrew scholar by the name of Yehudi Kaufman who not only would lecture, but he would sing the old Yiddish folk songs. Everyone sang and danced with him till one, two in the morning.

My father was the address for famous visitors. Ben Zvi, who became the second president of Israel, he stayed with us when he came to raise money for Zionism. Professor Warburg, the president of the World Zionist Association, he stayed with us too; he was a professor of botany and my father drove him up to Santa Rosa to meet Luther Burbank. Yossele Rosenblatt, the famous Yiddish singer, he stayed with us when he came to perform at the Center. Any Yiddish author who came, he got a room at our house and my father bought his book.

"That is the beauty of chicken ranching," my father said. "When you work for yourself on a farm you can make time for what is important."

My father was a very learned man. In the Old Country he had studied at *yeshiva* to be a rabbi. The *shul yidn* in Petaluma loved to talk Torah with him, but Torah was all they knew. My father preferred talking with other intellectuals. He'd get together with Mr. Feinstein or the Jacobs brothers in the afternoons and they'd talk for hours talking about literature, history, the state of the world.

My mother worked awfully hard on the ranch and my dad was the scholar. She was ambitious to do better, but he was not so interested in money. He preferred studying. Every morning, after he fed the chickens, he would study for a few hours. And after his studies he would lay down on the couch, put the *Forward* over his face, and take a nap. My mother would say, "Don't disturb him."

There were other Petaluma families like that. It was like in the Old Country where the women worked in the marketplace so the men could study Torah and pray. Only here the work was with chickens and the studies were in Zionism and Marxism and Yiddish literature and modern history.

My parents' generation were very cultured people. They would go all the way to San Francisco for it. On Sundays a whole group of them would crowd into somebody's touring car. They were taking their lives in their hands, because none of those men could drive. With a lurching and jerking of gears, weaving all over the road, they'd wind through the hills to Sausalito and take the ferry over to San Francisco. First they'd go to the big Jewish bookstore on Fillmore Street, and then to the opera at the Civic Auditorium.

They had a very cultural community here in Petaluma with all the activities at the Center. My favorite was when the Rosen brothers did public readings from Sholom Aleichem, Peretz, Avrom Reisen—the Yiddish classics—a beautiful literary Yiddish. The whole community would turn out for those readings. All us kids would crowd up front to hear. Those stories of Sholom Aleichem were so funny! And the food! Our mothers made huge amounts of food when we went to the Center. *Lokshnkugel* and blintzes and knishes and *tsimmes* and *piroshki*—tables and tables loaded with food. This was serious cooking. before the days of diets.

Our parents got together as often as possible. They were just a small group of immigrants living on these poor little chicken ranches outside a little country town. They felt like they were doing the right thing, they had a lot of idealism, but they needed each other's support. They needed a close community like the *shtetlekh* they came from. They would use any excuse to get together. One place, the Gardeners', had so many people every evening that my mother called it the *kretshme,* the inn. Being a kid, nobody paid much attention to me over there, so I'd just wander around the house. It was filled with books. I remember one big volume on the Civil War . . . Mathew Brady pictures . . . I loved that book. I read while my parents visited.

The days might be occupied with the chickens, but there was *always* visiting in the evenings. Then the tea and strudel would come out. They would drink tea the old way, with a sugar cube between the teeth. They talked, they argued, they told stories. Sometimes someone would get out a balalaika or a mandolin and they would sing. I think they were trying to recall what it was like in the Old Country.

4 "In the Darkest Days of the Depression, We Were as Kosher as They Came"

YOSSEL WOLIN [b. 1900; Cracow, Poland]

If you had a *yidisher kop* [Jewish brains], you could make good money in the chicken business. That was my problem. When I came to Petaluma in 1924, I thought I would learn fast and then go on a kibbutz in Palestine. But I had the nerve for business, I was expanding my ranch all the time. And, well, when you're making money it's hard to leave for Palestine.

The problem was, I started to speculate in the stock market. I had a friend named Kael, a leader in the Jewish community. He made money on Bank of Italy stock. So I went into the bank and said to Mr. Lepore, "I want to buy some stock."

"You have to go to a broker in San Francisco."

I learned fast. On the stock market it was so nice! They sold you the stock on 5-percent margin, no questions. It wasn't like the chicken business where you sweat in the chicken house and hock yourself to the feed mill for credit.

I was running my business on half air. With Kael I went to the stock market in San Francisco every day. I hired a man to work my ranch, and with the chicken profits I speculated. I made thousands of dollars in the market.

Meyer Levy, Secretary, Abraham Haas Loan Fund to Moses Brinkman, Petaluma Committee, December 7, 1928

Do you know if there is any way we can secure a payment from Yossel Wolin? Since last February we have received no remittance from him. There is a balance due on his loan of $500 without accrued interest, and although I have repeatedly written to him have received no response. Mr. Tompkins of the Golden Eagle Milling Co. spoke to me some time ago regarding him stating that he has the money but is spending most of his time in the city playing the stock market. Can you have any influence with him?

YOSSEL: By 1929 I accumulated over $80,000 in the market. On Fridays I would pull out a little money to live, but one Friday I had a cold and I didn't go down there. By Monday my $80,000 dropped to equity—around $20,000. I put in to sell on Monday. If I would sell at that price I would be all right. But in one morning I was wiped out of the whole thing.

I had to sell my ranch to pay my feed bill to the Golden Eagle feed mill. I got cleaned out! *Every dime!* And when you don't have a dime, it's hard to go to Palestine.

DR. MEYER FRIEDMAN

It was a pitiful thing. My uncle Ike Kael—that's the father of the movie critic Pauline Kael—he lost everything in the stock market. Until then he was a very distinguished man in Petaluma

PAULINE KAEL [b. 1923; Petaluma]

Chicken ranching? I can't remember a thing about it. But just ask me about the Mystic Movie Theater in Petaluma.

LOUIS KAEL

My sister Pauline was just a little *pisherke* when the tragedy happened. I already was working in San Francisco. One night I got a call from my grandfather Ben Zion: "Leybl, *groise gehakhte tsores*"—"there's a lot of trouble." We were wiped out.

You see, Pop had over $100,000 tied up in the stock market. Everything was going good until he decided to sell the market short. He invested a lot of money expecting the market to drop. But this was 1928 and the market kept rising. Every time it went up, Pop had to raise more money to hang onto the stock. He put up everything he owned as security, and still he was short. He went to the Haas family—Daniel Koshland and Walter Haas—and they put up $10,000. The Golden Eagle feed company lent him another $5,000. And it wasn't enough.

If Pop could have held out one more day, he would have been a millionaire. Augie Lepore was willing to lend him money from the Bank of Italy, but Giannini himself gave the order: "Ike Kael must turn everything over to us." They wiped us out.

Through the whole thing, not a one of those Jewish chicken ranchers offered to help. Pop helped settle those people. He built the Jewish Community Center. There would have been no Petaluma Jewish community without Ike Kael. But they walked on the other side of the street at the end.

Ike Kael left without a goodbye. He packed the furniture and the family into the Big Six Studebaker, and he drove us into San Francisco. He never went back to Petaluma. Hell no.

MENDEL RUBINSTEIN

It was very bad at the beginning of the Depression. At one time I could have lost everything. The Kuhn Brothers feed company was about to foreclose because I owed a $5,000 feed bill. My wife had to go back to Palestine to sell some land to pay the bill. They put a sheriff on my ranch to see that I don't run away with the hens in the middle of the night! I was lucky. Some lost their ranches and went to the city. What could I do in the city without a penny? I was in my forties, with a family to feed and no skills to sell. What could I do?

SID JACOBS [b. 1920; Petaluma]

Nobody told you about the fires? It happened through the Depression—especially at the beginning—for the insurance. Yeah, Jewish chicken ranchers. But it was a Russian who was supposed to be torching the buildings. They'd hire him, go to the Center for the evening, and return to find their house burned. Only the living houses. [Laughing.] They needed the chicken houses to raise the chickens.

Meyer Levy, "Report on Financial Transactions of Fiscal Year 1931," Abraham Haas Loan Fund

The loans granted this year show a considerable decrease in comparison with 1929 and 1930. I think it is better for the Fund that this was the case. Quite a number who were cleaned out by the Golden Eagle Milling Co. in December 1930, when the slump in the poultry business occurred, have been unable to make but very few payments or none at all, for the reason that they have nothing to work with. They have applications in, on which we have not acted and the raises of poultry that they have made have possibly given them just enough income to carry through with food. I think it has been very good for the Petaluma colony that we have not made it so easy for them as they had the idea that our funds were unlimited and that whenever they required money all they had to do was apply for it.

"The Jewish Farmers Community Aid Association of Petaluma," *Tenth Anniversary Souvenir Program*, Petaluma Jewish Community Center, 1934

Seven or eight years ago, several Petaluma residents felt the need for a mutual aid organization of some kind. A place where a member would be able to turn to when in a pinch in in need of a small sum of money; and where he would be able to obtain that loan without too many questions being asked and too much red tape involved. . . .

This desire finally crystallized into several meetings and discussions looking to the formation of such a mutual aid. . . . After these preliminary gatherings, a general meeting was called in November, 1927, and led to the formation of the Jewish Community Aid Association. By-laws were drawn up and a charter secured. A governing committee of five as decided upon . . . $10,000 stock was issued, of which $2,000.00 was immediately purchased by 37 shareholders.

When the crisis [the Depression] hit Petaluma, the need for this mutual loan was quickly apparent. This can be readily understood when it is noted that members availed themselves even of loans as small as $50 to tide them over. . . . No money has thus far been lost, although Petaluma went through a very critical period, many farmers being forced out of business.

HYMIE GOLDEN

Everyone was going broke in the Hoover Depression. No more help from the Haas Fund. There's not too much in our own Jewish loan society. Sooner or later, you're gonna be talking with that feed company.

See, the most people had to buy feed on credit from a feed company. The feed company takes a mortgage on your chickens—maybe on the ranch too. If you sell an egg, you gotta pay the feed company first. It's called a chattel mortgage. The feed companies was using this arrangement to rob the farmers. Sometimes its no credit. Sometimes its high feed prices. Sometimes they take the chickens—even the ranches they took.

They was hard on the Jewish farmer. One time, when I see I am charged more for feed than a Christian farmer, I go right into the office of the president of the feed mill. He says some Jewish farmers are selling the chickens and running away without paying the feed bill. Says when the feed company comes to take the chickens from some Jewish farmers, already they have smuggled the good hens onto another ranch and leave the tired old hens for the feed company. Says the Jewish farmer is a bad risk and they got to charge him more. I shouted the holy hell at him: "I'm here for five years now! I pay my debts and I'm not going nowhere!" He gave me that feed at the right price.

Another time, I had a problem with a manager of a feed house. He was a German, a Nazi. That feed house had a chattel on some of my chickens.

One day he puts a chit on my chickens that I can't sell them. Tell you what happened. Two Jewish bachelors rented a ranch on my lane. They borrowed feed from that German manager, sold the chickens, and ran away with the money. After they run off, that manager says to me, "Golden, why didn't you tell me they will do this?"

"How should I know?"

Said, "All you Jews is in with the others." He took some of the chickens and puts a chit on the rest. But the hatchery had a chattel on those chickens too. The hatcheryman was another German, but he's a good man. He says, "Don't worry. No one will touch those birds. They belong to me too. I will get you feed from another mill."

That's the way it was. I raised out those chickens and paid my bills. For a while everything goes good with the feed mill. Then I get an epidemic with my chickens. Same day, the feed company sends out a truck and takes every bird. Just like that. I tell them, "It's like the coal mines. The boss got all the money. The workers don't have nothing all their life. The only difference is that we don't even got a company store to feed us."

Meyer Levy, "Statement Concerning the Fiscal Year 1932," Abraham Haas Loan Fund

The payments during the past year have been extremely small in comparison with previous years. With about 50% of the Petaluma borrowers I have had personal interviews and they all claim and I believe their claims are justifiable, that they are unable to make any better payments than they have. 1932 was a hard year on the poultry producers. Rates were below the cost of production, and the Golden Eagle Milling Co. having restricted credit, their successive raises of poultry were made with smaller flocks, which produced less income.

A number of them have temporarily abandoned poultry raising and are making an effort to support their families by working at whatever presents itself. The various banks holding mortgages against our borrowers have been very lenient with them. We have quite a number of frozen loans against which the borrowers are unable to make either interest or loan payments and I presume we must have patience until conditions change.

BASHA SINGERMAN

In the Depression they were taking everything. I'm telling you, the feed companies and the banks, they wanted every cent you had. From Shimon and me they took half our land. Other people they were foreclosing and taking the whole ranch. Some of the progressive *khaverim* went back to live in the Soviet Union where they would find social justice. This was a terrible time! Terrible!

KHAYA FEINSTEIN

For ten years everyone was broke on the chicken ranches. Some of the Zionist *khaverim* left for Palestine. Batya Menuhin went in 1935—she carried Louis' ashes so he should rest in Israel. The Kravitzes, they were from my old kibbutz group, they went in 1935. In 1936 we were ready to go. We thought, "Why be poor in Petaluma when we can be poor in Palestine?" But then we heard there are pogroms in Palestine. So we waited. We waited and we had another son and we stayed.

In 1937, we bought this ranch. There were hundreds of farms on the market, cheap, but who had the money to buy? We were helped by a good friend of my husband, Augie Lepore at the Bank of Italy. He said, "Pay the interest on the mortgage now; pay the rest when you can." The bank and the feed company had confidence in the ability of my husband. All those terrible years they stood behind us.

AARON WAGNER [b. 1906; Petaluma]

I worked for the Bank of America all my life. When I started it was the Bank of Italy. I was the only Jewish person in the bank here. But it just happened that way. They didn't discriminate.

I never got too involved with the Jewish community. My wife was not Jewish. I was more active with the Lions Club and the Native Sons of the Golden West. I just so happens that I was the only Jewish fellow in the Native Sons.

You see, my parents were from Austria and they had a store here in town for many years. They never went into the chicken business. We didn't have much contact with the Jewish chicken ranchers from Russia.

I was never ashamed of being Jewish if anybody wanted to know. And if somebody said something against the Jews, I'd come right out with it: "I happen to be Jewish." But I never had any problems.

I worked for the Bank of America here for over thirty-seven years, from 1923 on. I saw it go from Sonoma County National Bank to Bank of Italy to Bank of America. I remember Mr. Giannini coming up here with his chauffeur when he was visiting the branches.

I knew a good number of the Russian Jewish people who banked with us. A lot of these people were green. They immigrated here thinking money falls out of the sky and you pick it off the streets. Until the Depression, they were making a living from raising a thousand chickens. Food was cheap, they did their own labor, they'd have a little job on the side. In those days, if a person had five or six thousand laying hens, he was considered a big shot in the chicken business. Some of them who had been here for a while were doing pretty well until the crash.

They complained when the hard times came. But you have to understand, the feed companies and the banks could have taken all the ranches in Petaluma if we wanted to get tough and foreclose. These little ranchers couldn't pay their bills. But what was the Bank of Italy going to do with hundreds of little chicken ranches? We worked with the more capable ranchers who hung on. Kept 'em going until they could make a go of it.

HYMIE GOLDEN

Bank of Italy was a robbin' bank. American Trust would foreclose and sell the ranch back to the owner. Bank of Italy sold it to someone else for half the price. They wouldn't give you the satisfaction of buying back your place.

I had a two-year lease when I was renting this ranch from Bank of Italy. One day some people come around and want to buy. I told them, "You can't take possession for a year."

The bank called me and said, "What's the big idea? That lease don't mean nothing!"

They think I'm a greenhorn. What I know? But I took that lease to the County in Santa Rosa, and I recorded it. Then it was cooked! They couldn't do nothing till the lease is over. They said I should buy the ranch. They want $8,000. I say, "$6,500." They say, "No, $7,000, no less." I said, "Listen, I'll give you $6,700." I bought it.

It was hard times, getting worse. When I bought I figured I could make the payments. Then Roosevelt came in with a moratorium: they can't foreclose on you without a good reason. Comes a time when I couldn't make a payment for three months. The banker calls me in: "We have to take action."

I says to him, "You have to take action! Listen! Do you know what's the difference between me and a janitor?"

"No."

I says, "I'll tell you. A janitor, he takes care of somebody else's property, he gets paid. I'm taking care of your property, you get paid!"

Just like that . . . and I walked out! Can you get blood from a turnip?

ANNA ROSENFIELD GOLDEN: He's some cookie!

HYMIE: Things change and I make money. Still the wife does not like the life on the ranch. In 1935 I give her the cure. I sell the chickens and we take a vacation to her family in Philadelphia. Was July. Was hot and sticky. Was dirty and noisy. After one week she says, "Let's go home." I say, "No, we stay longer." We stay the whole summer in Philadelphia. That cures her.

When we come home, we fix up the house for the first time. For eight years she wouldn't buy nothing because she didn't want to stay in Petaluma. After she got cured in Philadelphia, we bought furniture.

ANNA: Up to this day I would live in the city, but it got so that I liked the chicken life better than him. He didn't like the chickens cause they're always getting sick. He says the chickens will give him ulcers like the city. So I always take care the chickens and he gets more cows from himself.

HYMIE: I made good money after we decide to stay. Besides the chickens I got in some cows. The most Jewish people in here, they was afraid of cows. It's a more complicated animal than a chicken. But I started a dairy herd. I delivered milk to customers myself . . . in the middle of the night I'm delivering milk in my old touring car that I chopped down to be a pick-up truck.

I was successful because I did everything myself—the plumbing, the electricity, the carpenter. If the chicken is sick, I'm taking care of that chicken myself. If the cow is in labor, I'm there to stick the hand in and help. Every year I've got a big vegetable garden, with flowers too. Other Jewish people didn't do this with the flowers. It has to be in you. That's why I made pretty good in the Depression time.

SARAH SISKIN WEINSTEIN

Bernie got sick in 1930. One night they delivered a big load of feed. It was very windy, but Bernie was out there joking with the driver. I told him, "You better go in the house. You'll get sick." He said, "No, I'll be all right." And sure enough, in the morning he got a hemorrhage. He had TB from the lungs. When he came home from the hospital he still wasn't well. He was a big man, he looked healthy, but he couldn't do any work.

You can't believe all the aggravation I had. At that time it was the Depression. Seymour had to come home from college. You can't believe how hard I worked just to save the ranch. This was not the opportunity I was looking for when I came to America. We didn't get in trouble because I ran the ranch like a business. I cut back on the production for a few years. I got the best prices for feed and chickens. I got the most from the equipments. We weren't high spenders. Other Jewish ranchers went to the operas and bought fancy clothes. They remodeled fancy the living house, and before you know they were bankrupt.

Later in the 1930s when we was doing better, then I hired some help. This too I had to do, because Bernie didn't do it right. You needed people who are fit for farm work, and you had to tell them what to do. Bernie was afraid. I knew what I wanted and I said it.

I did so well that we bought the next property. I gave my son, Irving, our old house, but I wouldn't take the house on the new place. I told Bernie, "Listen! Since I came on the ranch in 1916 I wanted a new house. I worked hard for twenty-two years. I want a new house!" And *I got it!* The contractor built it just how I wanted. More closet space, more shelves, a big kitchen, a dinette. Everything was tight so there should be no earwigs inside. And out in front I had a lawn with flowers.

All the years we were in Petaluma I thought we were poor people. We always owed money to the feed company. But since we had that new house, I knew I had something.

MOLLY ROSENFIELD LIPSKY

In 1928 Isaac started to feel sick, sick. The doctor said it was tonsils. Tonsils! A man from thirty-seven, they should bother him so much tonsils? I couldn't believe it. But he went to Mount Zion Hospital in San Francisco and they take out the tonsils.

I came the next day, he was green, yellow, blue in the face. He says, "They want to take out the adenoids."

"What for?"

"For a crooked nose."

"I don't want they should do it."

Meantime the doctor comes in. Says, "Has to be done!" I didn't know what to do. I was green at that time. So they take out the adenoids.

I take Isaac home from Mount Zion, one morning he wakes up and screams, "I can't move! I can't move!" He was paralyzed. I took him to St. Francis Hospital in San Francisco. The doctor says, "He didn't need the operation on the tonsils. He was too weak for the operation on the adenoids. That's why he got paralyzed."

Four months in St. Francis, still he's absolutely paralyzed. Finally the doctor says, "Well my boy, we can't do nothing for you."

Isaac says, "Doctor, I can't go home! I'm a cripple! I can't do nothing. I have a family to feed. Help me!"

My in-laws say my parents should come to take care the ranch and I should take care Isaac. I say, "He married me. I'll do everything."

I brought him home in 1929. A big man, he can't do anything! For two years he was laying bed, didn't move a joint. Then he was walking on crutches a little bit, but still he's very discouraged.

While I'm taking care Isaac, I'm raising the chickens. Little by little, I made some good raises. [Laughing.] I had to make a living. My son helped, but it was bad in the Depression. The boys grow up with no dollar, no nothing. I dressed so I was ashamed for people to see me. We didn't have no radio. We didn't have no frigidaire. We was very plain.

One thing, we always had a lot of food. Sixteen hours a day we worked, eighteen hours, but we survived. [Laughing.] It's like when I'm escaping from Russia. When you have to survive, you survives.

MORRY FINKLESTEIN

We arrived in Petaluma with nothing but an old Ford and Stella's forty-nine-dollar Sears Roebuck sewing machine. We rented a ranch from a very romantic Yiddish literary gentleman, the kind of man who liked to look at the stars. He said he got disgusted with chicken shit and wanted to live in the city.

I first visited Petaluma in the 1920s, when I discovered all the vegetarians raising chickens, but I was back in New York when the Depression hit. I heard that it really hit them hard in Petaluma, but New York was a disaster too. I went to Los Angeles looking for work—that's where I met Stella, in a garment shop. Conditions were terrible in Los Angeles and finally I got disgusted. I said, "Stella, we're going to Petaluma!"

We made some money on our first raises of chicken, so we decided to rent our present ranch, which is a few miles from Sebastopol. When our Jewish friends heard about it, they said, "Where are you going?" They thought we will be away from civilization. Fifteen miles from Petaluma! Ben Hochman said, "The chicken dealers won't come out there to buy your chickens!" [Laughing.] The sophisticate . . . Hochman . . . they all thought we are crazy for moving onto this property.

You know what it was? They wanted to live close to one another. They were so provincial. Later I discovered that chicken ranchers lived fifty miles out from Petaluma! The chicken dealers came!

STELLA FINKLESTEIN [b. 1908; New York City]: There were stranger things. When we rented our first ranch from that "literary man," a friend explained, "You don't know why Chaim is leaving? He has to sell because Yentela can't do all the work anymore."

A lot of these Jewish men had it easy here. Petaluma had some very charming, totally irresponsible guys who read, visited, discussed world problems—who'd do anything but work on their ranches. They always had some perfectly good excuse—asthma or back problems or some such thing. So the wives did all the ranch work. It was this old-fashioned Jewish business of the men studying and the wives slaving their lives away.

Some of these guys spent their time hunting on the side, if you know what I mean. When I sold our first raise of chickens after we arrived, the chicken dealer who bought them was very nice and attentive. "I see you raise a good chicken," he'd say. I was flattered, until a few months later I learned that guy was a Don Juan. That was his line!

Some women rebelled. One had a husband who couldn't work the ranch and wasn't much of a man, if you know what I mean. A war injury. She needed consolation, and there was no lack of accommodating gentlemen. She wasn't living in sin—she was living in sin*s!* Everyone knew—there were no secrets. The wife of one of those gentlemen beat her up on Main Street one day!

Other women left their husbands and went to San Francisco. The Jews here had an expression to describe them: *froy mit an oyerring*—a woman with gypsy ears—with an earring. It meant that she was shrewd and calculating, someone to be dealt with, a woman and then some! But I thought that the ones who left were gay and vivacious. They didn't want the drudgery of the woman's life on the chicken ranch.

Those who remained with "sick" husbands were strong, hardworking, devoted women. They suffered terribly during the Depression. Their families were in perpetual debt. They were always begging the feed companies for more credit. They'd run the ranch, raise the children, and take care of these "sick" men. Take Isak and Fanny Laub. He read literature, talked philosophy, and built furniture. She ran the chicken business. How she worked!

MORRY: Well, he did have a heart deficiency.

STELLA: This is not the point.

MORRY: The point is that he dropped dead! None of us believed he had a heart condition. I didn't. But one day he was fixing a chair and he dropped dead from a heart attack. Fanny was left with the ranch and managed very well. She always was the mainstay of the work there.

STELLA: And that sums up the position of Jewish women in Petaluma.

MORRY: Come on. This is an exaggeration. In comparison to the gentile farm wives, the Jewish women were queens.

STELLA: No!

MORRY: And compared to the Japanese women . . .

STELLA: The only difference is that the Japanese women had no outside interests. The Jewish women not only worked on the ranches and raised the families, but they were active in organizations and they entertained hordes of visitors in the evenings. And when the women couldn't work anymore, the men had to sell the ranch.

MORRY: Oh, Stella, this is pure—I don't want to use a bad word—pure baloney! The women were very conscientious, but there were many competent men who operated ranches. You are building up a case of women against men! This is chauvinistic the other way! Some of the men worked themselves to death. Didn't they?

STELLA: Did they? Did they? I don't know of any.

MORRY: You think Ben Hochman didn't work? You think Yossele Gardener didn't work?

STELLA: What about Miriam? What about Emma?

MORRY: They worked too! Who had money to hire help? This was the 1930s. These were little family farms. Everyone was a slave on a chicken ranch in the Depression!

YOSSELE GARDNER

There was an expression the Los Angeles Jews had for Petaluma: *"Ligt afn couch, makht gelt"*—"You lie on the couch and you make money."

My eyes almost popped out with all the work. Starting a ranch in the Depression, you needed more than ideals that Jews should live on the land. Fortunately, Emma, being a former factory girl, she knew how to work, and so did I. I became a crackerjack with the chickens and she was the green-finger expert.

We never would have made it without help from the other people. When we arrived one let us stay in his house, another found us a ranch from someone moving to the Soviet Union. People showed us what to do with the chickens. Even money they loaned us, in the hard times, with no question that we will pay back. They were like family actually.

When I made good, I had a big part in expanding help for others. Besides the one-to-one help, I was active with our Jewish Farmers Community Aid Association. I cosigned for dozens of loans, and sometimes I had to pay for people who went bankrupt. In fact, one time, when I missed a meeting of the loan society, the board of directors made a resolution that they won't take my signature to back up any more loans. Because I was giving away too much of my money.

KHAYA FEINSTEIN

The new people that came here, they had to live up to our ways of life. It was the kind of place where nobody would cheat off anybody else. Our chicken ranchers were *erlikhe mentshn*—truly honest good Jewish people. Of course, the chicken dealers were trying to—well, I don't want to say anything bad [laughing]—but they were a little—well, they were a little not scrupulous.

MORRY FINKLESTEIN

If you didn't watch the chicken dealers, they'd skin you like the peasants they used to cheat in the Ukraine. Even when you watched, you couldn't have eyes all over. Such schemes! What these people did for money was extraordinary. When we first moved here, before our neighbors knew we were Jewish, they warned us about the Jewish chicken dealers. These chicken dealers gave all the Jewish people black eyes with the *goyim*.

Eli Nachman, he became rich buying and selling chickens, he would distract you by arguing with his helper while he did his counting tricks. Bella Sachs—she was really something with the swearing and the heavy hand on the scale. Jake Pinzur did his maneuvers with a fast pencil on the paper.

There was another crook, he had false weights in his scales. One time the *goy* who sold him chickens got suspicious after the sale and had the sheriff stop him on the highway to the slaughterhouse in San Francisco. They reweighed the birds and checked his scale. He got caught!

This guy was a left-winger, a cynic who said he was just making a living in a capitalist society. I don't have a grudge against a dead person—personally I liked him. But when he died, on the tombstone it said, "He Believed in Justice." I said to Stella, "Some justice he did to the chicken rancher."

STELLA FINKLESTEIN: You should go out to the Jewish Cemetery. You can see the tombstone! It's a scandal!

LOU GREEN [b. 1922; Petaluma]

My father was a chicken dealer, so I saw it all. The ranchers had a few tricks of their own to put extra weight on the birds before the dealer came: last minute feedings, salt in the feed to make them drink more water, sand in the feed. But you couldn't fool the chicken dealer. Sooner or later he came out ahead, like a used-car salesman. My father specialized in old leghorn hens. He'd buy 'em and "manicure" 'em, which meant clipping the spurs that had been growing since they were eighteen months. Then he'd sell 'em back to these German ranchers as yearlings.

Sometimes my father would go partners with Eli Nachman. This Eli had a reputation for being fast, and my father was no slouch. Once they bought a load of hens from a farmer out in the boondocks. When they started loading the birds, this guy pulls out a badge and says, "I'm a deputy sheriff. I've heard about you Petaluma chicken dealers. Don't try to pull anything."

That was a challenge to Eli. He started double counting, stealing hens right in front of this sheriff. So finally my dad says to Eli in Yiddish, "*Got in himl, loz im khotsch zayn* badge"—"For God's sake, at least leave the guy his badge."

BILL HAWLEY [b. 1921; Petaluma]

Herbert Sakan was one very loving chicken dealer. After my parents died, he saw that I was alone, just scrounging on the ranch. He kind of took me into his family and into the Jewish community. He was very good to me. Young people need family, and he saw that I didn't have any, and he supplied it to me. The Sakans were very protective of me.

It was pretty funny, an obvious gentile like me spending so much time at the Jewish Community Center with the Sakan family. At first the other Jewish people called me "the *goy*," but then they realized that I was learning Yiddish. And since the Sakans vouched for me, I was accepted.

The Jewish community were warm, fun-loving people with quick humor. They were mentally sharp people, especially in business—especially Herbert Sakan and his twin brother. The Sakans had more drive, more ambition, more *yidisher kop* than the others. Life had never been easy for them, and they liked nice things. They worked very hard and they were very shrewd. They knew how to find an edge and use it. Dealing chickens was a big shell game, and the Sakans never lost.

ELLEN MACKENZIE [b. 1903; Petaluma]

The Jewish people were sharp operators. They didn't do things on a small scale, even in the hard times. We weren't that kind—we were afraid of losing our ranches—but they had the push and the know-how. I never heard of any Jewish farmers going broke.

They were close-knit people, always helping each other. They were friendly to others too. They'd always give you a hand finding a good furniture deal in San Francisco. If you stopped over, they always gave you borscht or stuffed cabbage or something to eat when you went into their homes.

Another thing—they liked their card games. No, we didn't play with them. They asked us, but we weren't good enough card sharks.

JIM BAXTER [b. 1902; Petaluma]

The Jewish chicken ranchers were the most cooperative-minded people I've known. They came from persecution in Russia, so they had a tradition of helping each other. They had a socialistic viewpoint too. It figures that they were the ones who established the Petaluma Co-op Hatchery in 1936. They understood that by banding together they could produce better chicks at a cheaper cost to everyone.

Of course, you know how your people like to argue. At every meeting I thought they would break up the Co-op with their vitriolic statements against each other. The issues had to do with who got the best chicks and who was charged what, but they all made orations with biblical parables and world politics. And no one could speak sitting in a chair; each came to the front and delivered a fiery speech. The women too—they didn't take a back seat to anyone.

I was the assistant manager of the Co-op Hatchery for many years. I learned that arguing was just their natural way of life. After those hot meetings, everybody was just as friendly as can be over coffee and cake. Oh, the pastries they brought to those meetings!

I never completely understood them. The Jewish chicken ranchers were great idealists with their socialist philosophies and their cooperative spirit. But when it came to business, they were shrewd and enterprising realists. That's why the Co-op Hatchery succeeded. They wanted to know the bottom line on everything.

NORMAN HALLER [b. 1917; San Francisco]

My father, Mordecai Haller, was the spiritual leader and the business leader of the Jewish community. He was a learned man who graduated from *yeshiva* in the Old Country. He was one of the few people in Petaluma who knew how to read Torah and interpret Talmud. He was the *shoykhet* [ritual slaughterer] for those who wanted kosher meat and he conducted services every Saturday morning. He was like the rabbi.

My father was respected as a businessman too. He was a coppersmith by trade, so in the twenties he opened a little sheetmetal shop in town while he raised chickens on the ranch. He specialized in poultry implements—feed hoppers, incubators, pipe nipples, ventilation shafts. He invented some of it, like an automatic egg turner and a new gas stove for the brooder houses. And on the side, kind of quiet like, he built stills for these dairy farmers way out in the hills.

He was an innovator with the chickens too. When my father heard that Cornell University found a way to get more eggs in the wintertime, he tried it first. The trick was to make the daylight seem longer. To do that, he installed electric lights in the brooder houses and he rigged an alarm clock with a switch to turn on the lights at four in the morning. The other farmers thought my father was crazy. They said, "This is not New York where you can fool the chickens." But he got results.

During the Depression my father went broke a couple of times with the chickens, so he started the first Jewish feed business in Petaluma. He began on a shoestring. We'd pick up a dozen sacks of wheat and cracked corn out in the Central Valley and haul it back in an old touring car with the top chopped down. We ran it through an old feed grinder, attached to a mixer, all powered with an old car engine. We'd toss in some greens, maybe a little horsemeat, add some left-over skim milk and vegetables— you name it.

My father could sell that feed. He was a good salesman, very persistent and very convincing. He had to finance it day to day, swapping checks with customers, borrowing here and paying there, and before you know it he was giving feed on credit to a lot of Jewish ranchers. You never knew exactly what would be in our feed, but for those days it was good feed and we turned a good profit. That was the beginning of the Haller Feed Company.

Yossele Gardner

The *alter* Haller [elder Haller] started the first Jewish big business in Petaluma. That came after his sheetmetal shop [laughing]—every once in a while those brooder stoves he invented would blow up in your face! He was a *shul yid*—big white beard, very dignified, a learned man and very orthodox. But you had to keep an eye on him in business. Nothing dishonest—just a lot of maneuvering.

Well, Haller wasn't so different from the other Jewish feed merchants who started in the 1930s. Even with the Communist businessmen, it was the old-time methods with a lot of complicated deals and the records you kept under your hat. But if a rancher would owe a lot for a feed bill, the Jewish merchant always left enough to tide the family through the next raise. No Jewish merchant sent the sheriff after a rancher.

You know, the gentiles sometimes talked about the Jews in business here. And there were some Jewish ranchers and Jewish chicken dealers and Jewish grain merchants who pulled some tricks. But you have good and bad among all peoples. I would say that the Petaluma Jewish people, in the darkest days of the Depression, we were as kosher as they came.

Yossel Wolin

After I went broke in the stock market I was wondering, "How will I get back my ranch and my fortune? How will I get to a kibbutz in Palestine?"

A friend in San Francisco says, "Why don't you go into the burlap bag business? I need 100,000 bags a year."

All I knew from burlap bags is chicken feed comes in them. I went to the manager of a feed company in Petaluma, he says, "Joe, I have 80,000 bags for you, but you got to pay cash." He knew I was busted in the stock market. My credit was no good.

I went to another friend in San Francisco. He put on his glasses and he figured out 80,000 bags. We buy at four cents and sell at six cents. So we went to Petaluma and did the deal with his money. Figure it out—we made $1,600. Here I had been paralyzed, and suddenly I had $800! I was sitting on top of the world! First thing, I got me a shoeshine.

There was lotsa profit in the bag business, but you need money to make money. Goes along six months, I struggled. Until one morning I read the United States went off the gold standard. Being in the stock market already, I know what it means. I was completely busted, but I borrowed a car and went to the biggest rice mill in Sacramento. Nerve I never lacked. I told the manager I want to buy his bags for one year. If he asks where I will get the money, I couldn't answer. But at that time they didn't check credit. If you are in busines, you are in business.

He kids around: "What do you pay me?"

I says, "You know the price is 3 cents."

"I like you," he says. "I'll let you have them for $3\frac{3}{4}$ cents."

I said no. We were joking, but I really want the bags! I says, "Tell you what. I'll buy at $3\frac{1}{2}$ cents."

He says, "All right, I'll sell them to you for six months."

"You need a contract?"

He says, "Your word is good enough." I know my word is good enough, but I am wondering if his word is good enough! [Laughter]. I got home, right away I wrote him a letter confirming the purchase.

Next day I went into another rice mill and bought another six months' bags. In a few days I bought over a million bags! I didn't have a cent!

Next week, the price of bags went up to $7\frac{1}{2}$ cents. I already bought over a million bags for $3\frac{1}{2}$ cents. I made $40,000 without any money. That is how I established myself in the burlap-bag business.

When the price went up to $7\frac{1}{2}$ cents, the manager of the rice mill called me up, he says, "Who tipped you off?"

It was no tipping off. It was sheer desperation. In Hebrew—in the Book of Esther—they say, *"Ka'asher ovadeti ovadeti"*—"Since I am lost, I might as well be lost either way." I took chances because I had nothing to lose.

When I got going my bag business, I couldn't leave for Palestine. I stayed in San Francisco and made my fortune with burlap bags. From here I made my contribution to Zionism. I sent every year a big contribution to Jewish agriculture in Palestine.

Meyer Levy, Secretary, Abraham Haas Loan Fund to Yossel Wolin, San Francisco Bag Company, September 26, 1934

Again we beg to call your attention to the matter of your indebtedness to us which amounts to $500.00 principal and $113.33 accrued interest.

We have written to you previously regarding this matter without any response on your part. We have in the past, on a number of occasions, come to your assistance with financial aid when you required same. We feel that we are justified in requesting you show your appreciation by putting forth some effort to liquidate your indebtedness. As you know, we depend upon such repayments to maintain our funds for loans to Jewish agriculturalists.

LOUIS KAEL

After we lost everything in the stock market, Pop went into the produce business in San Francisco. First day, in one shot, he leased three stores. Without a license, without a scale, without any fruit! Just started right up!

But it was rough, and then the Depression hit. We needed help. Pop knew Dan Koshland and Walter Haas, but he didn't go near them after he lost their $10,000 in the market. Pop would send me down to the Jewish Welfare Federation for small loans. Ike Kael was a real businessman. He liked to do things on a big scale and he wasn't afraid to take risks. He still was the big sport, treating the salesmen to lunch and all. But he wasn't the same man after he was wiped out in Petaluma.

To be wiped out at forty-five! Pop was used to being a community leader. He was used to having a lot of money, driving a big car, making big contributions to Zionism. It was quite a blow to lose it all. Ike Kael never recovered.

MORRIS ROGIN

It just so happens that I am a socialist and an enterpriser. My sympathies were with the workingman since I saw the Potemkin uprising in Feodoisiya when I was a little boy. I participated in the movement to organize capmakers in Russia and America. But all the time I tried to improve myself—by leaving Russia, by coming to California, by starting a chicken ranch in Petaluma. I would not be helping any workers by remaining poor.

I made a living on my ranch, but I was restless to do something new. In 1933 I quit chickens and started up a feed mill. Once again it was that enterprising spirit—not to be afraid to do things. I began on a small scale with a *khaver,* and then I bought him out when he returned to live in the Soviet Union. For three years it was all right. Then I went broke in 1936.

It happened that I made a good speculation in grain. But the man who sold me short, when the prices went way up at the time for delivery, he would not deliver. I already promised feed to my customers at specified prices. When I didn't get my grain at the low price, I bought at high prices on the open market and made my deliveries. I considered it an obligation to my customers, but it broke me. My creditors, the big feed mills in here, they knew what happened. They told me to go through bankruptcy. If not, I wouldn't be able to stay in business. They testified to the bankruptcy court what happened. Then they advanced me credit to start over.

A year later, I brought one of my creditors one hundred dollars. He said, "What is this for?"

"I owe you money."

"You went through bankruptcy. You don't have to pay back."

"I consider that I owe you just the same."

He took the check to their board of directors. After the meeting he tells me they were so thrilled they decided to cut the indebtedness in half every time I bring a check.

I said, "I didn't have to bring that check altogether. I do not accept the decision of your board!"

I paid them one hundred percent! I paid all the others one hundred percent. Every time I made a little money I brought it to my creditors. Altogether it took me from 1937 to 1944 to pay back the fifteen thousand dollars I owed. I have letters from my creditors about it. One letter says, "I make it a point to show the younger elements of our company that there are still people who honor their obligations."

SID JACOBS

The rumor was that Morris Rogin paid everyone he owed, one hundred cents on the dollar. In fact, G. P. McNear, the owner of the McNear feed company, went as a character witness when Rogin became a citizen. Rogin was supposed to be a Communist. But when the richest man in Petaluma was his witness at the citizenship hearing, they had to figure Rogin was okay.

5 "Politics We Had Plenty"

ANNA ROSENFIELD GOLDEN

Once my children asked me, "What do you believe? You don't go in *shul*. You're not religious. What do you believe?"

I said, "I believe you shouldn't steal and you shouldn't lie. You should respect other people."

Another thing I told them: "You shouldn't be a strikebreaker. When the people strike, you should never cross the picket line."

PROFESSOR ELI GORDON [b. 1913; San Francisco]

Jews everywhere knew about Petaluma. They were on the map in those days, not simply because they were a Jewish agricultural settlement, but also because they had such deep cultural and political commitments. They were like every other American-Jewish immigrant community, only much more so. I would compare them to the early kibbutzniks in Israel.

I knew the Petaluma community in the 1930s from the special perspective of the Sunday school teacher. My first day there I was immediately thrown into the community's struggle between the Hebraicists and the Yiddishists. You could find the same ideological division in New York, but this conflict already was dying in the San Francisco Jewish community, which was assimilating. The Zionists were committed to Hebrew. It was the ancient language of the Jewish people in the Old Testament; it was to be the language of a new Jewish state in Palestine. Some of them were ex-*khalutzim* who still spoke about emigrating to Palestine. They all knew Yiddish, but they regarded Yiddish as the language of European ghetto life. A Jewish state in Palestine was the burning issue for them.

The Yiddishshists came from the tradition of the Jewish Bund, the Jewish socialist movement of tsarist Russia. After the Russian

Revolution some of them became Communists and progressives, while others remained social democrats in the Arbeiter Ring, the Workmen's Circle. But they were united in their love of Yiddish as the language of the Jewish common people, and they dismissed Hebrew as the language of religion. They opposed Zionism as a bourgeois nationalist movement which would have Jews go to Palestine instead of uniting with the working classes to build socialism wherever they lived.

None of these groups had much use for religion—that much they could agree upon. Any celebration in the Sunday school *had* to be secular. A couple of families went to religious services, usually on the High Holidays, in a small synagogue part of the Center building. But they had difficulty raising a *minyan,* quorum, for a Saturday-morning service.

The Petaluma Jews were split over many finer ideological lines, and you could easily tread on someone's toes if you forgot the divisions. Most of them trusted me because I was in Hashomer Hatsair, a left-wing Zionist organization that was trying to build a bridge with communism. But still there was the problem of whether to teach Hebrew or Yiddish in the Sunday school. After much debate they compromised and had me teach both languages, along with history and culture. It was quite a load [laughing]—the kids were miserable.

Don't misunderstand me. It was a delightful community precisely because they were all so political. You don't find many political communities in American life.

Despite their ideological differences, they had more in common than they ever realized. They were all *khaverim,* comrades, in one group or another. They were mostly secular- and socialist-minded. They ignored local Petaluma politics, they voted for La Follette in the twenties and Roosevelt in the thirties, and they were all consumed by burning global issues over the future of the Jewish people in the Soviet Union, Palestine, and America.

They were deeply committed to a labor ideology, to people living off the work of their own hands. They had contempt for the Jewish business people in nearby Santa Rosa—people who lived off sick things [chuckling] like trade and commerce.

They all had large libraries, basically the same. Zionists, Bundists, Communists—they were interested in the same writers, the same literature and history and politics. Everyone had, oh, say, a Yiddish translation of Babel's *Women and Socialism*—because it was an important work you had to read and keep in your library.

Their commitment to an agricultural way of life had a great deal to do with the high quality of their community. Because they worked *so hard* on those chicken ranches, they were all the more committed to an active political and cultural life. I have never met greater idealists.

You take Khaya and Aron Feinstein—I thought they were so unsuited for that type of life. I always imagined them as university professors. Aron had a delicate, subtle mind—he was the last person in the world you would expect to cope with chickens. Yet he did all the physical labor, studied all the latest chicken-raising techniques, and they stuck out the life they chose, against all obstacles.

The only thing similar I have seen was the generation of early kibbutzniks in Israel. They too were farmer-intellectuals who maintained the dual character of an agricultural and intellectual community. In fact, the Petaluma people were of the same stock, the same generation, and many ended up in Petaluma on the way to Palestine. For them Petaluma was a *hachsharah*, a place to prepare for life in Palestine, and they built the same kind of agrarian cultural community you found on the early kibbutzim.

I never was certain just how many people were in the Petaluma Jewish community, but they were active far beyond their numbers. They came from a political and cultural atmosphere in upheaval in Russia. In their Russian youths they first tried to break out of traditional *shtetl* life, into the modern world of secularism, socialism, and nationalism. This great transformation was their "Old World," and they held onto it in Petaluma.

Khaya Feinstein

I grew up in a home where the idea of building our own Jewish state was on the agenda. This was the dream of my parents. This was the dream of the Jewish people for two thousand years. That we will go back to live on the land, on *our* land in Palestine. My parents sent me to *kheyder* to learn Hebrew with this in mind. In order to build a Jewish nation, in order to keep up a Jewish life, it must be connected with the roots. Our roots are in Palestine, in the Torah, in the Hebrew language.

Yiddish was my language to begin. That is what we spoke in the *shtetl*. But Yiddish wasn't considered a fit language for education. The Yiddish language is *zargon*—a collection of different languages. Hebrew was the cultural language. Hebrew *is* the cultural language. Of course, the Yiddish language grew up with the Jewish people in Europe. It developed into a cultural language with great poets and novelists. It *became* a language. But with me, with our Zionist movement, Hebrew was our roots, our future. With a language there must be a land, a nation. I always dreamed the day will come when our Jewish people will be free in our own land. I always thought I will live in Palestine and build our Jewish country. Some of my *khaverim* went. Those who remained worked for Zionism in Petaluma.

Enfert Yidden af mine kashe
Vi'z mine brider, vi'z Abrashe
S'gayt ba im der traktor vi a bahn,
Di mi-me Laye ba der kosilke
Bayle ba der molotike
In Zhankoye, dzhan, dzhan, dzhan

Now if you look for paradise
You'll see it there before your eyes.
Stop your search and go no further on.
There we have a collective farm
All run by husky Jewish arms
At Zhankoye, dzhan, dzhan, dzhan

Ver zogt as Yidden kenen nor handler,
Essen fette yoich mit mandlen
Nor nit zine kine arbeitsman
Doss kenen zogen nor di sonim
Yidden, shpite zay on in ponim
Tit a kik of dzhan, dzhan, dzhan

Aunt Natasha drives the tractor
Grandma runs the cream extractor
While we work we all can sing our songs
Who says that Jews cannot be farmers?
Spit in his eye, who would so harm us.
Tell him of Zhankoye, dzhan, dzhan, dzhan

Here is another verse that was made up in the United States. This too we sang:

Work together, all as brothers
Jew and Gentile, white and Negro;
for that better world to come.
All must work, for work is good,
In work may man find brotherhood,
As in Zhankoye, dzhan, dzhan, dzhan

You see, this is what we sang. This is a folk song—*folkslid*—a living song. This was our progressive Yiddish folk chorus.

STELLA FINKLESTEIN

Most of these people, especially the left-wingers, lacked any sense of humor. They were very serious about their cultural work.

Take this business with the Jewish chorus. I sang with several Yiddish choruses before I came to Petaluma. I know music and I could learn my part in two rehearsals. The other Petaluma singers couldn't read music. It was fantastic how Uri taught them by rote, but all those rehearsals were horrible for me and I just came when it was convenient.

Uri understood, but the other women resented it. One of them comes over to me in town one day and says, "What kind of prima donna are you? You're too good for rehearsals?" You see, with them the chorus was a political duty. You went to all the rehearsals as part of Communist party discipline. They were so serious about it that I had to drop out.

Political duty even extended into their family lives. A lot of these women would not legally marry. It had nothing to do with free love or promiscuity. Quite the opposite. They were perfectly devoted to their husbands and families. It's just that they refused the sanction of capitalist law. The didn't need a piece of government paper for a devoted Communist marriage. They had a *shtile khupe*—a silent wedding—a common-law marriage. But it never occurred to me to think of them as anything but married. It was a purely ideological thing.

That's how it was with these women in Petaluma. Not just the left-wingers. They were all very loyal to their principles and their organizations. It was a mixture of political duty, cultural interest, and social life. You cannot imagine how religiously they attended meetings, prepared food for affairs, and contributed money beyond their means. I just wasn't comfortable with that.

MORRY FINKLESTEIN: I didn't get along so well with these left-wing men either. They were so Yiddish, so narrow. I never became a *Yanke*—I still have an accent—but since I got off the boat I used only English. In New York I became a internationalist; I believed the answer to the problems of the Jewish people will be solved by building socialism, not by preserving a separate Yiddish culture. Here in Petaluma the left wing claimed they were internationalists, but they stayed with Yiddish all the way. They kept their Jewishness close to their hearts.

Well, for years I went to the left-wing meetings anyhow. I paid my share! [Laughing.] At my first IWO meeting here, they took up a collection for Tom Mooney. In Los Angeles, if you gave a dollar it was okay. If you gave five dollars you were a prince. Who had money then? But Stella says, "Okay, they're big givers; give ten dollars."

Then one of them calls me over and says, "It's not enough."

I tell Stella, "You're making a fool of me! I have to give twenty-five dollars! I don't know where we'll get it, but that's what we have to give!"

They broke me in! [Laughing.] They raised huge sums that way. They had us giving to half a dozen left-wing organizations. It was the same fifty people, but we'd meet six times in six organizations and give six donations for each cause. [Laughing.] So the impression went out that we had three hundred left-wingers! Because look at all the money we raised!

It was *dis-gust-ing!* In Jewish law, the greatest thing in giving *tsdoke* [charity] is that your name shouldn't be known. But here in Petaluma they had experts working you over in front of everyone. These *shnorers,* money raisers, would say, "If Shlome gives fifty dollars, can you give less?" It was public blackmail!

STELLA: They carried it over from the Old Country. This was how their fathers auctioned off the honor of reading from the Torah in *shul!* [Laughing.] The Communists were very traditional, just like the Labor Zionists and the Arbeiter Ringers and the rest of the "radicals" here.

BEN: I told him, "I worked with American workers in New York. We are organizing farmers here in Sonoma County. We want to place the Communist party on the ballot in our local elections. We are fighting the fascist organizations here. A lot must be done before it is time for the Revolution."

JACOB FELDMAN

We were afraid that the Yiddish Communists will make trouble from the *goyim* here. The Communists wanted to change the world over. They was telling everybody, "The American government is no good. America exploits the workingman and tries to dominate the world. We got to have something like in Russia." The other Jews in here, we said, "America is our home. America is good to the Jewish people. Whatever the government is doing is for the best. We got to support it."

But the *goyim* was thinking all the Jews in Petaluma is Communists. Was dangerous. I say this: the Jew shouldn't be first in line when it comes to changing the world. Let the *goyim* be the radicals. Maybe it's different if you live in San Francisco, but in a small town everybody knows you. The Lefties was going right into the stores collecting money for communism! The lefties were nice, educated people. But one time they acted like bums with my store. They came to me selling ads for the book they put out with the concerts of their chorus. I give five dollars right away, but not for advertising my store. I want to put it in the book: "From a Friend."

No! They won't take the money unless I put in "Feldman's Store," so everyone will know who. They refused my five dollars. Then they held a big meeting and boycotted me that I am a reactionary capitalist.

It didn't make no difference cause I never had no business with them nohow. They went where they could buy for a nickel cheaper. But I didn't like them putting my store in the spotlight. You know, we had Nazis marching in the streets in them days. You had to be careful.

BEN HOCHMAN

You would be amazed at the fascist organizations we had in this area. Many people were frightened. The German Bund was meeting at Hermann Sons Hall, just two blocks from the Jewish Center. They would parade right down Western Avenue past the Center. In black shirts they marched with swastica armbands and hats with straps, yelling out, "*Sie Heil, Sie Heil.*" Behind the Nazi flag and the American flag they marched. At the very front was a fellow named Anderson, a neighbor of mine. He rode a white horse.

In Santa Rosa you would find the Silver Shirts. On Sunday mornings they did military training in the hills. Saturday afternoons they distributed the Protocols of the Elders of Zion at the courthouse in Santa Rosa. If you talked to them, they told you that Jews are capitalist parasites living off other people and Jews are Communists trying to take all the property. The atmosphere was so hot, they got away with saying this is public.

The Communist party fought them. We tried to convince the people that the fascists are against the interests of workers and farmers. Door to door we went with this message. We organized mass meetings. A few times we held demonstrations right in front of Hermann Sons Hall.

This was the left wing, Jewish and gentile. Most of the Jewish community stayed out of it. But the fascists knew that the Communists will give them a fight.

KARL ANDERSON [b. 1903; Petaluma]

The Jewish people were accepted in Petaluma. One of my best friends was Jewish when I grew up here. I was friendly with all my Jewish neighbors. I did business with the Jewish people for many years. The Jewish people were no different than anyone else. They had the same love of freedom as Americans. They're family oriented people . . . race oriented—like every group they kept to themselves mostly.

They're people who like to change things—socialist-minded people. And they're good business people, you know, good business people. They made money when the rest of us lost it. I never met a Jewish person who didn't know how to make money.

My folks were German. The German people in Petaluma congregated with themselves too. All the nationalities faced some problems until they had roots in this area. There was some feeling against the German race here during the wars. After that we were more tolerated.

No, there were no problems between Germans and Jews. There was never anything. Not anything I knew about. No. Nothing.

HYMIE GOLDEN

In the United States, too, they said the Jew is lazy, the Jew is a cheater, the Jew is dirty. Anything they could say—the Jew is a Communist and the Jew is a capitalist. At the same time! Stupid!

Course it wasn't like in Russia. The Russians, the Ukrainians, they Jew-haters. They killed us! I got good treatment in a German prisoner-of-war camp. The day I come home to Russia, they killed 530 people in

Revolution encouraged Yiddish culture and promised a Jewish homeland in the Siberian province of Birobidzhan. They did not see what I saw in Riga at the beginning of the Revolution. I witnessed the Soviet terror against Jewish religion and Jewish property, with fanatical Jewish Communists leading the terror against Judaism to show they are kosher Communists. I knew that our Communists in Petaluma were the same. If the Soviet line would shift, they could not be trusted to defend Jewish interests.

But for many years all our Petaluma organizations were in this Popular Front to raise money for Jewish settlement on the land in Palestine and Birobidzhan. From the business point of view it paid, because the Communists were ordered to give a lot. But it was more than money raising for them. It was political maneuvering to show that the Petaluma Jewish community supports communism and the Soviet Union.

The Communists were maneuvering to build up support in the Jewish community. When they made a move to take over everything in 1934, some people thought this was a danger to Jewish life in Petaluma. Then we had some trouble over who is leading the Jewish community.

Ben Hochman

The majority of the Jewish people in Petaluma became more inclined to the left. That's how the left wing became the leaders. We had just a few who were actual members of the Communist party. Most of our left-wing people in the International Workers Order were sympathizers of the Communist party. And even the not-so-left people in the Jewish community sympathized with our program in the early years of the Depression.

The people appreciated how the Soviet Union was solving the Jewish problem. They saw how the left wing supported the struggle for labor organization and the defense of the people's rights here in the United States. We led the resistance to fascism in this area. The people liked how we brought life into the Center with our cultural organizations and affairs.

We built a Popular Front coalition with many supporters who were not left-wingers. Then came the counterattack by reactionary leaders of other organizations. At that time we called them social fascists. They started a fight over who will run the Jewish Community Center.

Jacob Katz

The left wing elected a majority to the board of directors in 1934. But it happened that a lot of people who didn't hold voting shares in the Center were voting in the election. Some of them were elected to the board of directors. So some others took it to court. You see, some people were afraid that the Communists would sell the Jewish Community Center and send the money to the Soviet Union. There was such a case in New York. When the International Workers Order split off from the Arbeiter Ring in the 1920s—this was a part of the great world split between Communists and socialists after the Russian Revolution—the IWO seized many Arbeiter Ring offices. I wouldn't say the Communists would do the same thing in Petaluma, but some people were afraid they were fanatic enough to do this.

That legal action was done very silently. [Chuckles.] No, not by me. We had a very active man here by the name of Joe Holtzman. He had a big department store and he was a politician in town. He got that lawyer LaSalle who was always helping the Jewish community. They got a judge in Santa Rosa to send an injunction that the election was illegal.

The left wing complained they are being cheated. But the by-laws of the Center say it: you must have a share to vote or sit on the board of directions. That is the law. That's all. The new board of directors resigned and there was another election with only shareholders voting. The left-wingers could not win because they had just a few shares.

Why? When the Center was built in 1925, many of them wouldn't buy shares because there was a *shul* in the building. [Chuckling.] They thought religion is the opiate of the people. That was the line of the Communist party.

STELLA FINKLESTEIN

What a scandal! They actually had a gentile judge solve a Jewish dispute. It was like going outside the *shtetl* to the tsar's courts! Holtzman didn't know what was going on. They fast-talked him into doing it with that silly rumor about Communists selling the Center. And that lawyer LaSalle, he was in on all the anti-Communists dirty work here.

I'm sure Katz was in on that injunction; it was his kind of dirty work—you should see what he did twenty years later during the McCarthy period! But the Arbeiter Ring were the ones behind this thing in the thirties. They were socialists, but they were fanatic anti-Communists and anti-Soviets. They were anti-Zionists too [laughing]; for years they controlled the library at the Center and refused to buy any Hebrew books. They were anti-everything, except Yiddish.

They hated Holtzman's B'nai B'rith too. The B'nai B'rith was purely American-oriented—assimilationist oriented—and decidedly conservative. The B'nai B'rith looked down on immigrants as greenhorns. But the Arbeiter Ring needed Holtzman's political connections in Sonoma County to overturn the 1934 election.

Communist. He became dedicated to Communism like his grandfather was an orthodox Jew. It was no change!

Same thing with the *rekhte,* the right-wing *khaverim.* Right-wings [chuckling]—they were socialists too. Katz, the Jacobs brothers—they were steeped in the orthodoxy of their parents and grandparents too. They were just as fanatical believers as the left-wings. And they were afraid of how the gentiles will react to Communists running the Center. That's why they went outside the Jewish community to the judge.

Me? I never was an orthodox in politics. From the time I fought in Palestine during the First World War, I was in the struggle for workers' rights and for Zionism. But the belief was never instilled in me like those who came from a orthodox background. My father was religious a little bit, but he didn't have the long beard. He had a trimmed beard! He didn't take it too serious. I inherited the trimmed beard from my father.

I was friendly with the *linke* and the *rekhte* all the way through. But let me tell you, it's not so easy keeping a trimmed beard when everyone wears a long beard.

RABBI SOLOMON PLATT [b. 1905; New York City]

That first political split in Petaluma was just a hint of the really big battle that came later with McCarthyism.

I know the story well, because I performed many of the rabbinical functions for the Petaluma community since I came to San Francisco in the thirties. I officiated when it was a *bris* [circumcision], a *bar mitzvah,* a wedding, a funeral. Almost all of them were secularists, but they appreciated my presence. Even the *linke,* who swallowed the Marxist line that religion is the opiate of the people, would have me marry their children under the *khupe* [traditional wedding canopy].

They would have me, a rabbi, officiate at their funerals. Of course, whether it was a *linke* or a Poale-tsion or an Arbeiter Ring, during the service a *khaver* would get up and say, "*Geven a guter mentsch . . . a getrayer . . . a libhoberfun sholom*"—He was a good man, a loyal person, a lover of peace." They had these stock phrases for his contributions to their movement. But they wanted me to officiate at this memorial, without too much emphasis on religion. They wanted a rabbi at these significant moments in life. You see, there was a hangover from the Old Country. They couldn't completely dismiss the religious and cultural traditions of their youths.

They were rebels. They went through a period of intense hostility to religion. You know, instead of fasting on Yom Kippur, you eat soap [pork by-product] in front of the synagogue. To show not only that you are not fasting on Yom Kippur, but that you are eating *treyf* [impure food]. To double emphasize your emancipation! Of course it is juvenile. It shows how difficult it is to get rid of the burden of tradition. They never really did.

This is how you must understand their politics. I call them sentimental socialists—romantic socialists. Those in the *linke,* the Poale Tsion, the Arbeiter Ring—they committed themselves in their youthful rebellion in Russia to the idea of bringing salvation through communism, Zionism, socialism. They were idealists who believed that Jews were too much in the world of business—*shakher makher,* wheeling-dealing, and that kind of thing. They were determined to live on the land and break with the Old World Jewish life.

In Petaluma they formed a highly cultured community—a political community. Their ideologies and their political battles were modern. Yes. But their community was like a *shtetl* and they believed with all the religious fervor of their parents and grandparents.

in the audience. We talked about the contributions the Jews have made to the morality of the world, to science, to literature. We defended American democracy against these alien fascist ideas. When we challenged the Silver Shirts to come up and tell their program, they stood up and left without a word. That's all, but they remembered this humiliation. They were in with the vigilantes later.

Another thing . . . at that time we conducted a campaign to put the Communist party on the ballot. We were supporting the labor movement, collecting money for the longshoremen's strike, holding meetings. A lot of people in Sonoma County figured, "It is a new party for the working people. Let's give it a chance."

MIRIAM HOCHMAN: Not everyone was so friendly. [Laughing.] One Sunday morning I was going house to house with leaflets in Santa Rosa. At one house a young guy answers the doorbell, I tell him, "It's about time we put a workers' party on the ballot."

He says, "If you don't leave this porch, I'll get my rifle and shoot you down!"

I moved, believe me, I moved! Turns out he is a commander in the American Legion!

BEN: They were frightened of our support. We collected enough signatures to put two Communists on the ballot. They were shocked when one of our candidates, Bellini, he polled over one thousand votes for the state assembly. That's when the newspapers warned that the Communists are subversive traitors. That's why they didn't hesitate to use violence to get rid of the Communists. Terror and violence.

It began with the apple orchards in Sebastopol. There were migrant workers who picked the apples in August. They were called Okies—you probably read about them in *The Grapes of Wrath*. About three thousand came with the families in jalopies. They camped in tents. For twenty-five cents an hour they picked apples. They couldn't live on that! One came to me and said, "I am a Communist. The people want to strike, but we need help."

We helped the strike. What was their demands? Forty cents an hour, settle for thirty-five. But the apple farmers wouldn't give in. They were almost ruined themselves. They wouldn't pay another ten cents an hour.

From the left we put out a leaflet that it was an intolerable situation—the farmers and the workers are both depressed—but the workers must have a raise in wages. We helped the strikers with food and clothing and money. We held public meetings. We did a lot.

The violence started at one of our strike meetings at Germania Hall in Santa Rosa. All of a sudden the hall filled up with men carrying guns.

Vigilantes! They ordered the people out of the hall. I stood up and said, "This is a legal meeting!" Some of us refused to leave, so they beat us up. The Santa Rosa police just stood there outside. After the meeting they followed me home. In front of my house they yelled out, "Benjamin . . ." They knew my name. "Benjamin, give up this work." I didn't pay much attention to it.

MIRIAM: I did! That night I burned all the Communist leaflets in the house!

BEN: Finally they terrorized the workers. The apple farmers, the sheriff, the vigilantes—the highway patrol set up machine guns around the workers' camp! The workers left and found work somewhere else. The apples were not picked. The crop was ruined!

So you see, the vigilantes had a chance to set the farmers against the Communist party. The vigilantes said, "See what the Reds have done to you? They want to destroy the farmers here." That was how they got support from the people, even though the Communist party in here was started by the farmers.

Still, the attack was like a bolt from the blue sky.

MIRIAM: No, they had headlines in the newspapers the week before: "Death to the Reds!" That is why you bought the shotgun.

BEN: One night—August 1935—Mike Adams came to our door at one o'clock in the morning. He was a friend, a very good fellow. At one time he was the chairman of the Central Labor Council of Sonoma County. My son Nathan heard the knocking. He comes over to the bedroom, he says, "Pop, Mike Adams is outside." I was wondering why the heck is Mike at the door in the night. I open the door. Mike fell in the kitchen! He says, "Ben! The vigilantes! They want to lynch us!"

Two of them stood at the door. In masks, with guns. They grabbed my arm, but I pushed them back and closed the door. I told Nathan, "Get me the shotgun."

We had rifles too—twenty-twos. I said, "Mike, Miriam, guard the front door with the rifles. Nathan, stay with me. Keep down."

It was maybe one hundred people in the back. They yelled, "Benjamin! Come out!"

I yelled, "You just try to come in."

I opened the door and fired twice in the air. Not to hit people—I was worried I might hit somebody—but to show them I mean business. That I'll do what I can if they come in. That lasted for two hours. They yelled

He thought for a few moments and he said, "I'm very sorry Mrs. Hochman. I cannot help you."

An hour later I heard you were in Penngrove. The word spread quick when you were found.

BEN: The vigilantes told us we should get out of town. The others went right away to San Francisco. But I got some medical help and I decided, "No, I will stay on my place. I will take care of my chickens."

In a few days they called me into the golden Eagle Milling Company. The manager was active in the Republican party, and some leaders of the Republican party were in this affair. He called me in and said this way: "I got bad news for you. We can't give you credit anymore." For eleven years I had credit there. Everybody got feed on credit. But he says, "We can't give you credit anymore."

After that I got my feed from Rogin's feed company. Then all our insurance was canceled. They were in a conspiracy to get me out of here. But I decided to stay! The heck with them! I had the Communist party print up some leaflets: "We Will Stay!" I spread around those leaflets!

I swore out complaints against the vigilantes I recognized, but there was no prosecution by the Sonoma County district attorney. After a year's time there were editorials in the San Francisco newspapers: "Why is there no prosecution?" Finally the state attorney general put them on trial.

I was the chief witness for the state at the trial. The lawyers for the defense—they were very influential people—they tried to show that the vigilantes were good Republicans who wanted to get rid of communism. They read to the jury *The Communist Manifesto* and the preamble of the Comintern. They tried to turn it upside down, that I was the guilty party because I was a Communist revolutionary.

I fought back. I told them, "Yes, I am a Communist. Communism is true Americanism. The United States was born in revolution. The people turned against an oppressive government. The Declaration of Independence states that the people have a right to change the government if they are dissatisfied." I told them, "This is true Americanism."

During the trial they tried to prove that I am an enemy of the country. They had the nerve to say that my refusal to kiss the flag for the vigilantes shows I am a bad American. But it wasn't so easy. I was a soldier in World War I. I defended the United States.

Their lawyer says to me, "I see you are a veteran."

"Yes."

"When did you become a citizen?"

I knew what he was driving at. When they drafted an immigrant in the army, they made you a citizen in twenty-four hours. I made believe I don't understand the question. I wanted him to come out so the jury should hear. I said, "What do you mean?"

"You went into the army to become a citizen!"

I said, "No sir! *First* I became a citizen and *then* I enlisted in the army!"

He retreated like a beaten dog. He said, "Lots of water has flowed down the river since then." Meaning, once upon a time I was a good American, but now I am no good!

I hit them back hard when they questioned me. But nothing came of the case. Not guilty. Then the American Civil Liberties Union—they were not friends of the Communist party, but they made a second trial, a civil case for damages. It didn't do any good either. Again the defense lawyers turned it into a case against communism.

NATHAN: Pop had another day in court ten years later. It seems that Will Bates, the leader of the vigilantes, was an immigrant too. One day we heard that Mr. Will Bates was coming up for his citizenship. Pop showed up to testify at the hearing. And Bates did not get his citizenship papers.

BEN: I'll tell you, it was unbelievable—in a town like this, such violence. I actually dramatized what happened to labor organizers all over the United States. It's because of the defense I put up—for two hours I fought them off. That's why it was in the New York newspapers, in all the papers, even in the Soviet Union it was news. It was a sensation, the struggle that took place here.

MIRIAM: *Ich volt dir moikhel geven dem sensation*—who needed such a sensation?

BEN: She don't care for it. She can't forget it. Now she's more used to it, but for two years after, at night she would scream out.

MIRIAM: I couldn't sleep. I couldn't sleep.

ARTHUR LaSALLE

We had a little incident here. There was a poultry farmer called Hochman. He was accused by a group of hotheads of failure to follow American tenets. He was brought to a place where he was asked to salute the American flag. Whether he refused or not, I don't know, but his behavior was interpreted to mean a refusal. Then he was tarred and feathered. He wasn't seriously hurt in any way. Naturally that kind of conduct was in

So I called the sheriff. I call once, he says he's coming. I call twice, he says he's coming. I call again, he says he came and didn't see nothing. Then I know what's happening: "Oh my God! The police and the sheriff is in with the vigilantes!!!"

Petaluma *Argus Courier,* August 22, 1935

Mrs. Hochman claims that she called the sheriff's office at Santa Rosa after the vigilantes arrived and that there was no response to her appeals for help. She also claims that she called the Petaluma police department and was told to call the sheriff's office as the district in which the Hochman home is located is out of the jurisdiction of the department.

Santa Rosa *Press Democrat,* August 23, 1935

Local police revealed that no calls had been received for aid during the time the raids took place. Sheriff Reardon said that one call was received from a rural route at three o'clock in the morning with an excited woman shouting that "one hundred and fifty men are surrounding my house with guns and clubs." Reardon and deputy sheriffs sped to the route number given in the telephone message, but found no signs of trouble of any kind, the sheriff said.

GAYE LeBARON [b. 1936; columnist, Santa Rosa *Press Democrat*]

I've researched the history of the tar and feathering of Ben Hochman. I am convinced that many of the leading citizens of Sonoma County were in favor of it. This was a very anti-Communist place.

Certainly, my newspaper was involved. The *Press Democrat*'s stories were inflammatory. More than that, I've heard it told—and I'm sure it is true—that when the vigilantes were trying to get Hochman out of his home, the *Press Democrat*'s reporter went to the sheriff's office for the tear gas. Which is not exactly the role of a reporter in a free society.

There was anti-Semitism involved too. When I researched this incident, I interviewed a Santa Rosa man named Samuel Schwartz. He was a World War I hero with the Lost Battalion, he was leader of the Santa Rosa American Legion, and he was a Jew. He knew what the Legionnaires were going to do. And he knew it was because some of the labor organizers were Jews—Communist Jews. It was a hard choice for Sam. He was a real American patriot. He hated Communism, but he was a defender of the Jewish people. He told me, "When my Legionnaire friends told me what they were going to do to the Jewish Communists, I didn't know what to do. I closed up my store and went home early." He didn't participate and he didn't try to stop it.

Sam got very emotional telling me about it forty years later. He felt like he hadn't defended his own people.

"Doc Bill" Rutherford

They didn't do it because he was a Jew. It was because he was a Commie. Some of these young fellas from the Junior Chamber of Commerce were behind it. They came to me and said, "The Commies are trying to overthrow the government. We've got to stop 'em."

They wanted me to join their secret committee, but I didn't like the set-up. I said, "No thanks, I'm not a joiner."

When I saw Hochman the morning after, I felt sorry for him. My brother's nurse called me over: "Doc Bill, you gotta see this guy who came in for help." The poor devil was covered with tar and feathers. We had a heck of time getting it off. Thank God I stayed out of it. The whole thing was a bunch of hooey. These young fellas kinda went nuts defending democracy. You know how the Commies give some people a bug up the . . . [chuckling].

Yossele Gardner

A lot of people said it was an attack on Communists, not on Jews. It is true that Hochman was the only Jew among the five who were kidnapped. It is true that one of the gentiles was tarred and feathered with Hochman. But everybody in the county knew that everything moving under the apple pickers strike was Jewish and everything moving behind the left wing was Jewish. It was an attack on Jewish social conscience. We were Jewish farmers helping out impoverished farm workers who were striking for a few pennies more. It was just a few Communists among us and no plan for a revolution. But the powerful people in the county wanted to break the strike and scare all the supporters.

People in the Jewish community took it as a warning. Yes. Most Jews don't like to be connected to such things, especially in a small town. The Jewish community was very scared.

Jacob Feldman

He happens to be a very nice man, Hochman. A gentleman. Intelligent. But in them days, my god, that Jewish people should make such trouble! In a small town! Everybody knows who you are! I say, why do the *yidn* have to help the farm workers? Why the Jews?!! It makes for anti-Semitism. I say, let the *goyim* help the farm workers. Let them do that kind of work.

go out looking for brawls, and I was big enough to make it stick. But I'd learned to take a powder sometimes. I stepped on the gas and pulled out.

The tar and feathering was a few weeks later. I had to go into San Francisco on a Thursday, and Hochman wanted a ride. I went to pick him up that morning. When I got there I found the whole ranch ransacked and deserted. The windows were busted out, furniture was turned over, clothing was strewn everywhere. I found tear-gas shells on the kitchen floor.

Soon enough I heard the whole story from some of those jackasses with the vigilantes. They snuck up on the ranch in the dark of the night. They thought they'd grab Hochman right away, but he surprised 'em by fighting back all the way. They did everything they could to intimidate him. When they finally got him in the back of a car, they stomped him all the way to Santa Rosa.

They took him to the Rosenthall warehouse. The Rosenthalls were Jewish—the richest people in the county. Now I'm not saying they were involved, but it makes you wonder. There were some real Jewish reactionaries in Santa Rosa.

A woman wrote a letter to the Santa Rosa *Press Democrat* a year ago, describing how she served coffee and cookies to the vigilantes that night. She was proud of the tar and feathering. No doubt she really believes they were on the verge of bloody revolution and her man was in there savin' Sonoma County from the God-damned dirty Bolsheviks. She believed it, but she couldn't have been worse wrong.

I heard what happened from men who were at the warehouse. The Hart's Brewery supplied a barrel keg of booze. It sat there, head knocked out, with a tin dipper for any vigilante who wanted to wash out his guts. I was told this from men who drank it—men who had no reason to lie to me—fellow workers that I knew. They sincerely believed they were saving the country from the Bolsheviks. But they were just a bunch of God-damned drunks being encouraged by the big shots of Sonoma County.

The word was that Sheriff Reardon was involved. There is only one place in Sonoma County where you could get tear-gas equipment, and that was the sheriff's office. The word was that the vigilantes were deputized, so that if anyone got injured, they were protected as deputies cleaning out a radical nest. That was all denied later.

The next election Reardon got defeated because he worked hand-in-glove with the vigilantes. The American people are basically good people. They have the concept that "I might not agree with what you believe, but I'll defend your right to say it and think it." Then apathy set in, and a year later they put Reardon back in as sheriff.

But I say this without qualification: the whole power structure of Sonoma County was involved in this thing. Newspapers, law enforcement, courts, politicians, businessmen, the big farmers—they might not have actively participated in the tar and feathering, but all the official people knew what was happening. Hell, they created the atmosphere for it, they let it happen, and then they ignored it.

It's no wonder the fear was runnin' out of people's ears after the tar and feathering. Especially among the Jewish people. They were right in the middle of this whole thing. Everybody was frightened, terrible frightened, for a long time.

MICHAEL FELDMAN [b. 1920; Petaluma]

There are *still* some old-time gentiles who think it was all right to tar and feather Hochman. Every few years you come up to a group who's talking about, what happened in those days with the vigilantes. They don't know who you are, but you hear them say, "Too bad they didn't get all of 'em."

You look at those fellows and you think, "Jesus! These guys could be talking about me!" Now, does he care because Hochman was a Jew or because he was a left-winger? Who in the hell is "all of 'em?" It's hard to know! What do you do? Start asking? And open up what?

GAYE LeBARON

A few months before I wrote my historical column on the tar and feathering, I talked about it to a woman's club as an example of the frontier character of Santa Rosa in the twenties and thirties.

After the lecture a woman came up, looked me straight in the eye, and said, "I was among those who made coffee and sandwiches for the Legionnaires when they tarred and feathered those men. We were proud of it then and I'm proud of it now!"

Whe-eee-ew! Forty years is not long enough for these things to be taken out of the realm of personal prejudice and put in the realm of social history.

When I wrote my column on the tar and feathering, I explained my reasons for doing it:

> Why bring it up? Because it happened. It's soon to be the fortieth anniversary of the event and I'm not of the mind that believes that history means recording what's pleasant and pretty about by-gone ways and leaving the ugly interred. Santa Rosa history is interesting and vivid, but it's not always pretty. There was racism and violence here too. I don't think it would be wise to try to pretend otherwise.

I didn't use any names in the column because the Hochmans didn't want publicity. But I showed the mob terror, the complacency of law-enforcement officials, and the inflammatory role of my own news-paper. And to my surprise, there wasn't much reaction at all.

It's funny. You write something and you think, "Oh, boy, this is really going to get me in trouble!" Then you publish it and nothing happens.

MICHAEL HOCHMAN [b. 1948; Petaluma]

My grandparents would not talk with Gaye LeBaron when she did re-search for her column on the fortieth anniversary of the tar and feath-ering. Grandpa Ben was willing, but Grandma Miriam said no. She still has bitter, painful memories about what they went through. That's why you waited three years for an interview with them. The family convinced them to talk with you because we feel strongly that the history should be recorded accurately. In fact, my aunt was writing on it for her M.A. the-sis. And my mother wanted to do a psychological novel about the scars it left on the family. She was going to call it *Ripe Green Apples.*

My grandparents are very proud of their history. Anyone who comes over, they show their album with all the news stories on the tar and feathering. Just looking at those old photographs makes me angry. Those outrageous pictures—right on the front page of the *Press Democrat.*

A few weeks ago I saw *The Grapes of Wrath* on television. Those mean crowds in the movie got me going again. I could just imagine those people with their sticks and guns at my grandparents' door. I could see it right there in front of me!

The tar and feathering always has been a part of my life. When I was a teenager I did a folk-music show on the radio, and I got telephone threats about it: "You're playing down-in-the-throat Communist music from Israel. There's no room for you in Petaluma." These rednecks around here didn't know about folk music, but they knew who I was. It was a personal attack from the vigilantes who went after my grandpar-ents in the thirties.

The callers never showed up, but I had encounters with some of the grandchildren of the vigilantes who tarred and feathered Grandpa. Those redneck kids didn't like my activities against the Vietnam War. They were known anti-Semites. It got to the point where I let it be known that I kept a lead pipe in the back seat of my car. I figured the thing to do was to meet them on their own turf and say, "I have as much right to be here as you."

The history of my grandparents in Petaluma gives me strength. They were just awesome. The tar and feathering is still a very frightening thing for them, especially for Grandma Miriam, but they continued to live in Petaluma. They walked down the street with heads held high, and when they passed the vigilantes they looked them straight in the eye.

BEN HOCHMAN

We stayed for two years after the tar and feathering. Still, you know, the tension. They used to run by, the vigilantes. They ran by fast in the cars as a warning. They told a neighbor to watch how I behave. I kept my gun ready.

NATHAN HOCHMAN: We'd see the vigilantes in town sometimes, but what could we do? Beat them over the head with a club?

BEN: Finally I said, "Let's get out of here. I'll try somewhere else. I'll go back to work as an electrical engineer." We sold the chickens and we went to New York, Miriam and Nathan and me. My other son, Joe, was fighting in Spain at that time.

First I wanted to go in the Soviet Union. One of the editors of the *Freiheit* was just there and he told me I should go. Because they needed electrical engineers for the building of socialism. He said. "What for do you stay here?" I actually bought tickets. But then they canceled the trip. Because of the trials of the old Bolshevik leaders took place at that time. Stalin ordered no new immigrants. They told me I couldn't come.

NATHAN: Thank God, *thank God,* I didn't go there!

BEN: So I went to the Brooklyn Naval Yard for a job, because I am a veteran from the First World War. I showed them I knew generators, so they said all right. But Miriam and Nathan wanted to come back to Petaluma. In Petaluma we had friends. They were used to the life here.

MIRIAM HOCHMAN: Not only this. Our friends kept on writing, "They wouldn't dare do a thing like this again." You know, the tar and feathering business. So it quieted down and we came back.

BEN: Before we left New York I met a man from Western Electric, one of the biggest electrical companies in America. He wanted me to come to Indianapolis to change their system from two phase to three phase, to show the workers how to do it. But my wife said no.

MIRIAM: Because you would try to organize them into Communists the first day! [Laughing.]

BEN: She wouldn't let me go through Indianapolis on the way back to California. She was afraid I will stop off at Western Electric. [Laughing.]

MIRIAM: Because he would be tarred and feathered a second time! I knew that if he'll go there and take that job, it'll be bad for us all. Because he wouldn't be able to help himself. He was such a hot Communist in those days! He would start organizing the workers and there would be trouble. I made him drive the jalopy straight back to Petaluma. We rented another ranch, we worked hard with the chickens, and we made a good life. Here we stayed.

BEN: Here we got used to it. And, all right, we made out pretty good. Well, that's all about that, Now what I was going to tell next?

MIRIAM: About the Anti-Fascist Emergency Committee.

BEN: Oh, yeah. It happened around 1938, right after we came back from New York. We organized . . .

7 "There Was No Such Thing as a Babysitter": The American-Born Generation

SHURA EASTMAN COMPISI [b. 1920; Chicago]

The kids in left-wing families grew up asking our parents, "Can you help me with my homework, or do you have a meeting tonight!" [Laughing.] Usually, it was a meeting. They were busy making "the Revolution."

As kids we had twenty-four-hour exposure to politics. Before my family moved to Petaluma, it was the the labor movement in San Francisco. I was taken along to union meetings, picket lines, and demonstrations. If we went on a picnic, it was a picnic to hear a speaker and raise money for the movement. You were never alone, never a wallflower, in the left-wing movement. In Petaluma my parents were busy every evening with organizational meetings, affairs, and informal visits of the *khaverim*. The Petaluma *linke* went down to San Francisco for more movement activities. And any broken-down left-wing sailor could always find a bed, all the chicken he could eat, and all the politics he could talk in Petaluma. The homes were open to everyone on the left.

Our parents believed in politics. They came from orthodox religious backgrounds in the Old Country, but they were totally disillusioned with a God that would allow pogroms and sweatshops. So they replaced religion with socialism. It was a total commitment to socialism, just like their parents had followed religion back in the *shtetl*.

They included the kids in everything. And we were involved not just because our parents said it was important, but because they made us *feel* it was important. I was proud that I knew people who were jailed in the 1934 general strike. I felt special that I knew people who went to fight in Spain. And it was special! It was important! But I think we kids missed something. It wasn't enough to be part of a movement to build a socialist world. We felt deprived of something—attention, individuality, family identity—I really don't know what it was. But whenever I talk about it with others from left-wing families, we just nod our heads in agreement.

FRAN RUBINSTEIN GINSBERG

All the company at our house, all the visiting Zionist leaders who stayed with us, all my parents' Zionist activities, it was nice, but I felt— well, left out a little bit.

It's not that they didn't include the kids. When my parents went to a meeting at the Center—and they *both* went to *all* the meetings—they took us along. If they stayed late, they put us to sleep on benches. There was no such thing as a babysitter. We were a part of everything. But we were just kids, and they were—well, they were very busy with their friends and the movement to build a Jewish nation.

My parents raised me as a Zionist, and I am a Zionist, but that was never enough for me. It's funny—but I always wanted a religious ritual in our family, and my parents would have nothing to do with religion. My mother refused when I asked her to *bent likht,* to light the candles on Friday night. We'd have a big meal at Pesach, but my father would not do a *seder* or explain the celebration. At Rosh Hashanah and Yom Kippur my parents kept me home from school, but they would not take the family to services. My father stayed inside and meditated all day. No work, but nothing religious.

I felt like I was missing something. So when I was a teenager, I'd walk over to Bessie Haller's ranch on a Jewish holiday. I'd go to *shul* with the Hallers. I don't think my parents liked it, but they didn't stop me. I had a good feeling there—a warm feeling.

MILTON RUBINSTEIN [b. 1924; Petaluma]

I had a run-in with Mordecai Haller that I was partially proud of and partially ashamed of. I must have been ten or eleven. It was on Yom Kippur. Since it was a holiday, I rode my bike over to the Hallers to see if Ike could play. And there I found the whole family dressed up for *shul.* In fact, my sister Fran was there too.

Now you must understand that Mordecai Haller was the religious patriarch of the Jewish community. He kept the *shul* going for a handful of religious families. Mordecai thought of himself as an intellectual and a scholar, but he always had to come to my dad for explanations of the Torah. And even though my dad knew Torah from his rabbinical studies as a boy, my dad was a Labor Zionist and no longer interested in Torah.

On this particular morning, Mordecai took one look at me and *he gave me hell!* "What are you doing on a bicycle like a *goy?*" he yelled. "Why are you dressed like a *goy?* Don't you know this is Yom Kippur?"

I was not one to talk back to my elders, but I was a *farbrenter* [red hot] secularist like my father. I really took offense at what he said. So I did a terrible thing. I said, "At least there is no *khazeray* [impurities] on my father's ranch—we don't raise pigs! And my father does not hire *goyim* to feed any pigs on Yom Kippur. And my father does not hire *goyim* to keep his feed mill running on Yom Kippur."

Then I got on my bike and rode away.

SID JACOBS

I didn't set foot in that little *shul* at the Center until I was fifteen. I was hanging around with Michael Feldman at Feldman's store one day, when old man Haller came by. He wanted to say a *kaddish* [a prayer for the dead] and they needed two more men for the *minyan* [quorum necessary for a service]. Mr. Feldman sent Michael and me. That's the first time I was in the *shul*. You know, we'd always peek in to see the old men praying, but I'd never been to a service before. They had to show me what to do with the *talis* [prayer shawl] and how to pray.

My parents were socialists, Arbeiter Ringers, and they didn't observe religion. My father really got angry at me one time when I chopped down a cypress branch and brought it home as a Christmas tree. He thought it was terrible, but it was hard being the only kid who didn't celebrate Christmas in the little country school. We didn't even light candles at Channukah. My family was *completely* secular.

I don't think I really wanted to be Christian. I wanted to be American! For as long as I can remember I was interested in guns and hunting. When I was nine years old I got my father to buy me a twenty-two rifle, even though he had an ingrained fear of guns. To him guns represented authority—the tsar, the Cossacks. For me guns were a way to make the transition into America.

You know, my father was a little guy, under five feet—they called him *der groyser Jacobs*, Big Jacobs, as a kind of joke, because my uncle was even smaller. But all our fathers were little guys who were afraid of authority. You could see it when they came to school. They were much better read and more learned than our teachers, but no matter what happened they deferred to those teachers as authority.

Our fathers couldn't give us much help with being accepted in America. That's why I became interested in guns, cowboys, the West, the whole bit. I figured if I could hunt like my gentile friends, I would be more American.

JULIA SHIFFMAN SEGAL [b. 1927; Petaluma]

Jewish kids need Jewish holidays and Jewish rituals. You need one day to be different from another. I didn't have that when I grew up in Petaluma. And I didn't know who I was. My parents were *totally* unobservant of anything religious. They didn't light candles on Friday night, they didn't fast on Yom Kippur, they didn't have a menorah for Channukah. They didn't need it because they had it as kids in the Old Country. They had rebelled against it.

My parents just assumed I would be Jewish because we spoke Yiddish at home and we went to all the Jewish community affairs at the Center. But believe me, they did expect me to be Jewish. If a non-Jewish boy came to pick me up for date, Pa would show up in the living room in his filthiest overalls. He would stomp around muttering Yiddish about my going out with a *sheygets*. I would die with embarrassment when he did that.

All the Jewish kids felt uncomfortable about Yiddish. We learned it from our parents, but we never spoke it. We were divesting ourselves of that. When our gentile friends came to our homes, we would die with shame if our parents spoke Yiddish in front of them. We were embarrassed even then they spoke English with their Yiddish accents. When our parents came to school to confer with teachers, they seemed so foreign. It wasn't just the language. It was their clothes, their smallness, their timidity with the American teachers—they just stood out! Or so we thought. I suppose it was the same for the Italian and Portuguese and German kids, but it seemed like *our* parents were the ones who were different.

There was a contradiction. I wanted to be more traditionally Jewish, yet at the same time I wanted to be more American. I didn't know what I wanted. I didn't know where I belonged.

Lou Green [b. 1922; Petaluma]

I had no doubts about who I was, because there was a tremendous amount of anti-Semitism in our area. I was chased home from school every day for years. It was routine to be called "Christ killer," to be stoned, to be beaten up. From the age of six I knew I was Jewish.

I grew up in Penngrove, a little community about five miles north of Petaluma. There were a lot of Germans in Penngrove, and some of them were Nazis. Their kids persecuted the Jewish kids. There were a couple of outstanding teachers who tried to stop it. They lectured students about tolerance and about how Christianity evolved from Judaism. I was proud when they spoke about my heritage, but things still happened.

I don't know why these kids did it. I suppose it was something they picked up from their parents. But my parents got along fine with their parents. The oddest thing is that my father was the chicken dealer for a lot of these Germans whose kids beat us up. He got along fine with them, even when he pulled some fast ones. But those German kids persecuted us every day.

I was just a skinny runt. I couldn't fight them with my fists, so I learned how to cut them to ribbons with words. From an early age I could decimate them with an assiduous barb. I became the fastest tongue in the West.

IRVING GOLDEN [b. 1924; Petaluma]

It's baloneysville, this talk about anti-Semitism in the schools here. Sure, it wasn't easy being the only Jewish kid at a country school. You always felt self-conscious, especially at Christmas. I'd go along with the Christmas party and singing carols, but I'd never sing that Christ was "our Lord." I felt Jesus was really bad, so I'd fake it and hope nobody noticed. See, our parents never explained Jesus to us. They hardly taught us about our own religion, let alone Christianity. Our parents didn't mix with the gentiles; they kept to themselves at the Center. That was the problem. We had to find out for ourselves that Jesus and the gentiles weren't all that bad.

As for anti-Semitism, well, we had all these Jewish kids who were wise guys. They always had an angle. They were always making cracks. And then it would boomerang on them. They'd be called "Jew," and there was reason for it. I never acted that way. I never felt uncomfortable among gentiles. I mixed with the Jewish kids at the Center, but my closest friends were non-Jews. I felt alien to the Jewish wise guys. I felt alien to a lot of the Jews around here.

That's how it's been all my life. In fact, nowadays nine out of ten people will not believe I'm Jewish. They say, "Come on, tell me another one. You're half. You're a quarter. You're not Jewish at all."

JOE HOCHMAN [b. 1921; Montreal, Canada]

My school friends didn't give a shit that I was Jewish. They accepted me for who I was. The few times I heard anti-Semitic cracks at school, I settled it very quickly with my fists. This was one Jew who wasn't going to be pushed.

FRAN RUBINSTEIN GINSBERG

For years I didn't want anyone to know I was Jewish. Growing up in Penngrove, I never knew which big boy was going to call me "Christ killer" and throw rocks. A few times they threw lighted matches in my hair. Lighted matches! I still get the shivers about it. There was nothing you could do. If it wasn't the kids, it was the teachers. I still remember the day my high school English teacher said, "Class, I would like to talk about *The Merchant of Venice,* but because we have a Jew in the class I'll have to skip it." She then proceeded to tell the whole story of Shylock. I sat there and felt the red rising. Everyone stared at me.

No, I didn't tell my parents. I didn't want them coming to school and making waves. I wanted to lose myself in the crowd and be like everybody else. The only time I complained was after I was elected vice president of my high school class. The principal called me into her office and said, "Do you realize that you are the first of 'your people' to attain this office? You must set a high example." I was very upset, so I went to Mr. Holtzman. He was our standard-bearer in town. He told me he would take care of it. I never heard anything like that from the principal again.

Even as the vice president of my senior class, I still wasn't fully accepted. No Jewish girl was asked to join the Rainbow Girls and no Jewish boy was asked to join De Molay. You were Jewish, and you had to accept the fact that you were excluded from the top social clubs.

There wasn't much for Jewish girls in Petaluma. We organized a chapter of BBG [B'nai B'rith Girls], but all the Jewish boys were busy having fun with the *shikses.* Oh, they'd come if we put on a dance at the Center, but all the parents came too. It was like a ball in the Old South— the mothers sat around watching their daughters, while the father went into the club rooms to play cards. It was a nice warm feeling—but not for romance.

We mixed with the gentile kids at school dances. In fact, one of those little Nazis from Penngrove actually asked me to dance with him at a high school hop! This was a guy who had thrown lighted matches at me in grammar school, and suddenly he found me attractive in high school. I said, "No way!!" I wouldn't even look at him! I still remember those matches when I see him around town now.

I went out with a lot of gentile boys, but I had to meet them at the movie theater in town or at the softball games in Santa Rosa. Sometimes we'd hitchhike to the Russian River and meet the boys at a beach there. Everyone knew you were dating a gentile—you can't hide anything in a small town—but it was okay as long as no one went into the parents' homes.

The one time a gentile boy picked me up at the house, my father really humiliated me. I used to go dancing at the Russian River with Dominick Bertelli. It was nothing serious, but we didn't want to sneak around all the time. So when my father saw Dominick pull into our ranch one evening he yelled at me in Yiddish, "You're not going to the big bands with a *shaygets!*" And before Dominick got into the house my father yelled at him to get out and never come back and not to bother me again!

I'll never forget that. It was just prejudice by my father. It was prejudice by the whole Jewish community. I felt stifled in Petaluma. There was nothing here for Jewish girls.

IRVING GOLDEN

Oh, listen, you couldn't! If you brought home a girl who wasn't Jewish, good-by Charlie! None of us did it! Never! Just going out with a non-Jewish girl meant a fight. My mother would holler, "Why a *shikse?* Why a *shikse?* What's wrong with the Jewish girls?"

And I'd yell back, "There is none! There is none!"

ARLENE FEINSTEIN FELDMAN [b. 1923; New York City]

You want to know why the Jewish boys and the Jewish girls never dated each other in Petaluma? It was because they grew up in a kind of *kibbutz.* They were like brothers and sisters. It was impossible to date each other. I was an outsider. That's why I was able to date Petaluma boys. But I never felt like a real part of this community.

My life stopped when our family moved to Petaluma in 1938. We came from New York at the suggestion of my aunt and uncle, Khaya and Zev Feinstein, because my father took sick and couldn't run the delicatessen. I suddenly found myself isolated on a little chicken ranch ten miles outside of this little chicken town.

I missed the big city life. I missed the feeling of Jewish life in New York. My family wasn't orthodox religious, but we observed all the Jewish holidays in New York. My father would close the store, my mother cooked kosher, and we'd have a big holiday dinner with all the relatives. There was a holiday atmosphere in the whole neighborhood. Everything was closed. Everyone went to *shul,* a real *shul* with a real rabbi. Everyone strutted around in their best clothes; you could smell the mothballs in *shul!* In New York you were *surrounded* by the holiday. You had a *feeling* of a Jewish holiday. In Petaluma it was just your little old family driving to that funny little chapel at the Center for services led by Mr. Haller. You hardly dressed up. After services you drove right home, changed clothes, and fed the chickens. That's no holiday!

Living way out on a chicken ranch, I missed everything. Not that there was much to do in Petaluma, but I couldn't even get into town for the school dances. I never learned how to dance! I missed it all. I was stuck at home because nobody ever thought of teaching me how to drive. If I got a ride to a BBG meeting at the Center, I'd just sit there like a bump on a log. The Petaluma Jewish girls had their own little clique and I couldn't get in. They drove, they went dancing to the big bands at the Russian River, they dated gentile boys and they [laughing]—well, let's just say they got around a lot more than me. Compared to my old girlfriends in New York, they seemed like gentiles! I was completely out of it here.

SID JACOBS

I was different from the other Jewish kids. I wasn't much of a joiner and I didn't do much dating either. I liked hunting and fishing and hiking. I played football and ran cross-country in high school. I did all these things that Jewish boys don't do. My Jewish friends always got on me about hunting: "Why do you kill animals? Why do you like guns?"

They never understood the sociability of a hunting group. They didn't understand how satisfying hunting could be. There was this neat unbroken chain: their fathers didn't do it and they didn't do it. Jewish boys did not hunt! But I hunted. I loved the outdoors. Very few of the other Jewish guys did. Most of my friends were gentiles. They always said to me, "You don't act like a Jew."

MIKE GOLD [b. 1921; Petaluma]

Prejudice? Yeah. I saw prejudice as a kid—from the Jewish community—for being too Jewish, for being religious. Rube Lipsky—he went to *shul* every Saturday morning with his father. Since his father was crippled up and didn't have much to do, they put him in charge of collecting *shul* dues, getting the right wine, hiring a cantor for the High Holidays; and Rube helped him. They were in the *shul,* and most people in the Jewish community were fanatically antireligious.

Rube's Jewish friends gave him a lot of problems about going to services. The prejudice was so strong that his father actually canceled Rube's *bar mitzvah.* A *bar mitzvah* wasn't a big deal in those days. They did it simply, like in the Old Country. You learned your *haftorah* [ritual reading from the Torah] in a few months, you went through the ceremony at a Saturday morning service, and afterward there was cakes and *shnaps* [whiskeys]. Simple. But all Rube's Zionist and socialist friends made so many snide remarks that his father finally canceled it.

Compared to that harassment, the anti-Semitism around here was nothing. I wasn't bothered by a little teasing from gentiles—calling me Jerusalem or something. I didn't much care when I couldn't get into De Molay, the top boys' club in high school. They never let you forget you were different, but the prejudice worked both ways; we Jews didn't have a very high opinion of the gentiles either.

The Jewish kids stuck together. The guys had a chapter of AZA [Aleph Zadik Aleph, a B'nai B'rith boys' organization] and the girls were in BBG. We had our own sports events, dances, hay rides, you name it. Of course, you didn't date a Jewish girl from Petaluma, but you didn't seriously date a gentile girl either. For serious dating you'd meet someone at a dance at the San Francisco Jewish Community Center.

The gentiles weren't any problem. The *linke* kids were the problem. Their parents wouldn't let them join "reactionary" B'nai B'rith youth organizations. The *farbrente* [red-hot] left-wingers wouldn't even let their kids walk into the Center after the 1934 election controversy. It went on for years that way: one kid was *rekht*, another was *link*, and there was no more contact than an occasional hello.

That's why the Jewish community always was in danger from the gentiles. Here we were, trying to make a place for ourselves in Petaluma, and these left-wingers caused nothing but trouble. After Hochman was tarred and feathered, the gentiles were convinced that all the Jews were Communists. So what did the *linke* kids do? Stick to sports and cars and dating like every other kid in Petaluma? No. They started a chapter of the Petaluma Young Communist League!

David Adler

The guys from left-wing families were late bloomers. Where the guys from *rekhte* families went to AZA dances, we'd go to San Francisco to hear a speech by Mickey Lima, the Communist party organizer for the Pacific Coast.

My father discouraged me from entering the Center after he was kicked off the board of directors by the judge in 1934. AZA was taboo to him because B'nai B'rith was a right-wing organization. I missed all the Jewish youth activities here in the thirties.

We had a Jewish orientation in our home, a progressive Jewish orientation. You know, Moses, the Prophets, Judah Maccabee [chuckling]— the Jews were always fighters for social justice. When we had a *seder,* we had all the traditional foods and my father told the story of the Jewish revolutionary struggle against the oppression of the pharaohs.

When it came to anti-Semitism, I think the *linke* parents were less afraid of the authorities and more willing to rock the boat. My father had a very hot temper about anti-Semitism. When a teacher once called me a dirty Jew, I ran home to my father and he took me right back to school and barged in on the classroom. The teacher sent the kids out for recess, but we all listened at the ventilator. My father read that teacher the riot act, in Yiddish and in English. And that was the last anti-Semitic remark I heard from her.

There was a lot more anti-Semitism in the schools in those days, but it wasn't very serious. All the Jewish kids went to two-room country grammar schools with gentiles as our closest friends. We were accepted like everyone else at Petaluma High School. There were occasional anti-Semitic remarks, but I was able to join De Molay, the top social club for boys.

Actually, I was more interested in progressive organizations. I identified with my father's politics when I grew up, and I joined some very liberally oriented organizations. All us *linke* kids were in the American Civil Liberties Union and the Young Democrats. We didn't actually do anything in Petaluma except hold meetings, bring in speakers, and have weenie roasts at the beach. But we considered ourselves very enlightened in our support for the labor movement and the struggle against fascism.

JOE HOCHMAN

I went to work on the docks in San Francisco when I was fifteen. I left home because I couldn't get along with the old man. The tar and feathering happened right after I left. My first job was standing up some God-damned oil drums laying on their sides. My partner was a great big Swede. He stands his first drum right up! I got a hold of the back end of my God-damn' drum and MFGGH! My arms are jerking, my ass is going up in the air, but the drum ain't moving.

The Swede says, "You having some trouble kid?"

"I can't stand this fucking thing up!"

"Watch." And boom! He stands up another barrel!

I say, "All right, I can do it now." Boom! And the barrel stood up. You had to rock it when you put a heave to it. But you still had to heave. By the end of that first day I knew I had worked! But I made it. I stayed for a year and a half.

The 1936 dock strike happened during that time. Picket duty! Tangling with the company goons and the cops was a big charge for a sixteen-year-old kid. And then the flush of victory. Nice—being a part of the whole thing and getting a pat on the back from guys that knew you'd been there.

Then the Spanish Civil War broke loose. When I decided to go, my folks were at the second trial of the vigilantes. I told them outside the courtroom, "I'm going to Spain."

My mother started to cry. Pop says, "You're not old enough."

I looked at him and says, "I've managed to survive a year and a half on my own."

"War is different. They shoot at you."

"I know," I said. "But if nothing else, you taught me fascists are no good. They've got to be stopped."

He looked at me: "I can't stop you."

I went, for two years. I was only seventeen when I arrived, but I got myself into the First Regiment of Transport. It was a special trucking battalion that went where they figured no vehicles could get in or out. We hauled troops, guns, ammunition. Where the ambulances stopped, we went in to bring out the wounded. Under front-line machine-gun fire. I've been there. Then a tank hit the truck I was driving, and I got fucking hit in the foot. They sent me back to a hospital in Barcelona. Then there was the agreement to pull all the international troops out of Spain.

The American Internationalists get a send-off with cheering crowds in Spain and all across France. We got royal treatment, until we reached New York. The FBI and the Immigration Department marched us right off the boat and onto Ellis Island. Welcome home. They tried to keep me out of the country. This bunch of fat slugs from the Immigration Department gave me the second degree, but all they learned was that Dick Tracy recruited me into the International Brigades. They were fuckin' livid when Secretary of Labor Perkins allowed me in.

That was it. I caught the next Greyhound bus west. There were probably a hundred people waiting for me when I arrived at the depot in San Francisco. Most of the Jewish kids I grew up with in Petaluma were there. The hero had returned.

DAVID ADLER

When Joe came back, he was like a hero. You know, here was this guy who had been on the track team at Petaluma High School. He had been on the hay rides of the Young Democrats. And now he was a veteran of the Abraham Lincoln Brigade.

I never left Petaluma. My father took ill with ulcers during the Depression and it was my duty to help out with the family. I was a good student. I could have gone on to college and been most anything. But in those days you did what you had to do. I remained on the ranch after I graduated from high school.

I became partners in the chicken business with my father. It wasn't easy because he would not change his ranching methods. For instance, we had a problem with chickens getting blisters while on their roosts and then being downgraded when we sold them. We could have eliminated the problem by moving the feeders closer to the roosts, but he wouldn't consider it. That's how it was made and that's how you did it.

I spent years trying to convince him to put gas lines and brooder stoves into all the chicken houses. Then we wouldn't have to move the older chickens out of the one house with brooder stoves each time we took in a new batch of chickens. It was the same thing with installing a water-pressure system or building more convenient access doors into the chicken houses. No changes. My father would not cut corners. He would not innovate. None of our parents would do it. They were as stubborn in their ranching methods as they were in their politics.

Julia Shiffman Segal

College? Leave the ranch? I suppose there were a lot of things I could have done, but I didn't know any other life. Class differentiations didn't mean anything to me. When I was a teenager I once heard someone speak derisively about a man who hauled chicken manure for a living. I couldn't understand it, because he worked hard and he was honest. What was wrong with that?

These were the values of the Jewish community. The kids were not expected to attend some fancy college, become a professional, and get rich. You had *yikhus* [prestige of ancestry] when your family worked hard and raised good chickens. My family was poor, but I had *yikhus* in Petaluma. I didn't know any better.

Sid Jacobs

My father was disappointed when I didn't go to college. He didn't think it was degrading to work in a garment shop or raise chickens, but he wanted me to take advantage of the opportunities he didn't have. He thought I should get a college education and live the good life in America. I don't know why, but I never was inclined toward that. My father was a self-taught Yiddish scholar and he believed very strongly in education, but I didn't do very well in school. I was more interested in the outdoors. My love of hunting led me to forestry work. After high school I went to work for the county doing rural conservation and fighting forest fires.

Since I wasn't going to college, my parents made me promise to return to the ranch in a year or two. My interest in nature made no sense to my father. You know, who ever heard of a Jewish forest ranger?

Milton Rubinstein

Our parents didn't want us working on the ranches like the non-Jewish kids. The Italians, the Portuguese, the Japanese—these guys came to school yawning. Some of them had been up since four in the morning milking cows. The girls too! You should have seen Stella Giardini—a great big girl—she milked those cows right along with her brothers. Our parents pushed us to do well in school. The Jewish kids were strongly represented among the grade grabbers and the scholarship grabbers.

Why? That's like asking "who is a Jew?" My parents expected me to go to college and get a good job someplace else. They never considered it possible that I would stay on a chicken ranch. My parents weren't planning to stay themselves. They lived in Petaluma for over thirty years, but it was a transient thing. When I was young they talked about going to Palestine. As I grew up they talked about moving to the city. My father was a Zionist and an intellectual; he did not want to put down roots on a Petaluma chicken ranch, and he did not want me to have anything to do with chickens.

I always knew I would go to college. By the time I entered high school I knew it would be engineering at U.C. Berkeley. It was unspoken, but I always knew I would leave Petaluma. I wanted wider horizons.

FRAN RUBINSTEIN GINSBERG

I wanted to leave Petaluma as fast as possible after high school. There were no Jewish boys and my parents wouldn't let me go around with gentile boys. I wanted some independence and excitement. There was no life for me in Petaluma.

My parents wanted me to continue in school, so I lived at home and went to Santa Rosa Junior College for a few years. I regret now that I didn't go further, but I knew my parents couldn't afford to send both me and my brother to U.C. Berkeley. Milton was very bright and, well, he was a boy, so he went to the university. I guess I was more interested in having fun anyhow.

I finally took a civil-service exam and got a government job in San Francisco. Living in the city was very exciting. I was on my own. There was boys, dances, a lot of hubbub. I really wanted to stay, but Leon wouldn't hear of it. Leon and I were the only ones who got married from within the Jewish community. We went together on and off, through high school and after. I wanted to stay in San Francisco, but Leon said he could never live in a city. You know, he didn't have an education, he didn't have a trade. He grew up on a Petaluma chicken ranch and all he knew was chickens. So what else could we do after we married? We rented a little chicken ranch in Petaluma.

ELAINE GOLDEN BLUMBERG [b. 1921; Riga, Latvia]

My mother hated Petaluma, but my father refused to leave. He said he'd get ulcers in the city. My mother always said to me, "Go to San

Francisco. It's too lonely on the ranch. It's too much hard work. You go find a nice Jewish boy in the city."

If you hear it enough, you pick it up. I planned to leave Petaluma right after high school. I was going to start something new in San Francisco in the fall. But that summer I met him.

MAX BLUMBERG [b. 1920; Vineland, New Jersey]: You started in September. You started on me! [Laughing.]

How did I get to Petaluma? Oh, boy, that is a big *mayse*, a big story! Her uncle, Nathan Rothman, he used to work for my father in Vineland, New Jersey, another Jewish chicken-ranching town. When I was bumming through California in the late thirties, I stopped to see Nathan in Petaluma. I did not intend to stay. I was bumming all over the country. But you know what happens.

I stayed with Rothmans and found it homey in Petaluma. It was interesting people, a friendly little Jewish community, a quiet small town. Nobody had much money and nobody worried about it. The people were happy with hard work and no worries.

Then the Rothmans arranged for me to meet her, and that was my nemesis! I liked her—she wasn't one of these put-on city broads. I liked her family. I liked the whole thing. We got married and started living the good life on a chicken ranch.

IRVING GOLDEN

If your concept is that we all just sat here and loved the chicken business and loved Petaluma—if that's your idea—then you're all wet! Yeah, my brother-in-law Max liked it, but ask my sister Elaine about chicken ranching. I didn't want to stay, that's for sure! I didn't like the chicken ranch one bit. As far as I was concerned, chickens were a fly-by-night business.

I got myself started in journalism at U.C. Berkeley in 1941. After little Petaluma High School it was tough at the university with all those big classes. I was just starting to get over the hump when my folks pressured me to come back on the ranch.

I came back, but I got really turned off. First it was more of this brainwashing that you must date Jewish girls. Okay, you could do it, you could date a gentile girl, but marry a gentile girl? You might as well have jumped off a cliff! A lot went steady with gentiles. I was involved with a gentile girl almost down to the ceremony. And then, whooosh—they chopped it right off!

Then it was more brainwashing about how wonderful the chicken ranch is and how wonderful the Jewish community is and how wonderful the small town is. I wanted to be a journalist, and there I was, stuck on a little chicken ranch. I got turned off from the whole thing.

SHURA EASTMAN COMPISI

I escaped from Petaluma as quickly as I could. I was sixteen when my family moved here, and I always missed the excitement of a big-city high school and the big-city labor movement. Petaluma was provincial, and the Jewish kids were provincial like everyone else. I didn't fit. I went straight back to San Francisco after high school.

If I hadn't married a Petaluma boy, I never would have returned. I was working for the government, which was the thing to do in those days, and I was active with labor defense committees. It was an exciting time, but I had to marry someone who had *roots* in Petaluma. Italian roots! And they dug deep!

Yes, it was unusual that I married a gentile man. The Jewish kids who grew up in Petaluma all married Jewish boys and girls. It seems to me that they were very limited and closed-minded. They were not ready to accept my husband as a part of the Jewish community.

It was fine with my parents that I married a gentile. To tell you the truth [laughing], I think my father preferred that I married a gentile over a *rekhter*. A lot of these old guys in the *linke* preferred that their kids marry anyone but a right-winger from the Jewish community. My parents weren't disappointed over who I married. They were disappointed that I gave my marriage more attention than politics. Politics was the center of their lives and they just assumed that's where all my energies would go.

They didn't want me to work in a factory, but they didn't want me on a chicken ranch either. My parents' generation took pride in saying "my daughter works for a union" or "my son is a teacher." You weren't supposed to open a delicatessan or work in an insurance office. You certainly weren't supposed to be like a Santa Rosa Jew, geared in one direction, money! It was best to be a professional, as long as you served humanity.

I can explain it with a riddle:

What's the difference between a needle trades worker and a social worker?
One generation!

Well, my parents didn't mind that I was back on a chicken ranch. They were troubled that I would not devote myself to saving humanity through all the *linke* political organizations and activities. I had a strong sense of social conscience, but I didn't want to drag my family off to meetings every night. I didn't want all our family activities to be part of the struggle to build socialism. I was a different generation and I made a different choice. I devoted myself to my husband, my kids, and our chicken ranch.

8 "When There's a War It Gets Busy"

We organized the Anti-Fascist Emergency Committee in 1938. At that time the Nazis carried out a pogrom against all the Jews in Germany. They called it Crystal Night. We looked upon this as the beginning of the destruction of the Jewish people. We knew Hitler; we read *Mein Kampf*. He blamed the Jews for all the troubles of mankind. Every Jew—rich or poor, right or left—it made no difference to the Nazis. We saw that Crystal Night is the beginning of the Final Solution.

The *linke* felt we've got to do something. Don't forget, here in Sonoma County there were fascist organizations too. You can never tell what will happen. Even in America we had to defend ourselves. The *linke* talked to all the Jewish chicken ranchers about a new organization to fight the fascist menace. The people agreed, but the leaders of the other organizations hesitated. So we decided to call a meeting just in the name of the IWO, our left-wing International Workers Order. And you would be surprised, the Center was packed! People took the floor and said, "There is a danger, even here. We must be united."

It was decided right there to create an Emergency Committee to defend Jews anywhere in the world, whether it's Germany or here. That night we collected over one thousand dollars. The other leaders had to go along with it because of the sentiment of the people.

Holtzman was the chairman, with two delegates from each organization. The IWO worked with the Arbeiter Ring and the Poale Tsion and the B'nai B'rith. In fact, at one time Katz and the Jacobs brothers took a position with me against the B'nai B'rith. Katz said to me, "You can see they are bourgeois." The Zionists and the social democrats were inclined toward workers' interests to some extent, so we could work together.

The Anti-Fascist Emergency Committee was the greatest political event in my life here in Petaluma. All the Jews were united. It made no difference what organizations you belonged to and what ideologies you believed in. This was something else. This was Petaluma's Popular Front to save the Jewish people.

JACOB KATZ

You could not trust the Communists and their "popular fronts." Just before the Anti-Fascist Emergency Committee, they were calling us social fascists. They said we supported the move by capitalist nations to turn Nazi Germany against the Soviet dictatorship.

Then the Communists almost broke up the Emergency Committee when Stalin made the nonaggression pact with Hitler in 1939. At first the *linke* laid low. Then they circulated petitions that the United States should not give lend-lease destroyers to England in the fight against Germany. They did it because the Soviet Union was not against Hitler at the time of the pact. The Communists here said that the United States should stay out of a capitalist imperialist war. Indirectly, they actually were supporting Hitler against England!

We never trusted the *linke* to defend Jewish interests, unless it happened to be the policy of the Soviet Union. Only when the Soviet Union was attacked by Hitler did these Communists become very great patriots in the war against Naziism.

BEN HOCHMAN

We had some problems in the Popular Front against fascism. When Stalin made the pact with Hitler, the *rekhte* could not see that the Soviet Union needed more time to prepare for a war with the Nazis. They said that anyone who supports the Soviet Union is a traitor to the Jewish people.

When the Soviet Union invaded Finland, the *rekhte* made a big thing about the poor Finnish people. We explained that the Finnish leader Mannerheim was making Finland into an arm of the Nazis and the Soviet Union was protecting itself by invading Finland. But the *rekhte* went all out to raise money for Finland. They actually helped the Nazis!

The *rekhte* was so anti-Soviet that they went against the interests of the Jewish people. Not until Germany attacked the Soviet Union did they see that the Soviet Union was the greatest opponent of fascism. Then the *rekhte* became great sympathizers of the Soviet Union.

JULIA SHIFFMAN SEGAL

The week Paris fell, our neighbors, the Webers, had a barn-warming party. All the Germans in town came. There was a lot of beer and they got very drunk. We could hear them yelling, "Heil Hitler" and "we'll kill the Jews" and things like that. My parents thought they would come over and burn down our house! We were up all night listening to them. We were *so afraid*! I'll *never* forget it.

ARTHUR LaSALLE

Our Jewish people actually won more community sympathy when Hitler started up. There were no statements that "the Jews deserve this." We thought it was ghastly when the Nazis said, "Well, the Jews aren't producers so we'll give them the gas." Oh, there were a few oddball German Americans around here who liked Hitler. They met out at Hermann Sons Hall in soldier costumes. But the local representative of the FBI came to see me about these people. They weren't dangerous, but we kept an eye on them.

STELLA FINKLESTEIN

The guest speaker at the Petaluma United Jewish Appeal banquet of 1940 was Manfred Ary, who had been a member of the Austrian Supreme Court. He had been degraded when Hitler took over Austria. In flawless English he told how he had been forced to go on hands and knees scrubbing the streets of Vienna with a brush. This was a giant of a man. He gave a tremendous speech. When Mr. Rubinstein started to make the financial appeal—in Yiddish, of course—Ary interrupted: "Excuse me. If I knew this was a Yiddish-speaking community, I would have spoke in Yiddish." He said it in a beautiful Austrian Yiddish.

A lot of the Austrian Jews had a cultivated appreciation for German culture; they had contempt for Yiddish as a bastard form of the German language. But not Ary. He made a tremendous impact on the community that evening.

MORRY FINKLESTEIN: He was exceptional. The Austrian Jews and the German Jews were snobs! I saw it for myself when I left Poland and crossed Germany as a boy. They did not like Polish Jews when we were refugees, and they still did not like Polish Jews when they were refugees. A group of them landed here before the war, but they never fit in.

The first of the prewar refugees, the Frandzels, they were from Prague—Czech Jews. They were okay. It's just that they were city people. I was on our committee that helped them settle on a ranch. Two hours before the first chicks were to arrive, I checked their chicken houses and found no straw on the floors. And where were the Frandzels? In the house sipping tea!

I said, "What are you doing? You've got to put down straw!"

"Relax. There's no hurry. Join us for tea." They had a lot to learn about chicken ranching.

There was another refugee, an Austrian Jew who came up here to check into starting a chicken ranch. He was a well-heeled business-man who wanted to know about "capital investment" and "profit margins." After ten minutes on my ranch he said, "No, I think I will keep my assets liquid."

STELLA: These German and Austrian refugees were much more advanced than the Russian and Polish Jews. They were well educated and culturally sophisticated. These people had real business and professional accomplishments in Europe. Those who landed on chicken ranches found it disagreeable. They had a hard time accommodating to life in Petaluma. Some of them would have nothing to do with the Jewish community. Others accepted a few of us. I met them as an intellectual equal. But they were very much more culturally advanced than most of the Jews here.

MORRY: I beg to disagree with you. You think too much of these people. The Frandzels were nice, Gans was a nice guy, but most of them were snobs. It was beneath their dignity to deal with chicken shit. They were real snobs—stinky snobs.

SAMUEL GANS [b. 1912; Vienna, Austria]

Thousands of Jewish people perished because America would not take them in. Roosevelt, with all his good qualities, was a bastard on the Jewish question. There was a lot of Jewish influence around Roosevelt—Morgenthau and the rest—but these affluent upstarts didn't want more Jewish immigration. They were afraid of the same thing we Viennese Jews faced when the east European Jews flooded in after World War I.

You know who helped a few of us get into America before the Holocaust? It was the little people—the garment workers in New York, the chicken ranchers in Petaluma. The Petaluma Jewish community helped me personally in so many ways. I don't know how else I could have survived the war years.

My wife and I were uprooted from Vienna when the Nazis invaded. I had no desire to leave. I had a large, close family. I had just received my doctorate in child psychology and was starting a career. I was completely uprooted. I lost everything. The Hebrew Immigrant Aid Society brought me to San Francisco with the understanding that I would get a job, but no institution would hire a refugee psychologist. The pressing thing was to raise money and get my family out of Belgium, where they had fled.

When I heard about the chicken people in Petaluma, I thought, "Perhaps that's a way to make money quick." We were taken to Petaluma in the back of a truck with our few possessions. That evening we were dropped at a ramshackle broken-down chicken ranch. No lights—no running water—nothing. My wife cried.

We got some broilers, we made a raise, and in ten weeks we had five-hundred dollars. Do you know what five-hundred dollars was in those days? We had the money to buy tickets and affidavits for my family in Belgium. The day we went to get it, May the 11th, 1940, the Germans invaded Belgium. We never heard from my family again.

So that's how we came to Petaluma. It was a small drab nonplace—hardly a town at all. Just a dusty little Main Street with stores for farmers. Not even a public park for walking. But there were all these Jewish people who were tremendously helpful to us. The Katzes, the Rubinsteins, the Feinsteins, the Jacobs brothers—they helped us not just with the chickens, but with emotional support. They were good people who did everything possible to help us join their warm community and their way of life. They became like our family. And they were aware—the immigrant generation knew what was happening in Europe. This was important to me.

When we came to this country, I had no mission in mind. I didn't particularly want to talk about what was happening in Europe because I didn't want to relive it. But when it sometimes came up in a discussion, many Jewish Americans wouldn't believe what was going on. They thought my stories were made up, particularly the younger generation in Petaluma. Their parents followed world events and understood persecution, but the children were terribly naive. They were typical provincial people from an isolated little American farming town. It seemed impossible that we could live there.

Lou Green

When they started drafting people, that's when I began to see there was something wrong in the world. Until then, I thought the whole thing would blow over. I had no idea what the Nazis were doing to the Jews in the concentration camps. No one told me. Nobody knew. Of course, I knew about the Nazis here because their kids had beat me up after school every day in Penngrove. In high school one of those Nazi bullies, Hans Koeller, would "Heil Hitler" instead of saluting the flag every morning. He openly boasted that his father sent money back to Germany for the Führer. They changed their tune after Pearl Harbor and the American declaration of war against Germany. A week later my father and I bought some chickens from one of these Nazi farmers. Now he was clucking his tongue about the Japanese sneak attack and the Japanese spies in Sonoma County.

I think the Germans around here were relieved when the focus shifted to the Japanese. But as far as I was concerned, they should have locked up the Germans. Why take all these innocent Japanese citizens and leave the German Nazis walking free? Well, some of us didn't forget the Germans. We specially remembered Anderson, the guy who had led the German Bund's Nazi parades here in the thirties. Like most Germans, he was very methodical. Everyday at ten o'clock he stopped at the newsstand near Gilroy's Bar, picked up a newspaper, and read the headlines. So we prepared a little surprise for him one morning. A few weeks after the war began, a bunch of the guys had a special newspaper printed with a false headline: that Anderson had been promoted to California leader of the Nazi party. We all watched that morning when he picked up the newspaper. He took one look at the headline, looked around to see if anyone saw him, and ran for his car! [Laughing.] We didn't hear much out of him for the rest of the war.

MORRY FINKLESTEIN

It is surprising how little impact the relocation of our Japanese neighbors had on the Jewish people. Because of the history of anti-Semitic persecution, the Jewish people usually are very sensitive to any attacks on civil liberties. But we didn't want to rock the boat in wartime. At that time we were 150-percent Americans.

It was a terrible injustice that happened to the Japanese. They were *all* taken, almost overnight! They were shipped out of Sonoma County so fast that they didn't have a chance to get a decent price for their ranches. And I am ashamed to say that some Jewish people were among those who took advantage and bought cheap.

On the other hand, the Haller feed mill took care of a few Japanese ranches and returned them after the war. Most of the Jewish people were fair and conscientious. We thought it was a terrible thing and we helped as we could. But we made no public outcry against their relocation. It never occurred to us to hold protest meetings or demonstrations. It was wartime and the military took them overnight. There was nothing we could do about it.

Most good people had the rationalization that the Japanese were better off going, because they would have been persecuted if they stayed. You can't imagine the poison that was spread around here! The *goyim*—excuse me, I shouldn't use that word—but some of them told me that this Japanese had machine guns hidden, that another was a captain in the

Japanese army, another was spying along the coast. Such rumors! Such lies! We thought the Japanese would be torn apart if they stayed.

Not even the left-wing movement said anything, not here and not in San Francisco. Because at that time the Communist party made an all-out effort to defeat fascism. The left wing accepted the Japanese evacuation as a necessity in the war against fascism. That was the rationalization of the *linke* here in Petaluma.

You must understand the tremendous patriotism in the Jewish community when the war came. In the Old Country it was impossible for the Jewish people to be patriots for those anti-Semitic governments. I knew boys who actually crippled themselves so as not to be drafted into the Polish army. I myself fled Poland rather than go into the army. But now we were proud to see our Jewish children go off to defend America against fascism. This was something new for us. It was a chance to show the gentiles that the Jews are not aliens and subversives. At the same time we would be helping our people in Europe. We all supported the American war effort. We gave huge amounts of money. This was one time I did not mind the community pressure to give.

BASHA SINGERMAN

Here is a picture of our Petaluma Russian War Relief Committee at the Soviet consulate. The consul and his wife are in the middle, with a group of our Petaluma *khaverim* around them. This picture was in the Petaluma newspaper with a report that we were honored at a consulate reception for our wonderful work.

We had twenty progressive women working for Russian War Relief in Petaluma. We opened a little shop in town to collect food and clothing. You would be surprised—all the Jewish people, even the *rekhte,* and a lot of gentile people too, they made contributions. We sent a lot to the Soviet Union.

We wanted to help the great Soviet struggle against fascism. It was such terrible suffering of the Russian people during the war. It was suffering of our own Jewish people and our own families in Russia. This is why we worked so hard for Russian war relief.

KHAYA FEINSTEIN

President Roosevelt did not go out of his way to help Zionism, so we doubled our efforts to send money. More than ever, the war made the American-Jewish people see that we got to have our own country in Palestine! Even some of the *linke* gave because they saw that we got to get the Jewish people from Europe to Palestine! This was *our families* that we left behind! This was *our people* Hitler was destroying!

SID JACOBS

The *linke* and the *rekhte* made a *sholom*, a peace, during the war. The whole community was united against fascism. Everybody socialized at the Center and everything was to support the war effort. You should have seen the money that was raised! We even had a big Russian celebration in the Center. Once a Russian ship came to San Francisco, with a woman captain! Her and her crew were invited up to the Petaluma Jewish Community Center.

The entire Jewish community turned out, except for a few die-hards like my uncle Rafoelke. He never forgave the Soviet Union for the Nazi-Soviet pact of 1939, when Poland was divided. We had family in Poland that we never heard from again. This Russian crew put on a real show. They sang, they danced, they did the *kazatski*! We joined in, clapping and singing and dancing with them! Then there was a big Russian feast, with lots of food and vodka and toasts. That evening everybody spoke Russian at the Jewish Community Center.

ARTHUR LASALLE

The Jewish people were accepted as good citizens during the war. They were very generous in our Petaluma fund-raising drives to help the American war effort. They were very hospitable to servicemen stationed in this area. And their boys went to war with all the other boys. They were good Americans.

LOU GREEN

I enlisted with the feeling that it was my duty. Agricultural deferments were easy to get, but I wanted to serve my country. We all thought the war was just and necessary. Every Jewish family was proud when a son went into the service.

I thought the war would give me material for the Great American Novel I planned to write. Well, I was overseas for twenty-five months, and I must tell you that the army helped me get a sense of reality. I grew up believing in the great American principle that you're rewarded if you do a good job. I thought the army would give me an opportunity to display what I really could do and be recognized for it. Boy, did I have a revelation! They couldn't care less about what I could do. The material

I got for my novel was all politics and ass-kissing and who you knew. The army was a microcosm of what American life is all about.

MILTON RUBINSTEIN

Lou Green was in on the invasion of Saipan. He had a hard time, to a degree, but by the time I got there he was maneuvering like he used to deal chickens with his father. Lou is a famous man [chuckling]—in the American occupation of Saipan.

DAVID ADLER

I enlisted in the army air force, because I was about to be drafted. I didn't expect much, so I was surprised by the new opportunities I grasped. I never had done anything but raise chickens and I never had been anywhere outside Northern California. While I was in the service I saw a good part of the United States and Asia. I was trained as a mechanic and I assumed a lot of responsibilities as an NCO in our outfit. It's hard to explain, but I returned to Petaluma with new confidence.

MICHAEL FELDMAN

You didn't pay much attention to the war before Pearl Harbor, and then suddenly patriotism was running strong. You figured this madman had to be stopped, so you wanted to do your duty. Of course, you tried to better yourself. I enlisted so I could get into radio engineering. I thought it would be useful in modernizing my father's secondhand store after the war, and I thought it would keep me on an American base during the war. But it turned out different. It turned out rotten! I wound up in a small hut in China with five uneducated guys from Mississippi. I had nothing to do but talk with these people for twenty-eight months!

MILTON RUBINSTEIN

My brother-in-law Leon shared a tent on Tinean with one of the guys who had thrown matches in my sister Fran's hair back in Penngrove. He turned out to be not such a bad guy. Kind of interesting.

JOE HOCHMAN

I hung around Petaluma for a year after I returned from Spain. It was a little too peaceful with no lead flyin' anymore, so I went back to work on the San Francisco waterfront until the war started.

When I tried to enlist the Petaluma draft board said, "No, you're in a nondraftable industry."

I said, "I don't give a shit. I'm volunteering. I ain't got no fucking use for fascists!"

I wound up in an armor training division. While we were out on maneuvers one day, they were hitting us with so-called machine gun fire—blanks. So everybody's playing soldier, only I'm not playing the way the other guys are playing. I'm playing like I'm really being shot at. I run, I cut, I hit the dirt and roll. Right after that I got called to see the captain. He says, "You ever been in the army before?"

"No sir."

"I don't mean the U.S. army."

So I knew my FBI dossier had caught up with me. I'd never told the army I'd been in the Spanish Civil War. I says, "If you mean was I in Spain, sir, yes."

"It was obvious in the exercises that you had been under fire before." He says, "Tell me about Spain."

That started a long bull session. When we finished he said, "At the next orientation period, I want you to tell the guys about your experiences in Spain. Tie it into the fact they they are being pushed in this training to save their God-damned asses some day." I gave the next orientation lecture, and when they got through with the questions it had lasted an hour and a half longer than usual. The captain said, "That's the first time those God-damned jackasses listened."

So that became my job in the army. They wouldn't transfer me into a combat group, no matter what I tried. I spent the war talking about Spain.

NATHAN HOCHMAN

There's nothing much to tell. I was a ball turret gunner on a B-17. Got shot down and spent a year in a German prisoner-of-war camp. A year and a day. Got liberated by the American army and came home. That's about it.

LEO HOOK [b. 1918; Petaluma]

My cousin Irving Rosenberg, he was the first Jewish boy from Petaluma to be lost. On Okinawa. I stayed out of it. You know how *yidishe* mamas are! They don't want their kids in the army. They came to this country to get away from the tsar's army. I got an agricultural deferment and raised chickens during the war.

HAL DRAPER [b. 1923; Petaluma]

Most of the Jewish guys did their duty and went in. Those who didn't—that was their problems. I enlisted because I'm sensitive about anti-Semitism. It bothered me when I grew up in Petaluma—and maybe it bothered me that we didn't do anything about it. I went into the air force and became an officer—a bomber pilot. I showed them that a Jew could do it.

IRVING GOLDEN

My draft deferment was another thing that turned me off about Petaluma after I returned from the university. People didn't realize that I was seventeen when I graduated high school. My classmates were all eighteen and they were drafted immediately. But by the time I reached eighteen there was a shortage of dairy workers, so they gave out deferments for dairy work. I was one of the few Jewish fellows left in Petaluma, and there was a resentment against me. People always asked, "Why aren't you in the service?" Which gets you sick and tired. We had those cows for years. They didn't make up this dairy deferment for me alone. It was just one of those things, but no one understood.

ARLENE FEINSTEIN FELDMAN

You know who went to war from Petaluma? Not the farmers' sons; they got agricultural deferments. It was the businessmen's sons! Michael was sent to a little hut in China just a year after we were married! And I was left isolated again. At least I was off the ranch. I lived in town with my in-laws, the Feldmans, and helped them out in the secondhand store.

But still I was not part of the Jewish community. Because I didn't have a husband! I was married, but it was like I was single. When I went to an affair at the Center, I was ignored. You needed a husband to be a real part of Jewish community life. The war years were boring for me: work, eat, write a letter to Michael, and go to sleep early. I didn't even learn how to drive because gas was rationed. And where would I have gone anyhow? There was nothing for me in Petaluma.

CELIA GLAZER HOCHMAN [b. 1925; New York City]

I didn't have much time for the Jewish community during the war. After I received notice that Nathan was in a German prisoner-of-war camp, I was completely occupied with working for the Red Cross and the YMCA prisoner-of-war program. I was allowed to send Nathan one package a month, and it was a big job just getting the things on the list of what could be sent. The war kept me very busy and very worried.

DIANE RABIN HARTMAN [b. 1925; Petaluma]

The war was marvellous! Absolutely marvellous!! Right near Petaluma was Hamilton Air Force Base, the Coast Guard at Two Rock Ranch, the cavalry at the Santa Rosa fairgrounds. Boys everywhere! I had a lot of fun!

The war didn't really hit me until my brother got drafted. Before that, when a girlfriend got me a date with a soldier from Hamilton Field, I was afraid to tell my mother. Jewish girls did not go out with soldiers! They were the dregs of the earth! But when nice Jewish boys from Petaluma became soldiers, it was entirely different. That's when this nonreligious Jewish community started holding Oneg Shabbat, Friday-night services. So the Jewish soldiers in the area would have someplace to go. It brought all the Jewish soldiers into the Center! Non-Jewish boys came too. Oh, we had a lot of boys around.

I met my husband at one of those Friday-night services. He didn't have a chance, poor guy. I met him in February of 1943 and we announced our engagement at the community *seder* in the spring. Joe Holtzman toasted us with champagne!

We had a huge wedding. Everybody came—four-hundred people. This was wartime, so the whole community gave sugar stamps for the cake. All the women helped with the cooking. Bill's parents flew out from New York for the wedding. They were very religious—sixteen sets of dishes—you couldn't mix anything—kosher kosher. When they arrived my mother-in-law asked, "Who is the *shoykhet* [ritual slaughter] for all this chicken at the wedding dinner?"

Bill says, "Me! I string up the chickens, take the knife, and whoosh— slit their throats!" [Much laughter.]

She almost had a heart attack.

We tried our best to have a real Jewish wedding. Rabbi Solomon Platt came up from San Francisco to marry us. We had the whole thing—the *khupe* [traditional wedding canopy], the banquet, music, dancing. We did it all after dark, so everyone had time to put their chickens to sleep.

BILL HARTMAN [b. 1921; New York City]: I was stationed as the dentist at the cryptography center outside Petaluma. Every Friday night, all of us Jewish soldiers went to the Jewish Center in Petaluma. The people were very hospitable, even to the non-Jewish boys we brought along. In other places where I was stationed, when you went to the local temple there was no special attempt to make you feel at home. But in Petaluma they invited you into their homes for the holidays, for Friday-night meals, anytime you felt lonely and wanted the company of a family.

Of course, the ulterior motive was to see that every eligible Jewish girl was presented to every Jewish bachelor in the area. Those Jewish mothers were quite active, and a number of Jewish servicemen married Petaluma Jewish girls. We never knew what hit us. It was kind of arranged . . .

MORT LEVINE [b. 1922; Columbus, Ohio]

When I tell people back in Ohio that our wedding was thrown by a whole Jewish community, they don't believe it. I show them the article from the Petaluma *Argus-Courier,* but they just can't believe it.

I was transferred to the Petaluma cryptography base in 1943. I already had gotten engaged to Sylvia over the telephone—we met while I was waiting for a boat in New Orleans—well, that's another story. She came out to visit me in Petaluma and we decided to get married before I shipped out.

Now, Sylvia was a typical Jewish broad. No little post wedding with the chaplain. She wanted a big affair with a white gown and all that jazz. Well, somebody in the Jewish community heard about it. And before we knew what was happening, the entire community was throwing us a wedding at the Petaluma Jewish Community Center. We ended up with five-hundred people at our wedding! It was all the Jews, all my army buddies, and the Petaluma VFW.

It was a real Jewish wedding. They brought up a rabbi from San Francisco. There were flowers and flower girls all over the place. They got a white wedding gown for Sylvia. There was a *khupe.* They even had a Yiddish chorus singing during the service! It was fantastic! Everybody brought food—what food!—and they all gave gorgeous gifts. There was dancing—drinking—toasts. What a crowd! What a commotion! The place was packed!

They were strangers, but they were like family. They put on one hell of a wedding for us.

KHAYA FEINSTEIN

So, all right, life went on, even during the war. If somebody bought a new ranch, right away we made a party for them. The Frandzels—they were the first refugees to settle in here before the war—when they bought a ranch, we all came in with presents and food and dancing. It was a *simkhe,* a celebration. Everybody was enjoying this party, when all of a sudden there is a knock at the door. They got a telegram: their son was killed in the war. They weren't even American citizens yet.

JIM BAXTER

I was delivering chicks from the Co-op Hatchery to a ranch one morning. Nobody was around the chicken house, so I knocked at the ranch house and a woman answered. The minute I saw her I knew something was wrong. There were tears streaming down her cheeks. She had just seen a picture in the newspaper of a certain street in Stalingrad. She said that many of her family lived on that street. And the picture showed nothing but devastation. All you could see was rubble.

MILTON RUBINSTEIN

Ike Haller was a real swashbuckler before the war. He whooped it up, drank it up. He was going into the U.S. Marines! He got the worst of any of us. He hopped the Pacific islands: Bougainville, Guadalcanal, a series of island fights.

I saw him in Guam, just after he quit. He was supposed to go to Iwo Jima, but he refused. He was not well at that point. He was having terrible nightmares. He slept with a cocked forty-five by his bed. He had some tomatoes planted near his tent—they were his pride and joy—and he had booby traps set all around them. He shot at anyone who came near those tomatoes.

I don't know the full story, but he was discharged soon after that. He came home early. He was never quite the same again.

LOU GREEN

The war was a bad experience for me. I went into the army with a lot of idealism and I came out disillusioned. I still don't regret having gone in. I couldn't have lived with myself if I had gotten an agricultural deferment. But I resented the ones who stayed behind in Petaluma and got fat in the chicken business.

MORRY FINKLESTEIN

The war rescued us all from the Dybbuk. No question about it. After all our suffering in the Depression, poultry prices rose in 1939, when the war began in Europe. It really got good when America entered the war. Agriculture is that kind of business. When there's a war it gets busy. The people who were already entrenched on their ranches for years, those who had the capacity and the know-how, they made fabulous money. Not fabulous like Wall Street war profiteers. But for such people to make $5,000 on a ten-week raise! To make $15,000—$20,000—$25,000 a year! They paid off their debts. They began to live comfortably for the first time in their lives!

HYMIE GOLDEN

First I pay off that Avrum Haas Fund. They was waiting patient all the years. They was very good to the Jewish farmers in here. Next I pay the feed company. They wasn't so bad. They always gave me enough credit for a small raise of chickens.

In 1943 I walked into the Bank of Italy, I said, "Mr. Lepore, I'm gonna pay off my mortgage!" All the years I couldn't pay a cent on the principal—I was just paying the interest—whenever I walked into the bank he says, "When you gonna pay on the principal? "Now I'm ready to pay everything, he says, "What's your hurry? We're not pressing you."

I paid him every cent what I owed. I went home I said, "This ranch is mine!"

Then I was the biggest millionaire, richer than Rockefeller! See, in Hebrew the saying is, *"Ha sameyach b'khelko"*—"the richest man is the one who is satisfied with what he has." I'll tell you one thing— money makes life more comfortable. Money, money, money! All the chicken ranchers made money in wartime. Everybody in here paid up the mortgage.

But I'll tell you another thing—some people was greedy. They was selling the chickens on the black market. Under the table they sold the chickens for six, eight, ten cents a pound over the government price. They weren't gonna be satisfied till they're the richest people in the Jewish Cemetery. We knew who they was.

SID JACOBS

One time I happened to find a sack full of money in a dresser at home! This was during the war. It scared the wits out of me! I asked my father what the hell's going on? He sort of grinned and said, "Everybody's doing it? Why not me?"

There was a lot of money to be made on the black market. Poultry wasn't rationed like beef, so there was a huge demand for it. The prices were controlled by the OPA [Office of Price Administration] at around thirty-cents a pound. But you could sell for forty to forty-five cents a pound on the black market. With twenty-thousand birds at two and a half pounds each in a ten-week raise, a difference of ten to fifteen cents a pound could add up to big money.

I saw it done. I was 4F during the war—I have a heart murmur and they wouldn't take me when I went to enlist—so I continued working for the forestry service, and occasionally I did some work for a chicken dealer. This guy operated on the black market. When he bought chickens, he paid the farmer by check, with a receipt, at the OPA ceiling price. He paid the balance under the table in cash. Then he'd sell the chicken at fifty to sixty cents a pound to stores and restaurants in San Francisco. They were tickled pink to get the stuff. This chicken dealer, by the way, was a *khaver*, a comrade, a *linker*. He had one of the worst reputations for cheating the chicken ranchers, and now he was dealing on the black market. I asked him about it once. He said he wasn't doing it because he wanted to, but because he had to—because that's what you had to do when you lived in a capitalist system.

SAMUEL GANS

The Petaluma Jewish people were very great patriots during the war. Most of them refused to sell chickens on the black market. When the temptation became very great, then they organized a poultry cooperative so they could make more money without selling on the black market. I became manager of that cooperative. I was instrumental in setting up the organization, building the processing plant in Petaluma, and renting the stores for retail outlets in San Francisco and Oakland. Everyday there were long lines of people waiting for our Petaluma chickens at the legal OPA price.

They made me the manager after the first manager, a chicken dealer, didn't work out. As one person explained it at a meeting, "Having a chicken dealer as manager of the coop is like hiring a wolf to watch the sheep! We'll keep better control over a Ph.D from Vienna. Let Gans be manager." I wasn't very enthusiastic about it. I detested the chicken business from the first. I daydreamed all the time about my profession. I should have joined the army, which was looking for psychologists. That was the route for me to reenter my profession in America. But we had a child, and pretty soon another child. And I still hoped to hear from my family and bring them over from Europe.

So I took that job as manager of the poultry cooperative. It was stimulating for a while. It was a large operation for those days—eighty employees. I gave it careful attention and made good money for them.

But it wasn't easy dealing with those Jewish ranchers, especially the left-wingers. They wouldn't sell a bird on the black market, but they'd argue prices, they'd try to pass sick chickens as healthy [chuckling]— they had all kinds of tricks. And even though I made thousands of dollars for them, I had to fight for months to get a ten-dollar raise. They were very tough in business. Very tough.

STELLA FINKLESTEIN

We were so patriotic it was pathetic! The wartime philosophy of the *linke* was: "Food prices must be kept down for the workers in the city." This was the line of the Communist party.

Everybody knew that the working class was doing damn' well during the war. And a lot of our little chicken farmers, especially the new ones like us, were pinched by the OPA ceiling prices. So some people sold a few chickens on the black market. Who could blame them? Nobody in the city stuck to the OPA ceiling price of thirty cents a pound. The chicken dealers and the San Francisco slaughter houses were cleaning up on housewives and merchants who'd pay sixty cents a pound. Why shouldn't the chicken farmers share in the profits?

There was a lot of bad feeling about it inside the Jewish community. You know, we lost a couple of boys, we had Nathan Hochman in a German prisoner-of-war camp, we had others fighting in the Pacific islands. And here at home we had some Jews in the black market. The *linke* actually brought a couple of these left-wing "black marketeers" up on charges before the Communist party. They actually called in a couple of party functionaries from San Francisco! There was a stormy meeting at which these people were charged with crimes against the working class. [Laughing.] They defended themselves—that they were just trying to make a living on a little chicken ranch. But Communist party discipline was invoked: "No selling on the black market. We can't overcharge the working class for chicken!"

MORRY FINKLESTEIN: That's when the *linke* started the poultry cooperative, so everything would be legal. And wouldn't you know it? When the OPA decided to arrest black marketeers, they went after the most honest people in town—those in the coop. They came after us! The Finklesteins!

STELLA: These two gangsters from the OPA came to see our records. We didn't have to show them anything, but Morry said, "Cooperate. We have nothing to hide."

We pulled out our papers—we didn't sell every chicken to the coop—and they looked for receipts from one chicken dealer, Jake Pinzur. They impounded everything and asked Morry to sign a statement that the information was correct. Morry said, "Why shouldn't I sign? I'm telling the truth!"

After they left I immediately called Jake and told him what happened. He said, "Oh, my God! I'll see what I can do!" As I heard the story later, he ran down to the hotel where those thugs were staying and said, "The Finklesteins are clean! There's nothing on them!"

Well, as those OPA hoodlums went through our papers they came across receipts from Ernest Wo, the new Chinese chicken dealer in town. On the back of one receipt was some figuring, some special bookkeeping. Ernie had an odd way of figuring. He wanted choice stuff for the San Francisco Chinatown market and he paid premium prices for it. Ernest Wo is one of the most responsible men in the San Francisco Chinese community. We just trusted him. But we didn't understand his method of computing prices, and that is what Morry got picked up on.

MORRY: It was a United States marshall who came for me! Jackson! A good American name! He demanded a thousand-dollar bond or I'd be taken in. He came on Sunday just so I couldn't get to the bank. He took me in! Me! Morris Finklestein! To jail!!! They booked me. Fingerprints! Pictures! Like a criminal!

STELLA: It was twenty-nine chicken ranchers who were arrested. All Jews! All members of the poultry cooperative. All left-wingers! There must have been a hundred Sonoma County farmers selling on the black market. But we twenty-nine Jewish progressives were prosecuted because we were the only ones who let the OPA crooks have our business records. Everyone else told them to go to hell. We cooperated because we were innocent! We cooperated because that was the line of the Communist party!

MORRY: It went out on the United Press that the government broke up a black-market ring in Petaluma. The OPA interpretation was that these little chicken ranchers controlled prices! You know how much we were in control. We took the prices the chicken dealers gave us. They took the prices they got from those crooks at the poultry-processing plants in San Francisco. Those crooks made the big money on the black market and they didn't like it when we started our cooperative. They got the OPA after us to break the cooperative! So the OPA put it out that we twenty-nine Petaluma chicken ranchers cornered the chickens and controlled the black market! Our names went out to newspapers as black marketeers! Friends in New York read it!

STELLA: We wanted to fight it. But the lawyer warned that if it went to a trial, irate housewives on the jury would throw the book at us. So we pleaded guilty. Ernie Wo was very decent—he paid our lawyer and the five-hundred dollar fine. Later it out turned that the one man who took his case to trial won it.

MORRY: It was a great embarrassment. It was humiliating. But there were all kinds of bigger problems then. We had boys from our community in the war. We had an aggravation with what the Germans were doing to our people in Europe. This was the least important thing in those days, but it hurt us terribly. We were such good Americans during the war.

HAL DRAPER

When the Jewish veterans returned from the war there was a feeling that we had done a heroic thing. Even the gentiles welcomed us back as heroes. We showed that Jews can defend our country as well as anybody else. As far as I was concerned, as a former bomber pilot I didn't have to put up with anti-Semitism ever again. Never! Unfortunately, our community's record was marred by these people who made a fortune on the black market during the war. They were real hypocrites. All the time they talked about how important it was to fight fascism, they cut a fat hog with the chickens. We Jewish veterans didn't forget who they were.

DAVID ADLER

I heard about the controversy when I returned from the war. I never blamed those at home who sold chickens on the black market. There was a huge black market everywhere in the service. Nobody gave a damn.

I won't say who did it in Petaluma. Along with the gentiles, they were from all parts of the Jewish community—some very pious religious people, some Zionists and Arbeiter Ringers and B'nai B'rithers, even some *linke*. I couldn't say who was most honest, but there is a tendency by those who are people-oriented in their politics to be more honest in business. My father never sold a nickel's worth on the black market. The only thing that bothered me was that some of these black marketeers were young enough to have been in the service like the rest of us. Instead of defending the country, they were home making a pile of illegal money. They were doubly unpatriotic. That was a sore spot.

But as far as I am concerned, the whole thing was exaggerated. The Jewish community had nothing to be ashamed of for our contribution to the war.

MORRY FINKLESTEIN

The poison was still here at the end of the war. When the Japanese returned to Petaluma, they were placed in a rented warehouse until they could find other places to live. Some lost their ranches while they were away. Others had trouble getting back the ranches they had rented out. We knew one Japanese boy who came back to his parents' ranch in an

American army uniform, and the guy who had the place came out with a shotgun. Such fear and hatred.

So Morris Finklestein—that's me!—as a demonstration, I drove to that warehouse and asked to hire temporary help. A middle-aged Japanese man came into my pick-up and we drove through town. You should have seen the people staring at us! It was like in the South were they hate Negroes. It was a fearful thing. But we drove right through town and out to my ranch. After all, we were Americans too.

9 *"Geknipt un Gebundn"*—"The Community Was Tied and Knotted Together": The "Golden Age" after World War II

STELLA FINKLESTEIN

The kids were getting married after the war. This community was a gold mine for outsiders, because the Petaluma Jewish boys and girls knew each other too well. They grew up together. You know, it would have been like incest. So the parents handled it like they were back in the *shtetl*. They made *shidekhs* [matches] from outside the community. One would call a friend in Los Angeles: "Oh! Your son is looking? Do I have a girl for him!" And then to the *mishpokhe* [family clan] in Philadelphia: "Sylvia's not married yet? Send her to Petaluma! We've got all kinds of *boyes!*"

DAVID ADLER

I met Esther when she came out for a visit from Philadelphia. Mordecai Haller was her uncle, and Mordecai's wife, Rukhele, was her cousin. See, Esther's parents were first cousins to each other in the Old Country, and Mr. and Mrs. Haller were first cousins. And it just so happened that Rukhele was my father's cousin from the Old Country. They were all related to each other from this little Polish *shtetl*, Dimatchiva. They kind of arranged a meeting between Esther and me, and one thing led to another.

JULIA SHIFFMAN SEGAL

I met my husband after his entire family moved to Petaluma during the war. Mordecai Haller was a *landsman* [countryman] and a distant cousin of Mo's mother from back in Dimatchiva. On a visit to New York for a meeting of the Dimatchiva *slovatchichka untershtitsung fareyn,* a fraternal organization of *landslayt* from Dimatchiva, Mordecai convinced the Segals that the streets were paved with gold in Petaluma. The whole *mishpokhe* moved onto chicken ranches.

Mo visited the family after he got out of the service. He planned to go to college in New York, but his father had a heart attack. As the youngest unmarried child, Mo was expected to skip school, move onto the ranch, and take care of this parents. He did it, not happily, but he did it. That's when we were introduced. We became engaged and we married— with big parties. At first we lived in my in-laws' house, which was not easy. Then we built our own place on my in-laws' ranch. Then came the babies and the baby showers. The older people called it *gesettled*—"the *kinder* [children] are getting *gesettled*." It all happened in short order. Mo suddenly found himself supporting a family by operating a chicken ranch. It was the only life I knew, but he was a city guy. His idea of a garden was to cement it and paint it green!

Mo had disdain for us naive Jewish farm folk who had grown up in Petaluma. The Easterners who came into the community after the war were much more sophisticated from growing up in the Jewish ghettos of New York. Mo took me to discussion groups and political meetings. He introduced me to Jewish history. He started me reading serious books and he challenged me to think about new things. He'd say, "You're not going to remain a Petaluma farm kid!"

That's when I took a different path from my gentile school friends. Most of them didn't go to college either, but they married and their interests stabilized at the level of Petaluma High School. For me, the world opened up through marriage and through involvement in the Jewish community.

Mo made me see that the Center was so interesting and so diverse, with all our parents' political organizations and cultural activities and meetings and affairs. We were there with our friends and our organizations every night.

My generation became involved at the Center. I wish I had a dollar for every hour I spent setting up tables for affairs. I spent countless afternoons making blintzes and *latkes* and *lokshunkugl* for community holiday dinners. It was a lot of work, but if we had done it just by writing a check, the closeness wouldn't have developed. We did it because we had to—because we wanted to. Our parents were passing the community on to us, and we wanted to pass it on to our kids.

STELLA FINKLESTEIN

I think of it as the Golden Age of the Petaluma Jewish community. You had the "pioneers" and their children and now the grandchildren. A lot of new families settled on ranches and brought in new life. Everyone was making money, and for once there was political harmony. It was golden [chuckling]—for a few years after the war it was golden.

The old-timers went on a binge with the *kinder*. They expanded the ranches so the kids could come into the chicken business. And as long as they were expanding, they figured why not help the kids build a house, furnish it, buy a car. The old-timers had a horror of debt from the Depression—they'd never buy something new for themselves but the kids they would indulge. They wanted the kids in the *shtetl*.

With all the community activity [laughing]—the gossip became impossible. Some of these old *yentes* [busybodies] would hear something, get on the telephone, and *who-ooo-oosh,* it spread like fire! You couldn't keep a secret in this community. But you had to be careful when you gossiped to somebody about somebody, because you never were sure if they were related. You couldn't keep track of all the family relationships. For example, after the war my brother Al Lyons married Rebecca Fishel. A little later I became connected to Morris Rogin through Rebecca's father, Noah. When Morris Rogin remarried, his second wife was the daughter of Noah Fishel's second wife—my sister-in-law's stepmother, if you can make sense of it. That's when we became closer with Morris.

You see how things worked in the Petaluma Jewish community? The relationships went round and round. We used to say, "*geknipt un gubundn*"—"tied and knotted." The community was tied and knotted together.

JACK LABOVITZ [b. 1918; Los Angeles]

The Petaluma Jewish community had the air of a *shtetl*. They were totally involved in each other's lives. Every Jew knew the business of every Jew. If one had *nakhes* [joy], others shared it. If one had *tsores* [troubles], another helped. Regardless of whether they were family. All Jews were family in Petaluma.

I lived there for a year after the war. There were about two hundred Jewish families making a good living on small chicken ranches. A lot of new people came in, but the older families made you feel welcome. There was a special closeness because everyone was in the chicken business and everyone talked about chickens. People worked hard, but there was flexibility for getting together. You could shake the feed hoppers, check the water, and take off the afternoon.

It was an informal way of life. People dropped by without calling. If you were busy, they left. If you were eating lunch, they'd join you. The women walked around in jeans and sweatshirts, with their hair tied up and caps on their heads. The men wore overalls and work shirts. You could see them walking around town in their work clothes during the day. You'd see them *shmoozing* [shooting the breeze] at the fee mill or at the poultry scales. You always could find a group of Jews outside the Purity Food Store. That was the big meeting place for the Jewish community. If you wanted to know chicken prices or if you wanted to discuss the Soviet line on Israel, you went to the Purity. When the *shul yidn* needed a tenth man to make a *minyan* [quorum for a service], they would draft him off the bench in front of the Purity.

One day I was in front of the Purity and somebody called, "Hey, *shmuch!*" Every person in sight turned to respond. That was Petaluma!

When I moved up to Santa Rosa I found an entirely different kind of Jewish community. The Santa Rosa Jewish people came to establish a business, they made money or they didn't, and they moved on. It was more of a transient community. In Petaluma the Jews set in roots. There was a feeling of permanence. They had a Jewish Cemetery that went back to the 1860s. Petaluma is where they lived and Petaluma is where they would bury their dead. That is permanence! They were more substantial people in Petaluma. The Santa Rosa Jews had no interests outside business and making money. Petaluma had working Jews— well-read mechanics. They spoke a literate Yiddish, the kind of Yiddish you get from reading the classics. They were culturally advanced, not just in Yiddish, but in *velt kultur*, in world culture—in politics and history and the arts.

And the money they raised for Judaism in Petaluma! At our first Israel drive in Santa Rosa, with all the business money in our community, with three millionaires, we raised two thousand dollars. From that community of chicken ranchers in Petaluma, they raised over twenty thousand dollars in one night. Young and old, *linke* and *rekhte*—a hundred people at the Center gave over twenty thousand dollars—a lot of money in those days! They used the old Jewish technique of calling out the names of who gave how much.

In Santa Rosa everything had to be soft sell with the Jews. They had a veneer of respectability which eroded Jewish communal life. They were moving into the greater life of Santa Rosa, but not as Jews. They wanted to be good Americans like the gentiles. They were embarassed by Petaluma *yidn*.

MANNY EPSTEIN [b. 1918; Santa Rosa]

I lived in Santa Rosa, but I established my hardware store in Petaluma after the war. I was successful because I respected my customers and they respected me. Of course, there's always a bad apple who'd give me a hard time, but I'd make him smile before he left the store.

Yes, I sold poultry equipment. You can't sell a swimming suit when it rains. You can't sell an umbrella when the sun shines! A businessman must feel the pulse of the community. You must please the customer.

Of course, some of my Petaluma customers would occasionally make a remark—unthinkingly—not knowing what it really meant. I didn't let it bother me. Because, well, being in business, that's the only way. I can truthfully say that in my whole life I've never tried to screw anybody. My motto was, "If you do right by the customer, the dollar will come to you."

I was successful because I learned how to do business growing up in Santa Rosa. I continued living in Santa Rosa when I had the Petaluma store. Jewish people from Santa Rosa were more—well, I hate to say "higher class"—let's say more "business oriented" than Petaluma Jewry. In Santa Rosa we Jews dealt with the public. And when you deal with the public—well, you cannot tell a customer, "If you don't like it, get the hell out of here." You can talk to chickens that way, but you can't talk to customers like that. The Petaluma chicken ranchers did not understand that doing business with the public, accommodating each customer, is the toughest thing in the world. Many times I wanted to tell one of those customers, "That, is impossible. Just *impossible!! Absolutely impossible!!!*" But I never said it! *Never!* I always was polite."

SI COHEN [b. 1922; Newark, New Jersey]

Some of these old *yentes,* they'd spend a few pennies in my store and they'd scream how they did me a big favor. I'd tell 'em, "Do me a real favor. Stay our of my store and I'll give you 50 cents a month!"

My general store was one of the big hangouts for Jewish farmers after the war. I had never heard of Petaluma until I read about it in a WPA guidebook—"Petaluma! The Egg Basket of the World!" That was for me! I had just gotten my master's degree in agriculture and I was looking for a small poultry town. Right away I hopped a train for California. This was 1947.

I didn't know a soul when I arrived in Petaluma. So I did what any Jew does—I looked up the Jewish-named stores in the telephone book. I got to Holtzman's department store, I ended up at Feldman's hardware store, and they took me in for the night.

To make a long story short, I bought a rickety old general store in Co-tati, about seven miles north of Petaluma. I filled every inch of that store with merchandise. It grew to maybe ten thousand items, everything from perfume to refrigerators. One of my suppliers said I sold more poultry vaccine than anybody else in the country. Most of my profits came from the poultry department, from volume, not mark-up. It was the opposite of most country stores, where you're miles from anywhere and charge high prices. I could have been rich from that store, but I always thought of myself on the customer's side.

Some of my Jewish customers were real *nudniks,* but most of them were great. They'd try to beat me down in price, but they knew I gave a good deal. They'd come to the store for supplies and they'd hang around to *shmooz.* I didn't have a cracker barrel, but I had an old soda fountain where people sat around talking—about chickens, sports, Birobidzhan— that kind of thing. It was a typical old-time country store.

IRVING GOLDEN

Any afternoon, you could find all these Jews standing around and talking. I'd warn 'em, "Any business where you just shake the feed hoppers a few times a day won't last. Chickens is a fly-by-night business."

I was after my father to expand into a real dairy ranch after the war. See, we were different from these other Jewish people—we raised chickens, but we had fifty milking cows too. Cows aren't like chickens. Cows are a complicated animal; you've got to know what you're doing. You can get to know a cow's personality—you can name it Bessie or Red or Big Eyes. And the bulls we had—mean—*mean!* A gentile would see me with one of those bulls and he'd say, "You couldn't be Jewish. You must be half. You must be a quarter. Jews don't have bulls."

My father just wouldn't go into dairy full scale. Too cautious. Instead, when I got married he said I could take the cows or the laying hens. I wanted the cows, but to make real money I needed new machinery and a sanitary cement barn. I thought, "Cows are a big risk."

I took the laying hens. Laying hens were more complicated than meat birds, which is why most of these Jewish people were afraid of them. It was a more substantial animal, but I didn't like the chicken business. I loved ranching, but I hated chickens. They kept me in a bad state.

All these new Jewish people who came in here after the war, they heard you could retire on a chicken ranch and live the good life. Good life! When I think of taking care of those filthy birds day after day for all those years! I had to teach those stupid chickens how to sit on roosts! I cleaned eggs on holidays! I breathed that black dust from those damn brooder stoves. I lugged hundred-pound sacks of feed all day.

And for what? For chicken feed! I should have taken the chance with cows. Dairy was a real business. There was money to be made in dairy.

HYMIE GOLDEN

Whatever you do, you have to like it. If you do it just to make money, you won't succeed. I liked raising the chickens. I liked my cows the most, but I gave up the cows after the war. Too much work. I don't need it.

A German neighbor—he was in the German Bund here—he says to me once, "You are a white Jew."

"Why am I a white Jew?"

"'Cause you are not just with the chickens. You are milking cows. You got bulls."

I told him, "Bulls don't prove nothing! You are still a Nazi anti-Semite."

I didn't need no big business with the dairy. I didn't wanna go in no hole with the bank again. I did good with the chickens. I even did good with the turkeys. In the poultry magazines it says turkeys is so dumb they can drown by drinking in the water trough. But still I made money from the turkeys. I made money from everything.

Research on turkeys? I'm gonna tell you about the "research," with your college education. Yeah, I read the poultry magazines. It said the only thing dumber than the turkey is the man who raises it. That's why the other Jews in here was petrified of turkeys. I was successful with the turkeys. I was successful with the chickens and the cows. I was successful with everything because I like what I am doing.

ANNA ROSENFIELD GOLDEN: He liked the turkeys, until they got sick with the sneezing. Then he says, "I don't want no turkeys. If you like turkeys, you take care of them." So I went nighttime to feed them turkeys hard-boiled eggs. You had to be patient with the turkeys.

MAX BLUMBERG [b. 1920; Vineland, New Jersey]

Chickens was a damn' good way of life. You vaccinated 'em, you fed 'em, you shoveled their manure. You had to work, but it was physical work. The only mental strain was matching wits with the chicken dealer. You didn't expect much, you didn't get much, and you lived an easier life.

When you got up in the morning you'd think, "Well, I guess I'd better feed my birds." But you could take an extra ten minutes to read the newspaper. Nobody was breathing down the back of your neck to do it right now. There wasn't any of that clock watching on your own ranch. Sometimes you'd be working out there and it was time for dinner. If you wanted to dump a couple more sacks of feed, you didn't look at the clock—the sun was still shining! And pretty soon, by golly, "Hey! I'm a half-hour late for dinner. She'll be mad as hell!"

ELAINE GOLDEN BLUMBERG: Max liked the ranch because he got a job in town as a butcher. I stayed home with the chickens all day. I fed them by hand when they got sick. Just like my mother, I got stuck on a chicken ranch miles outside of town.

MAX: I started working in town when I saw all these has-beens and misfits coming onto chicken ranches after the war. They couldn't hack it in the workshops, so they came here. Well, when a fifty-year-old guy could do a twenty-year-old guy's work, I could see that chickens wouldn't be a sound business very long.

ZEITEL KOLMAN [b.1898; Bratslav, Ukraine]

Murray couldn't stand it anymore with the painting trade. The fumes, the speed-up—it was terrible for his health. Our friends from Petaluma said, "Why paint? People are leaving the shops and coming onto chicken ranches. Everybody makes money with the chickens."

In 1945 I left a new house in San Francisco for a chicken ranch. No showers! No steam heat! It was *such a dump!* My friends said, "Zeitel is used to going out for lunch and playing cards in the afternoon. I give her four weeks on the chicken ranch." At first it seemed impossible to live in such a way. But I knew that Murray has good hands. Finally I thought, "If he's going to be in good health, I don't care. We'll make it nice on the ranch."

MURRAY KOLMAN [b. 1895; Bratslav, Ukraine]: It was the singing people from the Jewish Folk Chorus who helped us start up a ranch. We borrowed money from all of them. They were in seventh heaven that two more singers come to Petaluma.

There is a saying: "Today you lose one step, tomorrow you make two forward." The first year we lost money. We were in debt to all our friends. They were such good friends they said, "Never mind when you pay." But I *had* to pay back. So I rolled up the sleeves and sold out my ten fingers. I went back to work in the painting trade.

I was working on two fronts: eight hours painting and then I came home to ten thousand chickens. I had a very good partner—the wife took care the chickens in the day and she beautified the ranch. I did the heavy work at night and on the weekend. It's lucky I was only in my fifties and had the energy.

ZEITEL: *Oy vey,* how that guy worked, I'm telling you. But after a few years we got a little ahead and we had a good life in Petaluma. It got so good I had only one problem left. The progressive ladies, they played crazy poker with too many wild cards. I had to ride into San Francisco for a good game.

Samuel Gans

I detested Petaluma. We were cut off from the theater, the opera, from so many things you find in a city. It was an ungainly cultureless nowhere. I still shudder when I think about wasting the best years of my life with chickens in Petaluma.

My first mistake was during the war, when I became manager of the poultry cooperative instead of becoming an army psychologist. My second mistake was after the war when the poultry cooperative folded. Hospitals were looking for psychologists, and I no longer was a refugee who barely spoke English. But I knew I could make four times the money in the chicken business. So I became a chicken dealer and opened my own small poultry-processing plant.

I did well financially, but the chicken business was so tedious, with so much petty bickering, I always thought about returning to my profession. I joined the American Psychology Association, I read the journals, I attended conferences in San Francisco. If not for keeping up with my profession while I was a chicken dealer, I wouldn't have survived.

Lou Green

I hated the chicken business. I wanted to write the Great American Novel. I had all these creative dreams to fulfill, but it takes free time to write. With a wife and kids to support, I had to face economic realities. It was extremely frustrating. My father and I were buying and selling chickens for ten years after the war. I hated the constant bickering—the pettiness. I felt stifled.

I tried all kinds of nefarious schemes to write my way out of chickens. The worst was with a guy who I met in a little theater group in town. He had an idea for a documentary movie on the Papago Indians. He had visions of raising big money, national distribution, an Academy Award—oh, it went on and on.

He was just one of many con artists I've attracted—either because I'm gullible or I suppose because like attracts like. We formed a production company and I went out and sold all the stock in it to my friends. Eleven thousand dollars' worth! The movie turned out to be a complete fiasco. That's when I got my first ulcer.

That's the story of my years in the chicken business. I wheeled and dealed in chickens for a living, and in my spare time I tried every imaginable writing scheme: mysteries, novels, movie scripts, song lyrics, musicals. My only success was writing scripts for the Jewish community shows my generation staged after the war. They loved my jokes about the chicken business, but I didn't think it was very funny.

David Adler

I enjoyed chicken ranching. I built a solid business, I was at home with my family, and my time was my own. For a modern chicken rancher, those were good years after the war. I had to split up the partnership with my father to do it. He was a very stubborn man—especially when it came to chickens—chickens and politics. The chicken business was changing fast, and he was too set in the old ways.

I increased my volume up to forty thousand birds per raise by the end of the 1950s. I tested to learn which chick was best, which feed was best, which vaccines were best. I was among the first to keep records of the chickens house by house: how much feed went in, how much poundage came out. I made an arrangement with Ernest Wo, who was a new chicken dealer at that time, that I would provide him with the best-grade birds at a predetermined price. It took a lot of the gambling out of the business.

Poultry was developing into a real business—an industry—and my father never understood that. None of the old-timers did. I cleared twenty thousand dollars a year off this ranch in the 1950s, because my business methods were as modern as could be.

Ernest Wo [b. 1916; San Francisco]

When I first come to Petaluma to buy chickens, nobody knows me from Adam. In Chinatown everybody knows my father's chicken store, but in Petaluma I got to buy the chickens with greenbacks. You know, in those days the chicken dealers were the crookedest people. And I was even less trusted because I am Oriental. Was tough starting. The Italian and the Portugee people the toughest. They don't want to sell to another race. They think that *you* out to get them, so *they* try to get you. The Jewish people are like the Chinese people—you treat them right, they trust you. Businessmen. I build up my reputation with the Jewish people mouth to mouth. No monkey business with the scales when I buy chickens. Becomes friendly. After the business they invite me into the house. The Portugee people and the Italian people don't do that. The Jewish people say, "Come in for some matzo-ball soup."

A lot of times I take them to San Francisco for Chinese dinner. I make donations to the Jewish Center. I buy the Israel bonds. They invite me to the weddings and *bar mitzvahs* and funerals. I was like a brother in the Jewish community. Was like the Chinese community. Thirty years ago the Jewish people was family tight—marry your own race, stay close to the parents—close-knit families, close-knit community.

Good people. Friendly people. Understandable. That's why we do business together. When we know each other good, I make arrangements with the good young raisers who are expanding. I guarantee to buy all their chickens for premium prices. No written contract. Just the word. No problems. Good business people.

Shura Eastman Compisi

The younger guys ran their chicken ranches like businesses. They understood that the industry was mechanizing, the capacities were growing, everything was becoming specialized. When my husband and I developed a chicken-vaccinating service, with trained crews and specialized equipment, the younger guys immediately recognized it as a mutually advantageous business deal.

The old-timers resisted us. Even though we could do in three hours what took them three days, they wanted to do it like in the old days when you invited over a group of friends to vaccinate the chickens. They used to turn it into a party with tons of food. It was part of this tremendous cooperation they had over the years. And suddenly, just when they were older and it became harder for them to do physical work: "My God! Pay to have the chickens vaccinated? Terrible!" They hired us only because their kids badgered them into it. God, how I hated to work for them! [Laughing.] They were so chinzy about paying for this! And every time we came they spent the whole previous day preparing food for my crews. And every time I'd say, "Thanks, but no thanks. This is a business deal."

Norman Haller

There were tremendous scientific breakthroughs in the poultry industry from the late thirties on. Through genetic breeding an eastern hatchery came out with the "Bird of Tomorrow," the Rhode Island Red. Until then the chicken ranchers raised these small white leghorns for laying hens and sold the cockerels for meat birds at twelve weeks. This bird was a special fast-growing meat type. That was how the Jewish people moved more into raising just meat birds.

We could have a long discussion about changes in every part of the poultry industry: nutrition and feed formulation, management of chicken growing, design of chicken houses, mechanization of feeding and watering, disease control, government regulation. Everything was changing after the war. A few people kept up with it in Petaluma. Our feed mill put out over a hundred ton a day by the end of the war, Mike Gold put up a big new poultry-processing plant, and some of the younger growers were modernizing. But most people continued along with these old-time operations on undercapitalized little family-run farms.

The Jewish community continued raising chickens just like before the war. The only difference was that the families running the farms got bigger [chuckling]—more complicated.

LYNN AXELROD GOLDEN [b. 1927; New York City]

Irving and I lived very simply the first six months of our marriage [laughing]—we lived in a chicken house! We converted it into a cute little cottage, rather than move in with his folks. It was fun; you know, when you're newly married everything is fun. But I was glad to get the hell out of that chicken house.

That first year was very difficult. Irving just got started with laying hens and he had a lot of second thoughts about cows. He was working with those birds twenty hours a day, seven days a week. And I didn't like the animals and the manure—that's not my cup of tea.

It was difficult living on the same property with my in-laws. And then there was this social thing where everybody in the community was always together. Our house was like a hotel—constant visitors—with me running the restaurant. I wasn't used to so much mixing with family and friends—older people too. And the community gossip . . . that I hated, because I am a very private person, and the Petaluma Jewish community had the least private people I'd ever met.

THELMA BLUESTEIN WEINSTEIN [b. 1918; San Francisco]

Some of us threatened to write a book about it. Each daughter-in-law would write a chapter with her story about living and working with her in-laws on a Petaluma chicken ranch. The young couples had to do it because we had nothing to start with. The ranches were there and the older generation needed help. You didn't want that close proximity with them, but you had to share their ranch until you had some money. Some girls lived in bedrooms right in the homes of their in-laws! I was lucky. Seymour and I moved into the old house on the ranch when we married. But our house was so close to my in-laws that if I sneezed, my mother-in-law could gesundheit.

It was tense from the beginning. When I came to Petaluma as a new bride, I had nothing to do but take care of my husband and our little home. So I slept late in the mornings. My in-laws knew exactly how late

I slept because they could see our bedroom window from their breakfast room. Naturally, if my bedroom shades were down, I was in bed. It irritated them no end, especially Pop, who didn't work all that much himself because he had tuberculosis. When I first saw him every morning, there were daggers flying out of his eyes: "Oh! The princess finally got out of bed."

All the new girls clashed with their in-laws. The women of my mother-in-law's generation worked very hard on the ranches. Some of them actually ran the ranches, like Ma, because their husbands were ill. But the new daughter-in-laws were different. We puttered around the house in the mornings and played mahjong in the afternoons. [Laughing.] We were ladies of leisure.

IDELE RUBIN KOLMAN [b. 1927; Chicago]

I'm very opposed to a husband and wife working together. On the ranch you were with the same person day and night. It got pretty boring, especially with kids around all the time. If you don't bring something fresh into a marriage, what do you finally talk to each other about? Children and chickens, that's what.

Our families got us started on the ranch. Both Vince's parents and my parents moved to Petaluma after the war. They were all in the Jewish Folk Chorus and they kind of arranged for us to meet. When we married, we didn't just get each other. We got each other's family, we got the whole Jewish community, and we got a chicken ranch. It was a package deal.

I loved the chicken-ranching life in the beginning. I didn't like chickens. I didn't like borrowing money from every Tom, Dick, and Harry in the Jewish Folk Chorus. But Vince didn't have a college education or a trade. I thought the ranch was a great way to have a nice home and a good business all in one.

We worked very hard to pay all our debts. Vince ran the ranch during the days and worked swing shift over at a feed mill. I took care of the chickens while he was gone in the late afternoons and evenings. When the kids were infants, I just took them in the buggy when I fed the chickens. I never minded the hard work. But after our third child was born, I really felt trapped on the ranch. I used to say, "I feel like I'm in a factory all day. I have a kids and chickens factory, and I never get out of this factory." By that time I'd do anything to get the hell off the ranch for a few hours. I'd even pay a babysitter so we could go to the Center in the evening. But the funny thing is, when we got together with friends all we talked about was children and chickens.

SARA DICKSTEIN JAMESON [b. 1918; New York City]

As far as I was concerned, the idiocy of rural life really came home to roost with that second generation in Petaluma. Two things made up their social life: food and cards. You got together and you ate a huge dinner. Then the men congregated on one side of the room talking about chickens, and the women were on the other side talking about diaper changing and toilet training. Then they played poker, one game for the men and another for the women.

They were so nosy and gossipy. There was a saying in Petaluma: "Before the husband gets off the wife, the whole community knows she is pregnant." But it was worse with the children, because they were so prim and proper and moralistic. I remember when one couple was staying at his parents' house in Petaluma, waiting for his divorce to go through before they married. There was an enormous amount of community discussion over whether they were sleeping together. Not from the older generation—they just assumed this couple slept together. It was the younger generation—they thought it *might* be true and they made a lot of clucking sounds about it.

I don't know how those kids became so conventional. Most of their parents, at least in the *linke,* had lived together for years and years without being married. It was a life-long commitment. You didn't need a government document to show that you cared for each other! When Ben Hochman insisted that he and Miriam should marry for reasons of citizenship and property inheritance, Miriam came right home, tore up the marriage certificate, and announced that Ben was perfectly free to leave anytime he felt unhappy.

But the kids who grew up in Petaluma were so shallow and provincial. They grew up like lower-middle-class Americans with cars and sports and dating. They had what they thought were proper American weddings with formal invitations, corsages, and marching up the aisle just so. Then the "girls" kept busy with babies and mahjong. The guys were young businessmen, or at least they thought of their ranches as businesses.

I lived on my mother's ranch for a year, after my father died, but I never fit into the Jewish community. Not even with the older generation on the left. I felt suffocated by the constant socializing. No sooner would we finish dinner than cars started driving in. My mother felt it reflected poorly upon her if I didn't participate in entertaining these visitors. But it was *constant,* because if you were visited, you *had* to return the visit immediately! You couldn't protect yourself from these community demands.

I found the older generation's lack of privacy terribly oppressive. I loved and admired them, but there was no way for an individual to grow in that community. Even Ben Hochman, the community's scientist and Marxist theoretician, couldn't pursue his studies. It was *kalt,* cold, to limit others' access to you. There was no such thing as private study, private accomplishment on a musical instrument, private cultivation of a garden. Everything had to be collective.

I delighted in seeing them. There was a tremendous amount of talk every night—chicken talk, political talk, cultural talk—serious talk and funny talk. I would watch them and wonder if anyone listened, because they all spoke at once. And the women were so rude to the men, so bad mannered, at least by *goyishe* standards.

I especially appreciated the rituals. Ritual was so important in Petaluma—nonreligious ritual. When my father died, all the *khaverim* were there for the funeral. The Jewish Folk Chorus sang a song about the workers' struggle. Ben Hochman delivered a beautiful speech, partly in Yiddish and partly in English because there were non-Yiddish-speaking people there from San Francisco.

My sister's wedding was classic Petaluma. The entire *linke* group helped with the cooking. The chorus sang every Yiddish song you knew, including some of the old religious ones. All my sister's Berkeley intellectual friends were there, so it was an extraordinary mixing of cultures. And so warm—the *kinder* and the *alte.*

I appreciated it, but I really was part of another culture. The differences were fascinating. Once Anna Weissman was angry at me for a whole evening because I made the mistake of saying she looked beautiful! She was insulted because I didn't notice how tired she was after a day with the chickens. You know, if you told someone that she didn't look well, then you transcended politeness. You *really saw* the person! *That* was a compliment!

I accepted the whole thing with pleasure, except the total intrusion on my privacy. I quarreled over it repeatedly with my mother. By refusing to be swallowed up in that demanding social life, I rejected an important community standard. But I would have drowned if I did all that entertaining and visiting. I was not a *shtetl* girl. I also refused to join the . . . the infrastructure [laughing] . . . the community organizations. One time when I picked up my mother from chorus practice, Uri Lichtman, the chorus director, said, "Come over to the piano and let's hear your *stimme* [voice]." I refused. I couldn't bring my babies in baskets to rehearsals and meetings like my parents had done. I wouldn't make any necessary sacrifice for Yiddish political and cultural organizations. That wasn't for me.

They really didn't leave much room for the second generation. Everything they did was in Yiddish. They had a rich cultural life and they kept their political principles, but they didn't worry about continuity with the next generation. It was a great mistake. The kids who grew up in Petaluma saw Yiddish culture as something to escape. They saw their Jewishness as a burden. They wanted to be accepted as "proper" Americans.

The older women used to call the daughters *Amerikanishe zhidovka*—the American goose [assimilated Jew]. It means . . . well . . . someone you didn't value much, despite her pretensions. I think my mother understood that I wasn't one of these smart-aleck American girls who rejected everything Yiddish. I had been educated at a real urban *yidishe shule* [Jewish school] and I knew that whole secular Yiddish culture. I had *yidishkeyt!* That's why most of the older generation in Petaluma took me more seriously than their own kids.

It was the same with left-wing politics. Most of the Petaluma kids never had any real political involvement. In the thirties the Communist party had tried to establish a branch of the Young Communist League, but it never took hold. The kids tried to get away from their parents' politics after the war. So someone like me, active in the San Francisco labor movement, had stature with the older generation. I was one of the *kinder* who was making it *in the world*.

I mixed with the old-timers while I was living in Petaluma, but I kept away from that second generation. They were uncomfortable with their parents' *shtetl* community, but they hadn't left it, they hadn't changed it, and they hadn't got the best from it. Those children did not have the greatness of their parents.

IRVING GOLDEN

Nineteen forty-seven was the heyday of the community. That's when my generation made its move! We were young married couples with kids, a little money, and a lot of energy. We were the new generation coming into the community! My generation started taking over the social affairs. We put on a zinger of a New Year's party every year, with decorations and a band and a group of fellas tending the bar. Our Halloween costume balls were masterpieces—we turned the Center into a chamber of horrors with our decorations. We put on an annual Monte Carlo Night with gambling and a big spread of food: the guys would dress up as women and do the entertaining. It was really jumping at the Center.

The young people started the Havadim Club. We had over one hundred members. Politics didn't matter—we were getting away from the bickering of our parents. We put on dances and hay rides and weenie roasts. We fixed up a kindergarden room at the Center and dedicated it to Seymour Rosenberg and Art Frandzel, the two Jewish boys we lost in the war. We put out the first Jewish community newspaper.

It wasn't just oriented toward the young people. We put on annual talent shows for everyone in the community. It was all home grown. Lou Green, who wanted to be a writer, thought up most of the material. I directed with my brother-in-law, Max. We did skits poking fun about the chicken business. Three of the girls sang in a group called the Rancher Kids, and a couple of the fellas performed as the Crooning Cockerels. Stella Finklestein played the piano, Michael Feldman did magic tricks, Richard Mirsky played the violin. Ida Silverman—she was the chorus soprano who considered herself an opera singer—she sang. We had real talent!

Our Havadim Club shows brought the entire community together. It was standing room only at the Center. We put so much work into it because we wanted to continue what our parents had started. The older people came, and we played up to them. We threw in Yiddish words—they just loved it. Everyone was together.

SID JACOBS

I began drifting out of the community after the war. I never got too involved in the Havadim Club. I knew the kids all my life, but as you get older you change and your interests change.

I was back in Petaluma from 1945 on. I wanted to continue with the forest service, but I had promised my parents I would come back to the ranch. My father wanted me to take over. I participated in the Jewish community for a year or two. At that time they were taking younger people onto the board of directors at the Center—sort of passing it on to the next generation, like the ranches. My father was sick and he was very anxious for me to participate. I felt I should do it for him, so I ran for the board of directors. I think I was elected because my father was so popular in the community. After he died in 1947, I declined to run again.

See, I wasn't married, and in my leisure time I ended up with my gentile friends—hunting and that kind of thing. The Jewish kids all got married. For them everything was couples and families. The family enveloped all. Their group was family-oriented, and you were an outsider if you were not married. I don't know why. Maybe the women think you're a threat because you're going to take her husband somewhere. I don't know. But that's what I thought when I'd be at some guy's house and we'd want to go out. The wife would say, "Well, you can go, but . . . !" Then she'd point out various chores he'd neglected to do. And that was the kiss of death. It's a natural thing—when you get married you quit running with the pack. It's just like in nature. The buck deer, the bull elk—they hang around by themselves all season. Then they fight each other when the females are around for the mating season. It was the same thing in the Petaluma Jewish community.

ARLENE FEINSTEIN FELDMAN

If you were not part of a couple, it was hard to be active in the Havadim Club. I didn't become involved until Michael came back from the service and I was considered part of a couple. But even then it wasn't easy, because Michael didn't want a big social life after four years in the service. He wanted to build up his father's secondhand store into a real hardware store and he wanted to relax at home in the evening.

Again I was isolated. I was an old-fashioned *baleboste* [housewife] who spent all the time at home with the kids and the cooking and the sewing. I still didn't drive and I didn't get anywhere.

I finally started going to Havidim Club meetings at the Center without Michael. Ruth Skolnick, whose husband didn't like to socialize either, would pick me up. For years we were the Mike and Ike of the Jewish community.

SHURA EASTMAN COPISI

The Jewish community was not exactly ready for a Jewish woman married to an Italian man. One of the old *yentes* [busybodies] told my mother, "I don't understand it. Your daughter is not an old woman. She's not ugly. She doesn't limp. How come she married a *sheygets?*"

When the young people formed the Havadim Club, some of my old friends from the *linke* families asked us to join. We came to a meeting and there was a big argument over my husband. Some of these guys from *rekhte* families raised a big stink about a gentile joining the Havadim Club. We stopped going to the Center after that.

IRVING GOLDEN

The community was united and the second generation was making its move! I was the youngest person on the board of directors in the history of the Center. Twenty-one years old! Mr. Feinstein was president and he took me in a corner at an affair: "Hey, why don't you come on the board? We need a young guy like you."

A couple of us younger guys on the board fought for a new building. The Center was becoming an embarassment. A lot of the churches put up new buildings, and here we were in a building twenty-five years old. We needed a larger social hall. We needed some classrooms for the Sunday school and the coming generation. A swimming pool and tennis courts would have been nice. And how about a parking lot? Everybody was getting new cars, but we had to park right out on the street in front of the Center! What's wrong with parking lots? The churches had 'em!

If we had taken the bull by the horns then, we'd be sitting in clover now. The old-timers had the money, but they wouldn't budge. They'd say, "The Center was good enough for us, it's good enough for you. You want a new Center, you raise the money."

Max Blumberg

Aaach! I fought with these *alte kakers* for years to take 10 percent of the money we gave to charity and put it back into our own Jewish community. I don't know why I bothered. Once I went to Katz after our United Jewish Appeal committee collected twenty thousand dollars. I says, "We need five hundred dollars to get the Sunday school rolling. The young couples can't carry the whole burden."

He says, "They need it all in Israel."

I says, "Look, Katz, one of these days you'll be dead and gone. If you don't plant seeds, who the hell will collect for Israel in twenty-five years?"

"What do you know about Israel?"

Aaach! That may just curdles my guts! He was supposed to be a community leader!

We needed a strong Sunday school here. Nothing religious. Just something so the third generation would know who they were. The kids could accept or reject Judaism when they were older, but you had to give them a choice. If our kids were going to be called dirty Jews, they had to know why.

The *linke* didn't have any more sense than the *rekhte*. I went to Ben Hochman for help. I said, "Ben, you guys have got to support the Sunday school."

He says, "We've got to help rebuild the Soviet Union. We've got to help the Jewish people in Birobidzhan. The Sunday school is not necessary. If the grandchildren want to know about Judaism, they will seek it out."

"Sure," I said, "they'll seek it out, like they'll grow tomatoes in ice cream cones."

These old-timers were blind fanatics. If they could have taken the plaster off the walls of the Center, they would have sent it to the Soviet Union and Israel!

Aaach! Aaach!

Stella Finklestein

I told them forty years ago that they were not passing on a legacy to their children. I tried to tell the older people, the Yiddish-speaking people, that the Jewish Community Center was the logical place for them to have that communion with the next generation. But they were too damn' busy with their own organizations and their own causes.

I was on the Center's board of directors after the war, but the board's only function was to maintain the building and rent out rooms to organizations. Some of us wanted to modernize the whole operation. We wanted to put up a new building halfway between Petaluma and Santa Rosa, so we could combine with the Santa Rosa Jewish community. We wanted to develop a Center program that would attract the second generation and provide for the third generation. The Jewish Federation in San Francisco offered to help.

But you see, these old-timers were afraid of any change. They were stuck in their old organizations and their old ways. They were so provincial that they still considered the Santa Rosa Jewish community and the San Francisco Jewish Federation as foreigners. They were so isolated they still had nothing to do with civic life in Petaluma. They didn't even have a representative after the tragedy struck Joe Holtzman.

Holtzman's tragedy? [Chuckling.] The scandal! Domestic difficulties! He and his wife separated. Then, in the divorce, his wife reported that he hadn't paid any income taxes for years! Can you imagine? Between Uncle Sam and his wife he lost his department store, he lost every cent, and he had to spend six months in jail too! This was our own big businessman—our community leader—in jail for income-tax evasion! He never came back to Petaluma. I don't know what happened to him.

When the Jewish community was left without a leader—this will sound strange coming from me—but that's when I suggested we get a rabbi. I'm not the slightest bit religious, but I thought the younger generations needed some sort of traditional observance to maintain Judaism. I thought that a good progressive rabbi might unite the community— *linke* and *rekhte*, young and old—and represent us to the gentiles.

MORRY FINKLESTEIN: You're supposed to be a leftist! How could you want a rabbi?

STELLA: That's what I encountered. Most of the immigrant generation would not tolerate anything smacking of religion. The Center board wouldn't even give a few dollars so the *shul yidn* could have that decrepit little *shul* painted. [Laughing.] Not until I reminded those hypocritical cheapskates that they used the *shul* to claim the Center as a tax-free religious institution! So you can imagine the reaction when I suggested we hire a rabbi. I'll never forget Fran Ginsberg's mother, Mrs. Rubinstein, when she heard the word *rabbi!* She was furious! Those Zionists were as antireligious fanatics as the Communists. Even the *shul yidn* were against a rabbi [laughing]—they said they knew how to pray themselves.

I realize now that the changes I wanted were impossible. The old-timers couldn't understand why we needed a new building, a broad program, a real leader. It's true, their organizations were flourishing and the kids were quiet in the Havadim Club. But I'll tell you, these old-timers were scared to death of change, and they paid for it later. They were losing their children to America, and they didn't do a thing about it.

10 "The Grine":
Refugees from the Holocaust

JULIA SHIFFMAN SEGAL

Grine is green. Greenhorns. That's what we called the refugees who came to Petaluma after the war. They came from the bowels of the earth. From such horrors. Our community signed up with the Jewish Agricultural Society for thirty-five families. We took them in.

BERTHA LESNER [b. 1922; Minsk, Soviet Union]

A lot of nice people met us at the train station in Petaluma. We arrived cold and hungry. Mr. and Mrs. Rubinstein, when we came to their house, it smelled with chicken soup they made for us! Was like coming home! The Petaluma Jewish people was so good to us. Basha Singerman, she's from my home town in Minsk, she *gave* us her car, an old Nash. I'll never forget it as long as I live.

As soon as we could we rented a ranch and rolled up the sleeves. When we first came to America, in New York my husband worked on an assembly line. Here we worked for ourselves on our own ranch. Here was a good place for the children. Was hard work with the chickens, but we know how to work hard. After what we went through with Hitler, a chicken ranch is freedom.

ROSE YARMULSHEFSKY [b. 1921; Zgierz, Poland]

Petaluma was good to all the newcomers. The people who were survivors from the Nazis—we were taken in like family by the whole Jewish community.

There is no people in the world like American people. I'm not just saying so—it is the truth! The first day on the ranch the neighbor—very beautiful lady—she asked if I need some food. When I went for clothes for the children, at Montgomery Wards they knocked me down the price. I went to order a telephone—by that time I speak a few words English—and the lady who talked to me said, "You are doing beautiful." That is good for strangers. The American people make welcome.

Raise chickens? After you go through so much, you know everything! If you can make ammunition in a Nazi concentration camp, why can't you work with chickens? You need to make a living in America so you make a living. When you have no other choice, courage is big.

ESTELLE EDELSTEIN [b. 1920; Krasnovce, Czechoslovakia]

The first time I went to the Center, they looked at me like a *grine*—a greenhorn. I sat there very shy. But people came up to me. Right away they made me feel it is home.

Petaluma Jewish community is something special. We moved in here, Mrs. Feinstein came to see if we need something. If you miss an affair at the Center, right away Mrs. Katz calls: "What's up?" If you are sick, you can bet your life they will help you with the chickens and bring in food. It's like one bunch.

All the newcomers feel this. Still, we were always a separate bunch, the newcomers. We all went through the bad times with Hitler. We liked to enjoy in America. When there was a party at the Center, it was the newcomers who loosen up with dancing and singing. There never was a fight with the old-time community, but we were always together, the newcomers. It was not always mixing with the others. They sometimes looked at us kind of funny.

You know, they called us the "*grine*." The greenhorns. To this day, some of us do not like this name.

ELAINE BERGOWITZ HOCHMAN [b. 1950; Petaluma]

The *grine* were weird and uptight. They had tatoos on their arms, from the concentration camps, and they hid those tatoos. They never said a word about it, but the *grine* women always wore something to cover their arms. In the Jewish community we passed clothes around from one family another, but we had to be careful with the *grine*. We never passed a short-sleeved dress or a short-sleeved shirt to these certain women. The *grine* made the whole Jewish community uptight.

ELI SALZMAN [b. 1924; Bydgoszcz, Poland]

Later they got used to us, but in the beginning the Petaluma people were looking at us funny. You know, they read all kinds of stories about Jewish survivors from the concentration camps.

With me they saw a normal person. They wondered. They expected I would be different. One guy said to me, "My gosh! You have so much hair!"

I said, "Why shouldn't I have hair?"

He said, "I read reports that the hair was shaved off in the camps."

I said, "I'm no different than you. I was not in a concentration camp. I passed as a Christian for five years."

LARRY HIRSHFIELD [b. 1944; Petaluma]

There were all kinds of rumors about the *grine*. There were stories about what happened to them in the Holocaust. There were stories about how they all got so rich.

My father said the *grine* were sponging off the Jewish community. He said Petaluma took them in, loaned them money, cosigned for their credit at the feed company, and showed them how to raise chickens. The refugees kept demanding more help, and we felt sorry for them. Then, all of a sudden, they were operating three chicken ranches and buying apartment buildings in San Francisco. While the people who had been here for thirty years were still struggling to make a living, the *grine* became rich. My father said the *grine* came to Petaluma with money. They came out of the concentration camps with gold, silver, crystal, fine tablecloths, silverware, watches—people saw it! The *grine* came here rich, and then they stepped over people to get richer.

My grandfather said that I shouldn't listen to rumors. He said the *grine* deserved all the help we could give them. He said they were courageous people who survived the Holocaust.

SAUL HOFFMAN [b. 1916; Lublin, Poland]

We went through hell over there. I was not in a concentration camp. I was a partisan in the forest during the war. Ruth, my wife, she was with me all the way through. After the war, who was still a couple from before the war? But Ruth and I, we made it through hell together.

I was a veteran from the Polish cavalry. In 1942 it comes time for Jews to go to the death camps, the concentration camps. That's when I organized a partisan group. We were over eighty people living in the forest—all Jewish—women, children, men. I was the commandant. Whenever possible, we liquidated small groups of Nazi soldiers.

We lived like this for a year. Then the Polish nationalist groups and even the Polish Communist groups, they started to kill every Jew they could find. I wasn't afraid of the Nazis in the forest. But the Polacks, they can find you. You can hide from a stranger, but you can never hide from your own people. I had a few good Polaks what I could talk to. Still I didn't trust them. I could only ask them, "Do me a favor and sometimes

I give you back a favor." But I ask with my rifle in my hand. Always with the rifle ready. That's the way. Yeah.

From over eighty people in my partisan group were alive maybe eight at the end. It's a long story. We went through hell. That's why I say I don't owe nobody from nothing! Nobody offered me nothing. I didn't ask for nothing.

Let me tell you, when I came to San Francisco from Europe in 1947, and my wife is going to have the second baby, the Jewish Welfare Federation called us up—they want to help us. I told them, "I take care of myself! I never took charity in my life! I'm in the best country in the world, the richest country. I'm not going there in the bread line!"

That's how I did it. I learned the tailor trade fast. I got a good job in San Francisco making ladies' garments. I went up and up. But I wanted to settle down quiet somewhere. The best place quiet was a chicken ranch in Petaluma. This was 1950.

Did the Jewish community help me start with the chickens? Let me tell you! The first people what came over to visit, I was better off than them! Even then! They owed five thousand dollars to the feed company! The first chicken was sick, they said close all the windows. The chickens almost died from no air! He didn't know what he's doing.

I didn't owe nothing to nobody here. Some newcomers, they tried to get everything they can from the Jewish people here. Not me! I never said, "You owe me help! Do everything for me!"

I never asked for nothing. For three years I worked days as a tailor in San Francisco while my wife took care the ranch and the children. The heavy work I did at night and weekends. I accumulate me enough to raise chickens on a second ranch. When the third son was born, 1953, I increased to five ranches. I said, "Now I make a living just from the chickens!"

It was a challenge. After 1953 the chicken business was tough. You had to be a hard worker—it's not just feed the chickens and go to the beach. You must know what you are doing all the time. You must understand business. You must be honest. And *pashayet*—luck—I believe in *pashayet*.

Meanwhile, we make very good friends with the other newcomers in here. Picnics, parties, music—we live it up! We like the whole Jewish community, and we are told we are an asset to the Center. They pushed me to be president, but I told them no. In Europe, with the partisans, there was a necessity. Here is so many people that want the job, let them run the Center. I be the helper.

All the newcomers liked it here. But most of them left after a few years, when the trouble comes in the chicken business. I stayed here and did good with the chickens all the way. I did good with my apartment buildings too. But most of the newcomers, they went to the city and started a grocery store, a liquor store, an ice-cream store, a restaurant, the real estate. Whatever they did, they made a successful living.

Why? When the newcomers come to this country, we got that grit—to take something and make of it. We didn't sit around and wait for gifts. We didn't have no parents to leave us fortunes. We had to start from scratch and make good ourselves.

NAOMI BERENSTEIN [b. 1923; Berlin, Germany]

We was very lonesome when we came to San Francisco. We didn't speak good English and we didn't have no money and we didn't know what to do. We was completely lost because we went through the Holocaust. People don't realize what that means. You get out from the camps and you find out your family is killed and you are alone. And you come to this country and your fellow Jews don't understand. Even your relatives don't understand you. Because they *don't know* what it means to be lost.

I was working as a nurse at Mount Zion Hospital in San Francisco. My patients from Petaluma they told me, "Come to Petaluma. There are many newcomers. You will like it."

We went to Petaluma for a visit. We was greeted with open heart and open hands. They took us in like we would be family. All the old-timers who greeted us with such warmth, they found a farm for us, they loaned us money, they showed us what to do with the chickens. They gave us the love and understanding which we could not find in San Francisco.

Everybody laughed at how I worked with the chickens. Every time I had sick chickens, I made a hospital for them. I would not throw out a sick chicken. And I would not eat the chickens I raised. We worked very hard. We borrowed every penny to buy this place. And when the chicken prices went down later, we had to turn this ranch into a convalescent home to save it. But we did it, and by the way, we paid back every penny we owed.

I consider myself fortunate to live here. In Petaluma I made friends— and I *mean friends*. I gave of myself what I could to the Jewish community. And they gave me the love and understanding I did not know how to ask for. Not till years after I came here could I look in the mirror and say, "It's me. It's not somebody else."

ELI SALZMAN

We adapted easily to America. During the war I survived in Germany by passing myself as an Aryan, a Christian. I adapted. Jews as a people have a lot of experience adapting! Throughout the ages, from country to country, Jews developed this ability.

Let me give you a life experience. Immediately after the war I was in a displaced-persons camp with fifteen hundred Jews and fifteen hundred Poles. Within six months the Jews already were buying food and clothes, driving cars, doing business. You could see that people were hustling, advancing, trying to start a normal life. We created a library, we organized political groups, we had lectures. While the Poles were still totally dependent upon the camp authorities, we Jews had all kinds of schemes to make a buck and improve our lives. This was only a few months after the war, after what the Jews went through in the ghettos and the concentration camps. We came out half dead. More than half dead! Bare survivors! After this, America was an easy country to adapt to.

We came with nothing, but we were ready to take advantage of American freedom. Here we could build for the future, go where we wanted, do what we wanted. We found the true America! The land of opportunity! You really must be born someplace else to realize it! The immigrants in the Petaluma Jewish community, they came from persecution and they understood what we refugees found in America. But their children and their grandchildren didn't have this appreciation. My children don't have it either. They were raised under different circumstances. How could I explain to the American-born my feeling of seeing a Petaluma policeman without fear? I come from Poland where we feared people in authority. In this country there was nothing to fear. It was a great experience, a great experience!

Here there was opportunity for all! When I first came I worked at Rogin's feed mill, across the street from the Bank of America. One time I walked into the bank right after unloading fish meal. I smelled with fish meal, but Mr. Lepore invited me into his office to sit down and talk about the loan I applied for. And he gave me the loan! In what other country could this happen?

Of course, we had to work very hard for our financial success, but we didn't expect anything but hard work. I did not have the options of young people who are born in America. I started doing physical labor for the Rogin feed mill. Next it was a small chicken ranch, then a second ranch, and one day I expanded to five ranches. I raised chickens as a business operation. When the chickens were going into very big hands, I saw it was time to leave. We went to the city where there were greater business opportunities.

NORMA SALZMAN [b. 1924; Bydgoszcz, Poland]: I was heartbroken to leave. We loved the Petaluma Jewish people and the warm feeling at the

Center. It was like we are leaving home again. It was like leaving Anatevka from *Fiddler on the Roof.*

ELI: I missed Petaluma for a while. But it didn't take long for us to adjust to the new life in the city. Like I told you, we adapt to new situations very quickly.

MORRY FINKLESTEIN

Some of the survivors never recovered. As much as you hear the stories, you can't get used to it.

Levinsohn came from a very distinguished Lithuanian family. If you talk about Old World Jewish aristocrats, he was it. He told me the story of what happened to his family under the Nazis. He showed me the old photographs. And we both cried.

He was a solitary person. He didn't mix much with the Jewish community. His daughters grew up anti-Jewish—he didn't make any effort with them. He was married to a lovely German-Jewish young woman, but she developed multiple sclerosis and she was deteriorating. It was a horrible situation—very sad. He was a smart young man, but he was broken. Chicken ranching was too hard for him, so he found work outside at the shipyards in Vallejo. On one of those trips he was killed in an auto accident.

After he died I'd go over there to help out the wife. The place was in sad condition, but she insisted on staying: "This is all I have."

Once she sent me to do something in the chicken house and I found the old photographs thrown in a chicken bin—photographs of these wonderful old Lithuanian Jewish men with their magnificent beards. They were his relatives who had died in the gas chambers. Those photographs were laying in chicken manure, but I had no reason to rescue them. What would I do with them? It was the end of the road for a certain life.

LEO SEABORG [b. 1915; Warsaw, Poland]

I felt in my skin that the Petaluma Jewish community must remember what happened. Right after I arrived in March 1950 I told Mr. Katz, "We should have a Petaluma memorial meeting for the Holocaust. We should have a community commemoration of the Warsaw Ghetto uprising."

Mr. Katz said, "It's too late to get a speaker by the anniversary of the Warsaw Ghetto uprising."

I said, "Mr. Katz, I'll be the speaker."

That evening was the biggest crowd I ever witnessed in the Petaluma Jewish Community Center. I was the main speaker. I told about life under the Nazis. I spoke about the Warsaw Ghetto uprising. I reported on what happened after the Holocaust with the birth of Israel. Since then they continue this commemoration every year.

KANN: Could you tell me about your years in Europe during the war?

LEO: If I do that, you will leave with my story on your tape recorder, and I will be left with a concentration camp in my mind tonight. No, I would rather not.

But when I came to Petaluma, it was important that many of the Petaluma people were very much interested in what we went through in Europe. Not the young people, but the old-timers. They were people with deep roots in European Jewish life. They were very sympathetic to the newcomers. They extended us every helping hand. It was comforting to be among older people again. In the refugee camps everyone was between twenty and thirty-five—only the young survived the Nazis. Here in Petaluma it was like a big family with parents, aunts and uncles, cousins. You need that for faith in the future.

Once Mr. Rubinstein asked me, "How old are you?"

"Thirty-five years old."

He was sixty at that time. He said to me, "*Der mame's milkh is nokh af di lipn*"—Your mother's milk is still on your lips."

But we were not young "greenhorns" like when they came to America. When they left prewar Russia, they came from a different world. I came from Germany, which was as advanced as America. They tried to explain to me how to flush a toilet and how to operate a car. I said, "Nothing is new to me. I have seen it all."

They also were surprised that the newcomers did so well in the chicken business. When some of our newcomers succeeded, while the old-time Jewish chicken ranchers went bankrupt, there was some jealousy. When some of us newcomers left Petaluma and did well in the city, I heard several times a remark I did not like when I visited Petaluma.

Why did we do so well? There are many reasons. We knew how to conduct ourselves in business. We knew how to hustle. We were willing to work hard. And some of us had luck—never underestimate luck. There were many factors. There always are many factors which determine who shall live and shall die.

SHURA EASTMAN COMPISI

We were glad when they went on to bigger and better things in the city. I don't think they made a contribution to our Jewish community.

They felt that the world owed them, that *you* owed them, and they let the community know it. Maybe they were justified, but it wasn't pleasant to do business with them or to socialize with them. They didn't have much warmth for others.

I worked for a lot of the *grine* in my chicken-vaccinating business. They thought everyone was out to skin them, that *I* was out to skin them. It was totally uncalled for, but they felt they had to do you in before you did them in. That was their plight—they thought people were after them.

My parents felt the *grine* were entitled to what they could get. You know, my parents were part of the generation that wept for all mankind. I tried to think of the *grine* that way: "Gee, they went through this, that, and the other." But they learned some strange things from survival. Stra-a-a-ange things! They weren't very pretty people. They used the methods they learned in surviving the Holocaust to become rich in America. They made it by stepping on people here, and then they made it big by stepping on more people in the city. I recognize that that's how they survived the Holocaust, but I didn't like how they came out of it.

SAMUEL GANS

There were two kinds of refugees: those who came before the war and those who came after. Those of us who came before the war probably would have perished in the Holocaust. Because the ones who came after the war were the tough ones. The ones who survived were not the best of Jews, believe me. The *grine* were one group of people I could *never* get along with. I tried to work with them, but they wanted everything. Aggressive! Demanding! Greedy! Unethical! They were out for themselves and no one else.

They were hard people—stone hard people. That's why they survived.

HANNAH GANS [b. 1917; Vienna, Austria]: They were never our kind of people. *Never!*

STELLA FINKLESTEIN

The postwar refugees were a completely different element from the prewar refugees. They were not culturally advanced. They were very, very aggressive. They settled here, they were helped, they made money, and they left for greener pastures.

MORRY FINKLESTEIN: They became very wealthy in America, but they arrived with fortunes from black marketeering in Europe after the war.

The Jewish Agricultural Society presented them to us as poor, but these people knew how to fool officials. They got what they wanted from the Jewish Agricultural Society, and then they got more from the Haas Fund and from our committee here. They didn't need our money. They didn't need our advice either. Everything we told them about chicken ranching, they did just the opposite. They didn't trust us. If we had come to them for advice, they probably would have given us the wrong advice deliberately.

STELLA: The first time we went to help Yanowitz, he asked, "How long are you in America?" Morry answered forty years. Yanowitz says, "And you're still working with your hands?"

We had one of the refugee families for dinner. The woman takes one look at my knotty-pine walls and says in a disgusted voice, "Oh, a wooden house still."

MORRY: That whole family survived in a concentration camp. Poppa, momma, two children. Such things happened. I never asked how. I didn't want to hear. They came with a lot of money. One guy that came was a real pimp. He told me—in one of his exuberant moods he says, "Do you think I was so badly off in the concentration camp?" He says, "I had everything, including women!"

They had a category for such people. They called them *kapos*. Have you ever heard of it? It was a very feared word. It's those Jews who worked hand-in-hand with the Nazis in the concentration camps. He was one.

There was another young man among the refugee group—good-looking wife, gold rings on the fingers, quite a sport. He conned the whole Jewish community. We made a collection of five hundred dollars when his wife got sick, and he used it to buy a television set! Another skunk said to me, "That guy was a *kapo*." They talked about each other that way.

Well, you must go back to what they lived through. Terrible demoralization. The Nazis did that. They sometimes forced prisoners to beat each other and gas each other. The Nazis were insidious. A lot of people who came out from this ordeal were not very clean people. There were some ugly characters among the *grine*. Like one of them told me, "The good ones did not survive."

SHEILA COHEN [b. 1951; Petaluma]

It's hard for outsiders to understand the *grine*. I know them because I come from them. I come from an integrated marriage! [Laughing.] My father is American-born and my mother is *grine*. Right after my father opened his general store in Cotati, Julia Segal introduced him to this beautiful young woman who had survived the Holocaust. They made the only integrated marriage in Petaluma.

I know that a lot of the *grine* seem arrogant and ruthless. It's like when you go into a shop in Israel, the owner will treat you terribly and try to cheat you however he can. You'll think he's just a yukko person. But as soon as you get to know him socially, as soon as you come into his kitchen, he's the most loving, generous person you could meet.

Some *grine* are like that. They'll do anything to get money and security for their family. They won't let anybody stand in their way. The outside world is the enemy. It's because they went through the Holocaust. But some *grine* look at it another way. Mommy says, "We went through the Holocaust. We should know better than to treat others like that."

Mommy says people survived in all kinds of ways. Some became mean, some became kinder. Some denied their Judaism, some became religious, some became atheists. But everybody came out of the Holocaust different. Mommy says all the *grine* went through something unique, and it separates them from other Jews.

Estelle Edelstein

I call it a book. It is not even a hundred pages. I'll tell you why I wrote it. I used to watch "This Is Your Life" on the television. There was a lot of people from the concentration camps on that program. They brought them together with relatives. I didn't see my brother for twenty-six years. I thought, "I would give anything to get on that program."

Every week I watched "This Is Your Life." Then all my thoughts went through my mind. I'm very sentimental. I always feel sorry for the other people who were in the camps. I went through the same thing, but I feel sorry for the other people. After "This Is Your Life" I was sitting until two o'clock—thinking. So I put on paper all what I had on my chest—to get it out. That I would write my story and send it to "This Is Your Life." Maybe they would bring my brother to me.

I never sent in my book. I saw my brother later, but still I have my book. Maybe you can look and tell me what to do with it.

From Estelle Edelstein's Book
It was very cold when the Germans marched into Prague. March 1939. I was eighteen years old. I didn't take the streetcar to work that day. I preferred to walk. I saw German soldiers everywhere.

The Czech people loved their country and they knew something was going to happen. And it did. At my orphanage too. They had to relocate the children. I was sent to a farm at Korcycany in Moravia. There I was very happy. I was free and I liked the work. That is when I met the first boy. His name was Zdenek Roubicik, let him rest in peace. He was burned in a concentration camp. We were young and we fell in love. After work the young people would clean and dress. We sang and danced together. Of course it wasn't always fun. We feared the moment they would take us away.

In the meantime the Germans opened a ghetto in Teresienstadt, near Prague. I was sent there with a group. I lived in a room with forty-two women. We slept two on the bed. The men lived in another building but we couldn't see each other. Wives, husbands, and children were separated. The young people worked in the fields for the Germans. I liked working outside the ghetto because we could see other people. They couldn't talk to us, but sometimes they threw us food, which was very dangerous. That cost many people their lives.

The food in the ghetto was very bad and very scarce. We really were hungry. For us who worked in the fields, we always found something to eat. But the older people who couldn't work were starving. The teeth of the children became loosened because of lack of vegetables. Every group who worked in the fields tried to bring back vegetables. It was dangerous because of the check-up, but when you are hungry you get many ideas.

I was in Teresienstadt for two years. I had many good times with friends. We went together in the evenings and sang. We tried to forget the bitter moments. But there were many bad days and fear of what will happen next.

The worst was when they sent away a group. Nobody knew where. One day I had to go too. I went with many friends together. If we had known what was going to happen to us I am sure many would have tried to escape. They put us on a train, for horses, not people. There was no seats to sit down. There was no room to turn around and no toilet. We didn't know where they were taking us, but our hope didn't die. One played an accordian, we sang, we tried to be happy.

Finally the train pulled into a big railroad station. It was quiet and we couldn't see anybody. Suddenly we heard a noise and someone hollered "*raus,*" which means "out." We saw many people in striped clothing like you see in jail. We still didn't know what was going on. Then we saw the Nazis divided old people from young ones, and we didn't know why they did that. Many girls didn't want to leave their mothers but they beat us with rubber sticks. We met there men we knew from Teresienstadt, but they didn't care for us now. They looked to me like hungry dogs wanting to bite a piece of bread. They were not the same people anymore. Soon we knew why. We were in Auschwitz.

It was rough there. We slept six in a bed the size of a double bed here. Food was the same every day—no breakfast, for lunch a soup cooked with the kind of beets for horses, for supper black coffee and a piece of bread with one small spoonful of jam. Some worked in the kitchen, some cleaned streets, others worked in cellophane factories. Every day and sometimes twice a day we had to stand in formation in the rain and cold.

It didn't matter that we lived there like dogs, dirty and full of fleas. We knew it was our last station. We heard from friends what happened to the ones before us, and we knew it would happen to us too. I didn't care anymore. I knew we would all die.

Our camp was a special one with Auschwitz. What I remember is the children that stayed with us. Some children were born there. It was a pity to look at them slowly dying. They never had a smile, no laugh for others. They didn't know another life from that one.

Once I will never forget. A group of old people arrived. They were confused. They didn't know where they were—and the Germans threw them on the truck. I really mean threw them. There were two soldiers—one took them by the hands and the other took them by the feet, and they would swing them onto the truck. They were eighty-five years old and they were eliminated.

At Auschwitz there always was a smell of burning hair and bones. They burned people because they couldn't have such a big cemetery for all the people they killed. They burned dead people, but also live people. Four crematoria burned day and night.

I stayed in Auschwitz six months. One day it was said that the young people would go to work in Germany. We didn't believe it because of what we heard—that many times instead of going to work in Germany they went to the crematorium to be burned. But this time all the young people had to go in a building, take off their clothes, and march naked before five German soldiers. They looked at our bodies very closely to see if one had anything wrong. We had tatoo numbers on our left arm, and we were called by our numbers and not by our names. We had to pass a table where a man sat and wrote our number. The ones who passed on the right side of the table could go away to work. The ones who passed on the left side couldn't.

Many mothers left their small children. The husbands and wives agreed not to worry about the child because they could always have more. If they stayed there they would all die together. I never could understand how they could leave a child. But some people wanted to live, so they did it this way. Maybe they did the right thing. All the mothers who stayed were burned with the children and the old people.

Next morning we were marched to another camp that was different from Auschwitz. The people had been there already five years and they hated us because we just came. These people who spent five years there had very bad times—worse than we had. Their minds were not normal. I saw once a girl use another girl for her enjoyment. I don't want to write too much about that because I know those people didn't live a normal life—they couldn't help it.

What was worse was what the Germans did to us. They beat us up a lot and we had to kneel down for hours on the gravel and hold the hands up. If someone put the hand down they were hit on the head. Thank God we stayed there only a week. One day they put us on a train, of course the same kind of horse train. We arrived in the afternoon in a place called Kristienstadt, near Berlin.

When we arrived it seemed like heaven after the places we had been. We had clean rooms, clean bankets, and most special was a bathroom with a shower. The boss from that place was a lady, very friendly, and I must say she liked me. She looked all the time at my blonde hair and she mentioned how beautiful it was. We didn't believe our ears, that a German could talk so nice to us.

There were other people there too—Czech, Polish, but mostly French. Everyone worked in a bomb factory. I worked by the main machine and filled up the bomb with hot liquid stuff. Other girls mixed the hot liquid with a big stick until it got cold. Many of us who worked there got sick with something like epilepsy—it was ugly to look at the person.

In February we had to leave the camp and went for a big walk. Some ran away because they didn't want to go. They were lucky because in two days they were freed by the Russians. We marched for six long weeks in the snow to Bergen Belsen. Those who made the trip never forgot it. Some didn't have shoes and their feet froze. Some died on the side of the road because they couldn't walk farther. At nighttime the soldiers stopped us in towns and looked for a roof over our heads. Some German people were nice and cooked us a hot soup, but that was only sometimes. Some of my close friends ran away, but they were caught and sent to another camp, to German soldiers. There is a lot to write about, but no use to hurt the girls—they've been hurt plenty.

The ones who remained still kept on walking. They added more soldiers to take care of us and they beat us and kicked us. But in a short time they were also tired and hungry, so they gave up the beating. In six weeks we arrived in Bergen Belsen.

That was our last station. There we saw plenty of dead people on the road, dirt all over, and no water. We were weak, hungry, and waiting to hear what will happen to us. They put us in a house, if you want to call it that. It was a large chicken house, but my chickens in Petaluma had it cleaner. We slept on the floor and without blankets. In that house were five hundred people. It was so crowded we could hardly move. At least it wasn't too cold—we nestled ourselves together and warmed each other. The food was the same, soup and very little bread, but we didn't complain as we were lucky to be alive. After the six weeks' walk we didn't care what would happen to us.

I never saw in my life so many dead people as I saw at Bergen Belsen. There was one house in which they put all the dead people. I still see it before my eyes—they threw them one on top of the other. They were so dirty because most of them had typhus and some didn't have any clothes left on. But the worst thing was some people were still alive, and they put them also with the dead ones to make room for others. Nothing bothered me so much as this. I was afraid to go near that house because it smelled so much. Even now while I am writing it makes me sick.

Every day was the same—stand in formation or stand for food. Our clothes were dirty and we didn't have water. We wondered how long it could take until I or she would be the next to die. I was very weak and I started to get typhus too.

One day we were standing by the gate for food and suddenly we looked up to the sky and saw hundreds of parachutes that looked like little birds. We prayed so hard that minute for our freedom and I guess God heard our prayer. In a few days we got our freedom.

I remember the 14th of April. We couldn't sleep. There was bombing all the time and we heard tanks and airplanes. Next morning, April 15, we got up as usual and went to stand in formation. We stood for hours and we couldn't understand what was wrong because we didn't see any German soldiers. We knew sure something was wrong, and there was. Driving on the main road was a man talking with a loudspeaker telling us that we were free. He said everyone should stay in place and there would be plenty of food and medicine.

How true and how good it was. But the joy was too big. There was a panic between us all. Those who had strength started to scream, "We are free, free as a bird." That joy was so big, that many of them lost their mind and became real crazy. Other girls were ungrateful because they were dying. To them the freedom was black. Too late.

It was on April 15, 1945, that we were free. In the evening we got milk. That was the first milk I had in four years. To me it tasted like God gave us each drop to be stronger. . . .

I came to Petaluma skinny, but I didn't stay skinny. On the ranch I got fat from the milking cows! [Laughing.] I made so much butter, I ate bread with the butter instead of butter with the bread.

Now I never think about what I went through. It's out of my mind when I'm awake. But somehow it comes back in the dreams and I see everything. And I always say to myself in the dreams, "This time I am smarter. This time I will not go through it. This time I will hide."

MORRY FINKLESTEIN

The three Yarmulshefsky brothers survived the Holocaust. They were older—they lost wives and children—but somehow they survived. Isaac Yarmulshevsky is the one to talk to. We drove him home from the Center one time last year and he told us the whole story. It made us cry.

NATHAN YARMULSHEFSKY [b. 1946; displaced persons' camp, Germany]

I know almost nothing about how Uncle Isaac, Uncle Abraham, and my father survived the Holocaust. I just know that my father spent thirty months hiding in the attic of a Polish family. In America, when *Fiddler on the Roof* came out, "Sunrise Sunset" became his favorite song. He remembered that for thirty months all he could do was watch the sun rise and set.

My uncle Isaac told me that the daughters my father lost were the most beautiful girls in the world. I have *never* heard my father speak about them or his first wife. I didn't even know about them until I was a teenager. I don't know how he could bear such a loss without speaking about them all these years.

ROSE YARMULSHEFKSY [b. 1921; Zgierz, Poland]: First we say nothing. Then we tell everything. That's the *grine*.

ISAAC YARMULSHEFSKY [b. 1895; Zgierz, Poland]: Hitler came to *mayn* city 1939. Was September 5, maybe 6. Was Tuesday. The soldiers come: *Eins! Zwei! Drei!* One comed in my bakery: "Give me *emers!*" Buckets. To give a drink the horses. I give him. But I'm a baker—I need the buckets. I cross over the street where the soldiers are with the horses. I say I am a baker and I need the buckets. He give me. Okay, I went home with the buckets, I bake.

I bake maybe six months. Then they take my bakery. They put us all in a ghetto in our town, but not *mit* fence. Was not so bad. Because in the night we dealed with the Poles. We got potatoes. We got flour. My brother Chaim, who can deal like him! Nobody! If we be catched, they hang us. But we got to eat! We got children who are hungry!!

1941 . . . September—maybe October—the Germans take us. I don't want to go from my house. I bar the door! [Going over to the door, demonstrating.] We could stay! The Germans are not going house to house. I got a lot of Polish backers, they can help my family if we stay. But the Jewish *birgermayster* makes us go. We are the last ones from the houses.

They put us in the church. We were 3,500 people. My brother Chaim, he was downstairs. He went for water. They want water, his girls, two beautiful girls. The German soldier know Chaim. He told Chaim, "*Raus auf*—run away!!" Chaim go for water and run away. I don't know this. Because I am in the top of the church. I am with *mayn* wife and children—eight children. *Mayn* father was with me—eighty-six years—he still worked good. We are in the top of the church four days.

Friday they left the old people and the children in the church. They took the others to the train. We come 900 from 3,500 to the train station. My older son and daughter are with me. The other people they take to the ovens. *Mayn* wife, *mayn* children, *mayn* father—more from *mayn* family. We see the trucks come for them. We know.

We come to Lodz on the train. In Lodz we seen death! Fence! The ghetto in my town, no *gefenced*. We deal for food *mit* Polish, *mit* Germans. My brother Chaim, he was hiding thirty months in our town. He know who to knock on the door in the night. He knows the good Poles. He knows the good Germans. Don't think all Germans is bad!

In Lodz ghetto, they gives us a house. Was a lot of empty houses, empty beds, clothes. In Lodz was once a million *yidn*. When I come there is just thousands. We got to work in Lodz ghetto. I'm a baker, but you can't work in bakery unless you got *pleytses*—wide shoulders, influence. So first I carry *ayzn*, iron. Is bad. The *ayzn* is heavy. I got to walk twelve kilometer every day. Hungry. I can't do it. I say no! I find a job cleaning up—a janitor. This is what I do for a year.

Then . . . notices—they looking for a baker. I am a baker from 1908. When I take the flour in *mayn* hand, I know what for a bread be. Takes a week. Comes a paper. I need to take *eksamen. Eksamen!* Exam! For grade! [Laughing.] An *eksamen* for to be a baker! Me! In Lodz ghetto!

I come in the baker for *eksamen.* I see maybe sixteen people come to be baker. The other people, they look bad, swollen from hunger like me. But I am not so stupid! No! I were a whole day cleaning the lice and worms, because when the worms begin to eat you, then you finished. I come clean to the bakery!

When they told me to make *khale,* I'm a specialist from *khale.* I take eggs, flour a little, with the hands—no measure—I am a baker! But they don't let me finish the dough! The other boys, I see they don't do it right. But I don't know if I make good. They don't let me finish the dough! They don't tell me nothing.

Three days, a man comes to my house: "Your name is Isaac Yarmulshefsky? You make the *eksamen.* You work in bakery at Dvorska 6. Tomorrow."

Ok, Saturday I go to Dvorska 6. They work *shabes.* I don't work *shabes,* but this time I work *shabes.* Because when they give me a pound bread a day, it can be life! I go to work. Was beginning 1944.

I come in bakery, the boss says, "You work at the oven."

I was swollen. I was weak. The oven is burn *mit* coal. Is very bad. I told him, "No!!"

He told me, "Don't be afraid. You clean a little and you get your bread."

I got on my mind the same thing. [Laughing.] I clean. I finish work. The boss gives me a pound bread. Ai! Ai! I'm a *keyser,* a king. I got a pound bread. I wash *mayn* hands, I pray, I eat.

The next week comes in the bakery the small fish—small police—Jewish police. He stays in the bakery. The workers tell me, "Isaac, don't eat extra. If he see you, this is prison—then the oven."

I say, "Don't you worry. When he walks, you sing 'The Tikva.' " We make the extra bread. For everyone. For *mayn* children!

Happened one day I go home from the bakery, police catch me on the street. Jewish police. Bandits! They catch people. Take to prison—to the ovens. But I think, "You don't got a gun. You just got a piece wood." I run away.

Three days later Gestapo comes to bakery. Come for us. I think, this is bad. Jewish police, I can run away. But Gestapo have machine *gever,* machine guns. Is very bad. I run in the back. They *shisn*—bang! bang! I run to the toilet. I hide in there. They take the workers from the bakery. All the bakers, but not me. I run home.

This is a big story. A big story. I make shorter. They send us to Auschwitz. 1944—September. Went a day and a night on a train. Animal cars. Come to Auschwitz, the music is playing. Music! Music, then they burn you. I hear the screaming. But we was a special group of workers. *Mayn* two children are with me. We work in Auschwitz with machine bullets.

From Auschwitz we see the bombers. The Russians are coming. The Germans move the machines. Send us to Stutholtz. In Stutholtz was a Communist—sabotage!—we make no bullet right. Three months, not one bullet right!

They send us to Dresden. Dresden was a little better. We were living inside a building. Got a roof. In a camp. They send me working in a bakery in town. I get bread there. One night there is bombing. When I heard the bombs I got in mind to run away. I just want to be alive and save the children. We escape. We got to the bakery for help. These people [getting out pictures]—the baker *meister* and his wife—they saved us. They take us in their house. They give us food. They washed us up, changed the clothes. They got us passports, give me money.

We left the city. I start to walk from Dresden with *mayn* children and one more. This one was in Auschwitz with us. He says, "I don't go away from you, Isaac. You know how to stay alive." We walked a whole day. Friday. Was in May. A big day. Maybe six-thirty we come to a village. We say we are Polish people looking for work. They send us to work with a big farmer. The farmer don't know we are Jewish people. The other workers don't know. We sleep in the underwear so they don't recognize us.

I can never finish it, this story. This isn't the half of it! Not a half! No!

We work one day, two days, three days. Then the manager tells me Hitler is dead. Says Hitler was a good man. Hitler was a good man! This manager lost three sons on the front! Stupid! You think Germans is smart? You don't know. Russian is smarter. Polish is smarter. German is stupid! *Bitte sheyn—danke sheyn*—this is not everything! No!

Saturday. *Mai* the five—*Mai* the six. The manager is gone, the rich farmer is gone. I know the Russians are not far. In the night is shooting. Next morning we see German soldiers hiding in the trees. To the last the Gestapo fights.

We are another day in the house. Comes a Gestapo bandit. Asks, "What nation are you? Polish? Russian? Jew?"

I tell him, "Polish." We got Polish papers. He looks. He looks, and I kills him! Whenever I see Gestapo, now I kill! I got a right! I do the same as them! You understand?

The Russian fight with the German two days. Finished. The second day was *Mai* the eight. I were free. Free!

You never saw a guy like me! Right? You got enough?

KANN: I would like to hear about coming to Petaluma.

ISAAC: Oy yoy-yoy yoy-yoy! What you will hear about Petaluma is nothing! Was no war in Petaluma!

BASHA SINGERMAN

In Petaluma we remembered the Holocaust. This was our own family and friends who died. This was our people. We never forgot. Every year we had a Holocaust memorial. We did it at the anniversary of the Warsaw Ghetto uprising, to remember the heroic Jewish resistance to Hitler. We invited outstanding speakers—people who told the history of what happened. Every year we lit six candles, for the six million Jewish people who died. At these memorials our Jewish People's Folk Chorus sang "Buchenwald Alarm." In Yiddish we sang. In four voices. It is a beautiful song—very powerful. It is a message from the dead people in the concentration camp. They tell us to remember. It goes like this in English:

> Watch, watch the world.
> Take care of the world and take care of
> peace at last.
> All over the earth the wound is spreading,
> The alarm is running after each one's steps.
> Peoples! Countries! Take care of the world!
> Take care of peace at last.

NAOMI BERENSTEIN

The Jewish people who lived in Petaluma understood. They came from the same background as the newcomers. *They suffered.* In Russia they were persecuted. When they came to America they struggled to make a new life. They never had it easy. So they understood the newcomers. They identified with us, and they opened up their arms and their hearts to us. These were people who knew they were Jewish, like we knew we were Jewish. After my experience in the Holocaust, I know I am Jewish. I lived underground in Germany during the war, but you could have killed me before I would deny who I am.

All the people who suffered in the Holocaust became better Jews—not religious, not traditional, but better Jews. They know who they are, like the Yiddish-speaking Jews in Petaluma. When you have been persecuted, you never forget who you are.

The children and the grandchildren who grew up in Petaluma, they did not suffer . . . they did not know. I think it's good for a person to suffer. Because if you suffer, you become a bigger person. When you have life too easy, there is very little you can give of yourself. And if you can't give nothing of yourself, then you are not a very good person.

I want my children to be able to give of themselves. I don't want them to think they are alone. They have a duty to other people, particularly their own people, to give of themselves. I raised them this way, and I think to a certain extent I succeeded.

Of course I was very unhappy I had to suffer. It was un-normal, because I had to lose my family. It was a big family and a very close knit family. We was there for one another, and I lost them. That is what I found in Petaluma. The European Jews here had close-knit families and a close-knit community. They took us in and they gave us a lot of love. You ask me why we felt warm in Petaluma. Well, I think the Jews here had a lot to give of themselves.

SAUL HOFFMAN

For your information, the newcomers who moved away from Petaluma, even when they die they are coming back. They like to be buried here. Isn't that something!

Every newcomer who was moving away, we made a big party at the Center. One guy got up at his party and said, "Even when I move away, Petaluma will be home. In Petaluma I found family. In Petaluma I found understanding. On account of business I must move away. I have to make a living. But when I die, I come home. It is better to be buried in our Jewish Cemetery in Petaluma."

MORRY FINKLESTEIN

Arnold Lesner was a very good friend of mine. He's in the cemetery now. He was a refugee, a *grine*. Arnold was a leftist. He had been in the Polish underground during the war. He was a first-class soldier—very violent, very violent. His mother and brother had been executed before his eyes. He treated the enemy just like the enemy treated him. When his partisan group came into a town, they didn't think anything of taking a baby and swinging its head against the wall like we did with a chicken.

How he ever survived the war is beyond me. He said this to me about it: "All the Jews that survived the Holocaust are not the good ones. The good ones are gone." He came right out and said it: "Those of us who survived, somewhere along the line we weren't as good as those who died."

He was a close friend of mine. We argued like cats and dogs, but I loved that man like a brother. He was a very beautiful man. He remembered his friends—he never forgot that the Rubinsteins had chicken soup waiting for them when they arrived in Petaluma, or that Basha gave him a car. And he remembered his enemies—to his dying day, the only good German was a dead German. He was strong, very strong.

Arnold instilled something in his kids which to this day I admire. When he died, the family brought him back to our Petaluma Jewish Cemetery to be buried. After the service, when the workmen were going to cover the grave, his son David said, "No strangers will cover my father! I will do it!" That was like Arnold. David was reflecting his father. He felt his father should be covered by loving hands. He gave his little brother a shovel and said, "We're going to cover him."

We all stayed. We watched while they covered the whole grave.

11 The "Split":
The Cold War in Petaluma

MURRAY KOLMAN

It was a good Jewish community when we moved to Petaluma in 1944. Didn't matter what you believed. Everybody went in the Center. Our branch of the International Workers Order [IWO] met there. Our Jewish Folk Chorus sang there. All the Jewish people was together. But then the conservative movement . . .

ZEITEL KOLMAN: Murray darling, no!

MURRAY: There was a progressive movement and a conservative movement. And suddenly the conservative movement wouldn't let the progressive movement into the Center.

ZEITEL: It was nothing. Nothing! It was a couple of people that spoiled it. There was a little argument and then it was okay again. Now everyone is friends. Everyone!

MURRAY: It wasn't just a few and it didn't end so fast. It was a few leaders like Katz and it was all the *rekhte* who followed. They kicked out the *linke!* For years they wouldn't have nothing to do with us!

ZEITEL: Murray, please!

MURRAY: Keep cool. Keep cool. They did more than that. Some of them spread it all over Petaluma: "The IWO and the chorus is a bunch of Communists. We chased them out of the Jewish Center."

ZEITEL: It's recorded, Murray. It's recorded on the machine!

MURRAY: That's all right. He can print everything! It's the truth!

DAN ADLER [b. 1946; Petaluma]

My parents tried to be discreet when those jerks in the *rekhte* kicked the *linke* out of the Center. They wouldn't talk about it in front of me. But I remember laying in bed and hearing my father yelling about so-and-so. I won't mention names.

As for my grandfather, this was the *second* time he was kicked out. He'd yell, "I'm not going back into the Center. Never! The building is cursed!!"

BASHA SINGERMAN

The reactionaries threw us out of the Center! They couldn't stand progressive people. Katz, he was the leader. He was mfgh! Terrible, terrible against us! Hated us! Since then, I for one would not come into the Center for many years. We helped build the Center. We contributed over the years. It was terrible that a small Jewish community in a small town should turn away its own people. It was terrible—terrible!

FRAN RUBINSTEIN GINSBERG

The fighting at those meetings when the *linke* was kicked out! Mr. Katz argued for the right. Ben Hochman defended the left. Ideological debates—yelling, screaming, almost fist fights.

Crippled old Mr. Lipsky—he was one of the *shul yidn*—he'd make these terrible tirades against communism, and all the while he'd shake his cane as it to say, "If you let the *linke* meet here, I'll brain them myself!"

My father was president of the Center during that period. He was a strong Labor Zionist and he didn't want left-wing meetings at the Center. You know, McCarthy was witch-hunting and the *linke* had carrying cards—the were card-carrying members of the Communist party. But they also were old friends and my father didn't want to kick them out. It was a trying time.

STELLA FINKLESTEIN

I'm not surprised that Mr. Rubinstein wouldn't talk to you about it. The decent ones on the right didn't approve of forcing out the left. They didn't like it, but they didn't lift a finger to stop it.

The older Mr. Haller was one exception. Whatever his faults as a businessman, I respected him tremendously for opposing the Red-baiting. He was a *shulkhn orekh* Jew, a pious man with the old ideas that Jews should live by Talmudic law. He'd say at those meetings, "We have differences of opinion, but regardless, the Jewish people must stay together. All Jews should meet at the Jewish Community Center."

He was a wise man, but no one could stop it. The dirty work in this community lasted about five years, while McCarthy did his dirty work in Washington. This was the period when McCarthy charged the State Department and the army were run by Communists. The Justice Department was prosecuting Communist party leaders under the Smith Act. Right here in Petaluma my Grange chapter built a platform on a hill and manned it round the clock with Grangers watching for a Russian air attack!

The trouble in the Jewish community began when the International Workers Order appeared on the attorney general's list of subversive organizations. The Petaluma IWO branch, with over one hundred members, had been active at the Center for years. Just a few of them were actual party members because the Sonoma County Communist party had virtually died out after the tar and feathering of Hochman in 1935. But the Jewish reactionaries branded the entire *linke* as Communists and kicked out the IWO: "No Reds in the Jewish Community Center."

That was just the beginning. It really got vicious around here. It's a terrible thing when Jewish people starting *masering* [murdering] one another.

Board of Directors, Petaluma Jewish Community Center, Minutes, October 2, 1950

A committee from the Petaluma B'nai B'rith organization presented the following:
(a) a communication from the U.S. Attorney General dealing with the subject of subversive organizations
(b) a communication from Petaluma Post #20 American Legion on the subject of the Communist threat to America
(c) a resolution from the Petaluma B'nai B'rith Lodge dealing with Communist, Communist front and other subversive organizations as they reflect on and endanger the entire Petaluma Jewish community
Motion made by Jacob Katz and seconded by Isaac Lipsky that the board of directors go on record to deny use of the Center for a meeting place to any subversive organization so designated by government agencies. Motion carried.

STELLA FINKLESTEIN

What could we do? They had the votes. We sent a protest letter to the Haas family in San Francisco, reminding them that the Center was built with a grant from the Haas Fund for all the Petaluma Jews. We wanted the Haas family to pressure the board to rescind the expulsion of the IWO. We got back a letter from Mr. Stephen Tussman, a prominent Jewish community leader who represented the Haas family in philanthropic affairs. He wrote that according to his information the board was perfectly justified because the expelled organizations were nothing but a bunch of subversives.

STEPHEN TUSSMAN [b. 1910; San Francisco]

There was talk in San Francisco that the Petaluma Jewish community had a bunch of—well—"Commies," they were called. I didn't think anything of it. They spoke out against capitalism, but they didn't really do anything to subvert our American system of government. The problem was that this kind of radical activity brought on anti-Semitism. The left-wingers caused a tar and feathering up there in the thirties. They courted worse trouble in the McCarthy period. It's understandable that the Petaluma Jewish leaders would ban left-wing organizations from their Community Center.

MORRY FINKELSTEIN

First they kicked out the IWO. Then they kicked out the Jewish Folk Chorus. They said the chorus was a subversive organization. Subversive! [Laughing.] The most subversive thing the chorus did was to sing that nice Yiddish song about the Jewish farmers in the Soviet Union.

MIKE GOLD

The chorus sang *very* left-wing songs. One night, when they were practicing at the Center, they started singing "Happy Birthday" to Stalin. In Yiddish! The board of directors was meeting in the next room. We banged the gavel for silence, so they sang it again—in Russian! They had a birthday party for Stalin in our Center!

MURRAY KOLMAN

The chorus was kicked out when the bugaboo came in from McCarthy time. They pinpointed: "The Chorus is Communists." They threw us out of the Center a few years after they threw out our IWO.

ZEITEL KOLMAN: They made us all for Communists. I never was a Communist. I'm a sympathizer for the working people, that's all.

MURRAY: They brand marked the whole chorus to be Communists. What did we do that was so bad? No preaching. No agitating. We sang songs. At synagogues in San Francisco they invited us to sing. But in Petaluma they forbid us like we gave a Nazi concert!

Petaluma *Argus Courier,* February 19, 1953

Locals Protest Red Treatment of Jews

More than 175 persons met at the Jewish Community Center last night and took two steps in protest of the "infamy of Communist outrages against Jews behind the Iron Curtain." The group has been aroused by the recent trials of Jewish leaders in Russia.

One resolution denied the use of the Jewish Center to the "pro Red" Jewish Folk Chorus, a group which refused to help sponsor the mass protest meeting. The second resolution asked that "the people of Petaluma condemn the mendacity and viciousness of these Communist crimes against humanity."

Arthur LaSalle, local attorney, was the main speaker of the evening. He praised the Jewish Center as "a bulwark of American principles."

ARTHUR LaSALLE

We were in that "era of disappointment," as I call it, with the sharp charges of Senator McCarthy and the crusades to ferret out Communists. To maintain the high regard of the general community for the Jewish people, the more conservative elements among the Jewish people were careful to eliminate the alleged pro-Communists from the Center. They did that by using stock ownership as a weapon to prohibit certain organizations from using the building. I gave them some advice in this matter.

There was no deprivation of constitutional rights at the Jewish Center. The conservatives forced the alleged pro-Communists out of a private corporation. There never was the idea that these left-wingers didn't have the right to free speech. It's just that the Jewish leadership recognized the importance of separating those Jewish people who might be seen as troublemakers in the eyes of others. It was wise leadership.

Petaluma Jewish People's Folk Chorus, leaflet, March 1953

Do as We Say or Get Out

That, in effect, is the intolerant edict of the Board of Directors in expelling the Jewish Folk Chorus from the Jewish Community Center of Petaluma.

Despite its loud claims to patriotism, the ruling clique of the Center is actually desecrating the U.S. Constitution by undermining the basic rights of free speech and assembly, which include the right to silence or opposition.

The Jewish Folk Chorus was expelled for declining to co-sponsor the protest meeting against "Communism and anti-Semitism."

Yet members of the Center's Board are fully aware of the irrefutable fact that the Soviet Union has demonstrated its support to all minorities, Jews in particular; that anti-Semitism is forbidden by Soviet law and severely punished; that the USSR saved hundreds of thousands of Jews from Hitler and was a leading force in the establishment of Israel.

Why, then, all the fuss? Those under attack in the Soviet Union are a number of Zionist leaders who have been engaging in anti-Soviet intrigue. They want to make it appear that all the Soviet Jewish people are being attacked. In this venture they find willing accomplices in the pro-fascist forces of the world.

Their Petaluma accomplices new expel the Jewish Folk Chorus from the Jewish Community Center. The ruling clique at the Center has chosen to continue the shameful practice of the Judenrater [Jewish collaborators with the Nazis] and a handful of other traitors throughout our long persecution. The membership of the Jewish Center must repudiate this irresponsible leadership. Let us return to the Center *ALL* Jewish people in Petaluma!

JACOB KATZ

There was no place in our Jewish community for people who persisted with the view that whatever Stalin does is all right. They followed every twist and turn in the policy of the Soviet Union. By doing that they dissociated themselves from the interests of Americans and from the interest of world Jewry. They were American patriots only when it was convenient, like during the war when the United States was an ally of the Soviet Union. But when Stalin started up his aggression in eastern Europe after the war, the *linke* returned to the old attack against American capitalism and American imperialism.

It was the same zig-zag with Zionism. After World War II, when Russia tried to get a foothold in the Middle East by supporting the creation of Israel, the *linke* suddenly became super supporters of Israel. A few years later, when the Soviet Union decided its state interests rested with the Arabs against Israel, the *linke* followed the *Pravda* line that Israel is a puppet of American imperialism. They criticized Israel for its bad treatment of the Palestinian Arabs, a people that wanted to throw the Jews into the sea! The *linke* defended the enemies of the Jewish people!

The *linke* even supported Stalin in his attack upon Soviet Jewry. They swallowed the claims of a plot by Jewish doctors to kill Stalin. All through the years they glorified Soviet Yiddish culture, but they didn't say a word when Stalin executed Yiddish intellectuals and wiped out Yiddish cultural institutions after the war. They would not sign our letter denouncing the Stalin terror against the Soviet Jewish people.

If the *linke* believed that Russia is the Holy Land, they should have gone to live in Russia. There was no place for such Communist fanatics in our Jewish Community Center.

BEN HOCHMAN

The *rekhte* kicked us out because we would not join the Cold War crusade. It was not only an attack against the Soviet Union, but it was an attack on the trade unions and on the rights of the people here in the United States. It was an attack on American Jewish people—remember the execution of the Rosenbergs. The *rekhte* was scared by McCarthyism and they wanted to show that Jews are patriotic Americans. That is why they would not have us in the Center. At that time we believed that Soviet Communism paved the way for the solution to the problems of the Jewish people. We heard about Stalin's terror in the capitalist press, but the capitalist press always lied about communism.

MIRIAM HOCHMAN: This time the *rekhte* knew what was going on in Russia. We didn't.

BEN: Who would have thought it? We knew the great advances in standard-of-living and cultural development for the Soviet Jewish people. We remembered how the Soviet Union led the fight against Hitler. We knew it was the Soviet Union, not the United States, who gave the big support for the creation of Israel. We could not believe Stalin turned against the Jewish people.

The *rekhte* demanded that everyone believe Israel is the only solution to the problems of the Jewish people. We on the left supported the state of Israel, but we criticized how the Israeli government treated the Palestinian problem. We criticized the capitalist exploitation and the social inequality inside Israel. We took the same positions as the left-wing movement inside Israel, that Israel too must live according to the teachings of the Prophets. But here in Petaluma the *rekhte* would not tolerate a word of criticism about Israel—not a word of criticism about anything.

KHAYA FEINSTEIN

The *linke did not understand* what Israel meant to the Jewish people. I saw for myself in 1948. After Israel became a country, Zev and I sold the chickens and went to see what's happening. We got there right after the first war with the Arabs. The people was dancing in the streets.

Israel was a tremendous experience for me. It was a *Jewish* land. Wherever I went I saw *Jewish* people. Some were dressed like Arabs;

some were dressed like Russians; some were dressed like Americans. They was all different colors; they spoke all the languages under the sun. It was tremendous feeling when you were on the streets and you knew that whatever sort of person you saw it was a Jew. They were all Jews.

I felt like I was home in Israel. I was born in the Ukraine, where Jews were oppressed. We were strangers in a strange land. After the Ukraine, the United States was wonderful. But even after twenty-five years in the United States, it was not home. When I came to Israel I was among my own people, free in our own land. At last I felt I am home.

In Israel I met up with *khaverim* who did what I always dreamed about. Batya Menuhin, she left Petaluma in 1933 and moved onto kibbutz Ma'agam Mikhael. She helped start up a modern chicken industry on that kibbutz. She told me that her nephew Yehudi, the famous violin player, visited her a few months before, while he was on concert tour. She told him, "What do you know? Fiddle, fiddle—there's more to life than that." On that visit to Israel she taught him he was Jewish!

Batya wanted us to stay in Israel. Zev's family wanted us to stay. Back in 1936 we were ready to live there, but in 1949 it wasn't for us. We had a big ranch in Petaluma. Our boys had to finish their education. We felt like we must return to Petaluma and later we'll settle in Israel. But it never worked out. We should have gone to Israel in 1936. We should have stayed in 1949—we should have stayed.

Still, we gave tremendous help to Israel from Petaluma. Most of our Jewish farmers understood that Israel is the home of the Jewish people— Israel is the future of the Jewish people. They knew that Israel was the only home for the Holocaust refugees—orphans, old, sick, every Jew. They knew that since we got Israel, the Christian people looked up to Jews more in the United States. And like one of the *grine* told me, "If the Christians in America ever decide to give us a kick like from the Nazis, then we still can go to Israel."

All the Petaluma Jews looked to Israel except the *linke*. The social democrats in the Arbeiter Ring like the Jacobs brothers, they switched from anti-Zionism to support for Israel. The B'nai B'rith, who was for Jewish assimilation in America, they became Zionist supporters. Everyone was for Israel but the *linke*. The *linke* weren't *anywheres* as far as Jewish life was concerned.

Yossele Gardner

Never mind what the *linke* said they believed. Never mind that they followed the Communist party line. They still had a Jewish heart. All the *linke* had families murdered by the Nazis—families living in fear in the Soviet Union. They all had relatives who went to live in Israel after the Holocaust. Their hearts were with the Jewish people everywhere, even while their political ideas were still with the Soviet Union. They needed more time to adjust.

The *rekhte* would not give them time. That is why I quit the Center. Like I told you, I never was a political fanatic with the long religious beard, but I quit the Center on principle. I disagreed with the *linke* about the Soviet Union and Israel. But I disagreed more strongly with kicking them out of the Center. When they left, I went with them. I helped them fight for justice in America.

BASHA SINGERMAN

The most part of the *rekhte* believed in socialism, but they would do *nothing* to make social justice in America. Not a word would the *rekhte* say in public against McCarthyism. *Not a word,* even when it was the killing of the Rosenbergs—our own Jewish people.

You know what happened. The American government made a frame-up that the Rosenbergs gave the secret of the atomic bomb to the Soviet Union. The government wanted to scare all the people, that everyone should be patriots for McCarthy and enemies of the Soviet Union.

The progressive people in Petaluma stood up to defend the Rosenbergs. We raised money for the defense. We sent letters to the newspapers asking that the Rosenbergs should not be executed. Our Jewish People's Folk Chorus sang, together with Paul Robeson in Santa Rosa, at a concert to raise money in defense of the Rosenbergs. "Never Say That You Go the Last Road"—Paul Robeson used to sing that. He sang beautifully—in Yiddish—such a beautiful Yiddish. [Sings it and translates again:] "Don't say that you are going your last way."

Two innocent Jewish progressives the government was killing—oh, this case was close to our hearts. It was a terrible time—a terrible, terrible time! If you would sign your name to a letter in the newspaper, you would get bad telephone calls in the night—the neighbors would look at your different.

We needed a bigger movement to save the Rosenbergs. But every time we went to the *rekhte* for help, they would say, "It will be bad for the Jewish people if the gentiles see we are involved with Jewish spies."

JOE HOCHMAN

The *rekhte* was crapping in their pants with fear. They were terrified of being connected with the *linke*. I don't know why. What was the *linke* actually doing? Making "the Revolution"? Shit! The *linke* was doing the same things they always did—sing Yiddish songs, discuss Yiddish literature, put on Yiddish plays, bring in a few left-wing speakers, raise money for left-wing causes, hold a lot of parties, and eat a lot of food.

The gentiles didn't care. The government didn't care. The FBI didn't care. The FBI knew the *linke* was just a bunch of harmless *alte kakers*.

JACK LABOVITZ

Joe Hochman! He caused me a visit from the FBI. He was one of many people the FBI was checking into around here.

No, they didn't want to know about his participation in the Spanish Civil War. The FBI was checking into the Havadim Club! [Laughing.] They said they heard the Havadim Club was a bunch of subversives. They wanted to know about people like Joe Hochman and Leon Ginsberg. How they paired Leon with Joe I'll never know, because Leon was a very conservative guy. But these FBI men wanted to discuss the differences. I told them, "No, informing is not my cup of tea."

Why did they come to me? I'll tell you, there were some super-patriotic Jews in Santa Rosa. There was one in particular, Samuel Schwartz, the guy who was pals with the American Legionnaires who had tarred and feathered Hochman back in the thirties. Schwartz figured that since I was active in the Santa Rosa synagogue, I might betray my radical background and be decent enough to cooperate with the FBI.

Schwartz was one of those Jews who wanted to be five-thousand-percent American. He was a World War I hero—all crippled up—and he was the county's *makher makher* [big shot's big shot] in veterans' organizations. He's the one who revoked the charter of the Petaluma chapter of the Jewish VFW. They had publicly endorsed world peace or some such thing. Samuel went down there, called them a bunch of Communist traitors, and revoked their charter! They were furious! After all, Nathan Hochman had been in a German prisoner-of-war camp.

Schwartz was not alone. The entire Santa Rosa Jewish community feared any connection with Petaluma because of the *linke*. Rabbi Gross publicly advised the Santa Rosa congregation not to join Petaluma's Rosenberg Defense Committee.

But the ten-thousand-percent patriots like Schwartz went much further. They went out of their way to show that Jews could root out "subversives" just like the gentiles. They were perfectly willing to finger other Jews to the FBI.

GLADYS SAKAN [b. 1905; Oakland]

FBI men came to my house asking about the Commies! They knew we were in the B'nai B'rith. They knew my husband was a prominent chicken dealer, a big businessman in the county. They thought we'd talk. The FBI man pulls out pictures and says, "We caught them meeting at the Green Mill Restaurant."

I tried to explain. You see, we all knew that a group of them met together. But they weren't really Communists. One of them was married to my cousin—nice as can be. Do you think they *really* knew what communism meant? No, not the real thing. They just believed in it. I couldn't make the FBI understand. Finally I told them, "This is a hell of a thing to come into my house and ask me about! I won't squeal on my own people!"

You see, we had to get the Commies out of the Center. But we put a stop to them ourselves. We didn't need the FBI meddling in our community.

MORRY FINKLESTEIN

It was an era when neighbor spied upon neighbor. Anything that wasn't strictly kosher was *verboten*. There was a guy who lived near the Green Mill Restaurant in Cotati—he was an informer for the FBI. He kept a watch on Jewish left-wingers in Cotati.

How did we know that? Through the grapevine. We knew.

SYLVIA STERN KUROKAWA

The FBI came to our ranch on fishing expeditions. We had been active in the Communist party and the labor movement in San Francisco. We were active with the left wing in Petaluma the fifteen years we lived there.

Oh sure, the FBI knew our history, all the way back to when Karl joined the Wobblies when he emigrated from Japan in the 1920s. Karl worked to build the longshoremen's union in the 1930s, I organized for the International Labor Defense, we both ran for office on the Communist party ticket. They knew we were organizing the left inside the concentration camps when the Japanese were rounded up with World War II. Karl enlisted from behind barbed wire and I stayed in the camp with our son, Billy. Yes, I was a Jewish woman in a Japanese concentration camp in the United States.

We went to Petaluma in 1946 because Karl came back ill from war service in Asia and he couldn't work on the docks. My parents already had settled on a chicken ranch up there, and they and some of the other *linke* families helped us get started on a chicken ranch.

There is no doubt that the FBI watched us, investigated us, tapped our phone in Petaluma. We helped organize a Civil Rights Congress chapter that worked for Smith Act victims. We helped organize a Sonoma County branch of the Tom Mooney Labor School. We worked with the Progressive party campaign for Henry Wallace in Sonoma County in 1948. Every year we had a big barbeque on our ranch to raise money for the *People's World,* the West Coast Communist newspaper. Sonoma County always went over the top in statewide fund-raising campaigns for left-wing causes. There was a dedicated left-wing group in the county. That's why the FBI was investigating.

They came to us to find out about Harry Bridges and people we knew from the San Francisco waterfront. Karl would tell them—he was vaccinating chickens one of those times—he said, "Now I'll tell you why I'm sticking this chicken in the ass. But for anything else, I'll met you in my attorney's office."

The poisonous atmosphere of McCarthyism had everyone on edge. We had one comical incident as a result of the fear. During a longshoreman's international convention in San Francisco, we somehow invited the whole Japanese-Hawaiian delegation to our ranch for a luau. Come seven o'clock that evening a busful of people and a parade of cars pulled into our ranch. We had a real luau late into the night. But a friend across the road, when she saw all those people on our place, she got on the telephone and started calling the *linke:* "The FBI is raiding the Kurokawas! Be prepared!" The next morning the entire progressive community came over to our ranch. They were up in arms! Already they were raising money for us! The Kurokawa Defense Committee was ready!

ANNA ROSENFIELD GOLDEN

We was scared to death from McCarthy and Nixon. The FBI in here was asking the neighbors about Jewish Communists. They was stirring up the gentile people. You know what happened to Hochman in 1935. I never was a Communist, but we always sent money to help the Jewish farmers in Birobidzhan. We subscribed to a Yiddish magazine from Birobidzhan. When the persecution starts, I thought, "Maybe they'll attack all the Jewish people who helped Birobidzhan. We better get the *linke* out of the Center."

HYMIE GOLDEN: See, one time when Khrushchev was in the United States, one of these here German Nazis sees me and says, "Did you meet up with your cousin yet?"

"What cousin?"

He says, "Your cousin who is visiting America!"

Then I caught on quick—Khrushchev is my cousin! I was in the middle of Main Street. I said—excuse the expression—I says, "You God-damned dirty son-of-a-bitch! Khrushchev is my cousin? East Germany is communism! No communism in Israel!"

He shut up and climbed down fast. But see, that's why we told the Reds they can't meet in the Center. The whole country was against communism at that time. In Petaluma the gentiles were saying, "The Communists is meeting at the Jewish Center. The Jewish Center is the Red nest." That's why we told the Reds they gotta meet some other place.

SHURA EASTMAN COMPISI

I could understand why the old-timers in the *rekhte* were scared. McCarthyism, FBI intimidation, the memory of what happened to Hochman—it brought back old fears of the tsar, the peasants, and the pogroms. Who said it couldn't happen in America too?

I understood their fears. But I couldn't understand the right-wingers my age, the ones who were born in the U.S. and never experienced pogroms. Instead of fighting, they knuckled under to the forces that created the repression. They were ready to support any kind of reaction under the guise of Americanism. All they could think about was saving their own skin by kicking the Reds out of the Center. It reminded me of the attitude of the German Jews when Hitler came to power: "We'll show that we're good Germans and we'll be safe."

HAL DRAPER

We always had this problem with the left-wingers. Back in the thirties we had a tar and feathering. In the fifties the left-wingers were on the attorney general's black list of subversive organizations. It was bad for the Jewish community. When a Jew does something wrong, every Jew is blamed. In town they thought we were all Communist troublemakers.

Throughout history Jews have been crusaders for other people. Some say Jews have a responsibility to help others, but history will show that Jews have always gotten it in the neck for these efforts. I can see sympathizing with apple pickers, but let the gentiles lead the strikes. Jews have a responsibility to Jews. I would never take up a cause that would hurt my own people.

The left-wingers didn't see it that way. They made our problems worse in Petaluma. Growing up here, you never forgot you were different. You never forgot your parents were from the Old Country, Here we were, people without any roots, trying to make a home for ourselves, and these left-wingers were turning the gentiles against us.

The anti-Semitism bothered me very much when I grew up here. That's why I went into the service during the war. I wanted to show that Jews were good Americans too. After I came back I wouldn't tolerate any anti-Semitism in my presence.

My generation was just getting established in the mainstream after the war, but these left-wingers were more active than ever. They never stopped crusading for the workers. There was no doubt in their minds that America was wrong and we should change over to the Communist system. I couldn't understand why they didn't go back to Russia if they felt that way. But they stayed and they tried to impose their beliefs on the entire Jewish community.

Those beliefs were dangerous in the 1950s. The House Un-American Activities Committee and the attorney general put the *linke* organizations on a black list. None of us liked McCarthyism, but it became an issue of "where do the Jews stand?" Should we let the town know that if our brother Jews are Communists, that's fine. Or should we make them meet outside the Center so the town didn't think we were all Communists? We had to stand up and show where we stood. We took the initiative against the *linke* before most gentiles in Petaluma knew or cared about Communist meetings at the Jewish Center. Maybe there never would have been any trouble, but we had to be sure to head it off. That's why we had an "in-house" cleaning.

MIKE GOLD

Why look for trouble? That's what the younger fellows thought. This was a conservative area and the gentiles didn't like Communist activities. The *linke* didn't learn a thing from the tar and feathering of Hochman in the thirties. They were openly pro-Russian during the McCarthy business. They were anti-American during the Korean War! They brought well-known Communist speakers to Petaluma!

One time their Harry Bridges Defense Committee tried to get the Center for Harry Bridges to speak. This was when the government was deporting him as a Communist agitator! When the *linke* publicized that meeting, the whole town was upset. The police chief privately warned us that for the good of the Jewish community we shouldn't let Harry Bridges speak at the Center. Some of us younger guys had to take the bull by the horns. We stood in front of the Center with bats that evening. Harry Bridges did not speak at the Petaluma Jewish Community Center.

Some of us younger guys were building up a good name for the Jewish community in town. We were developing big ranches and businesses. We were entering fraternal organizations—winning respect for the Jewish community. We knew the gentiles were on edge in those days and we felt it wasn't advisable for the Jewish community to take sides so strongly in politics. It was a time to be quiet, but these Stalinist fanatics in the *linke* wouldn't back off. That's why we had to expel them from the Center. You had to show you were a good American.

ELAINE GOLDEN BLUMBERG

The things people did during McCarthyism! My own cousin!—he had my husband Max blackballed from joining B'nai B'rith. Just because we acted in the *linke* drama group, my cousin decided we were Communists! Believe it or not! Blackballed!

MORRY FINKLESTEIN

Some of the younger sons of bitches were among the worst of the *rekhte*. One of them actually sent a letter to the Santa Rosa *Press Democrat*. In the biggest newspaper in the county he announced that the Petaluma Jewish Community Center threw the Commie rats into the gutter where they belonged. To me that letter is like yesterday.

And—would you believe it?—he was married to the daughter of one of our own progressive people! When that letter was printed the progressive people wouldn't do any business with that guy. Better to give the business to the *goy*. The progressive father-in-law still gave him business—blood is thick in this community—but he was sick about that letter.

STELLA FINKLESTEIN: That letter to the *Press Democrat* was a disgrace! At the next meeting of the Center shareholders—a group of progressives came into the building once a year for the shareholders' meeting—I got up and talked about it. I said, "Every national group in Petaluma has had their conflicts. The Germans had their Nazis and anti-Nazis. The Italians had their fascists and antifascists. The Danes had their monarchists and socialists. But never did they make a public disclosure about it. Never did they wash their community's dirty linen in public. *We* had to be the ones to do *that!*"

DAVID ADLER

It was impossible for my generation to stay out of it. Everything became public and everyone felt like they had to take a stand. I was among those who thought the Havadim Club should steer clear of politics and the old fights of our parents. But some members insisted upon introducing petitions to support Israel, resolutions against atomic testing, that sort of thing. This brought about bickering, caucusing, counting heads for crucial votes. The Havadim Club went *kaput* and we ended up divided over our parents' politics again.

Esther and I tried to remain aloof from the split, but it was very difficult when my father was cursing the *rekhte* and the Center. How could we maintain friendships with people who had been active leftists and suddenly tried to make themselves lily white by attacking the *linke*. I wasn't about to denounce my past political affiliations.

The rift was almost total. It involved friends, families, entire family networks. A lot of these ties went back to the Old World, but here we were completely divided in Petaluma. It was stupid, but there was very little middle ground.

JOE HOCHMAN

One night I got fed up with the holier-than-thous in the Havadim Club. They were from left-wing families, but they'd scream, "No politics! No politics! We're not a political organization!"

That night I said, "I'm tired of listening to this bullshit. The mere fact that we're Jews makes us political. The Jews who died in the German concentration camps said they weren't political either."

I said, "Everything you do is political. You're actually afraid to show that you're anti-McCarthy. You're afraid that some gentile in Petaluma might think you're not pure red-blooded Americans!"

BETTY EPSTEIN HOCHMAN [b. 1927; Chicago]: By no stretch of the imagination could you consider the children of the *linke* to be lefties. They had no experience in the labor movement or in left-wing politics. They never understood the issues of the split. It was a family thing for them. It was their parents' fight.

JOE: They knew what McCarthy represented! They were shakin' in their boots!

BETTY: They were very courageous. It was a scarey time. Look what happened with the Rosenbergs—the American judicial system killed two people for what they thought. And through it all, the *linke* kids stuck by their parents.

VINCE KOLMAN [b. 1925; San Francisco]

It wasn't just because of my parents. I was like someone who isn't so involved with being Jewish until he's a victim of anti-Semitism. That's how it was for me when the *rekhte* branded everyone Communists and kicked the *linke* out of the Center. That's when I got involved with left-wing politics and the fight against McCarthyism.

IDELE RUBIN KOLMAN: It all happened so fast. For a long time it was respectable to be a leftist. I remember just after the war, when a group of Soviet dignitaries visited the grave of Luther Burbank in Santa Rosa, I was there with the entire *linke*. We gave roses to the Soviet officials as an expression of American friendship. The Santa Rosa *Press Democrat* carried a story about it with a picture.

Suddenly the McCarthy era came and we weren't good Americans and we couldn't use the Center. Good friends of our were calling for the expulsion of the *linke* from the Center. I never forgave some of them for defending the execution of the Rosenbergs.

We closed ranks in our own left-wing club: the Maccabeans. It was very political. We had fascinating meetings. Well—sometimes the meetings seemed more like an excuse to talk about chickens and kids. But there were political discussions too. I'd say to Vince after those meetings, "My brain is tingling."

By the time you got into the Maccabeans you were labeled a left-winger, so you might as well participate in left-wing activities. We gathered petitions for world peace, we raised money for the Rosenbergs, we sent protest telegrams all over the globe. We even put out our own left-wing newspaper, *The Maccabean*. It was scarey times, but we were vocal and active, and we were better for it.

FRAN RUBINSTEIN GINSBERG

At first I thought like the older people in the *rekhte:* "The Communists are a danger. They should be barred from the Center for the good of the Jewish community." But after we kicked out the *linke,* they rented meeting space at the most respectable places in the area. The IWO met at the Women's Club and the chorus held concerts at the high school. For big affairs, the *linke* actually rented out the Veterans' War Memorial Building!

I thought, "My God! Even the VFW doesn't care! No one else in Petaluma knows the difference between the *linke* and the *rekhte*. To them a Jew is a Jew."

SHURA EASTMAN COMPISI

Petaluma was so provincial that McCarthyism never reached it. Oh, that anti-Communist lawyer LaSalle kept tabs on the Jewish community, and there was the usual gentile redneck conservatism, but McCarthyism reached the *rekhte,* not the gentiles. It was all those Jewish social democrats and Labor Zionists and liberals at the Center who attacked the free speech of the *linke.* It wasn't because the *linke* did anything with great political consequence. It was enough that they had a different ideology—different convictions. The Jewish McCarthyites couldn't stand it when the chorus sang "Die Gedanken Sind Frei"—"Your Thoughts Are Free."

When I refer to "McCarthyites" in the Jewish community, I'm not talking about the whole pack of chicken-shit cowards who excommunicated half the Jewish community. I'm talking about the informers—the *rekhte* fanatics who tried to do in the *linke.*

When the chorus started rehearsing at the Women's Club, the woman who operated it called me once and asked why they had been evicted from the Jewish Community Center. It seems that someone had called her anonymously and told her she was renting to a Communist chorus. She had called the FBI, to see if Petaluma Jewish Folk Chorus was a subversive organization, and they said they never heard of the organization. She wanted to know what was going on. I told her, "People do funny things from fear."

That wasn't the only time it happened. Some of these right-wingers were so eager to prove Jews were patriots that they became FBI informers. I'm not talking about people who were intimidated by an FBI visit and talked a little. I'm referring to the ones who went out of their way to contact the FBI with names and rumors. To this day I wouldn't trust those bastards.

JOE HOCHMAN

Petaluma was like Hollywood. We had informers here too—people who did finger-pointing to the FBI. Some of these stool pigeons really knew, because some of them were left-wingers who turned. They became *farbrente rekhte,* red-hot reactionaries, trying to prove how kosher they became. There's a Yiddish saying for it: *"Afn genef brent dos hitl"*— "The hat on the thief is burning." Meaning, the guilty one reveals himself. They were the kind of people who were called *kapo* and *yeke* during the Holocaust.

BETTY EPSTEIN HOCHMAN: Oh, Joe, that's too strong.

JOE: They were like the Jews who collaborated with the Nazis in the concentration camps.

STELLA FINKLESTEIN

The final attack by the enemy was to destroy the Jewish Farmers Community Aid Association that had been established in 1934. The *rekhte* leaders argued that nobody needed such small loans anymore, but in fact it was just a few young left-wingers who used it. That's what galled these reactionaries. That little community mutual-aid society probably would have died for lack of use in a few years, but the *rekhte* had to murder it first.

Mordecai Haller stood up against them at one of the meetings. He said, "Where is your righteousness?" He used the Hebrew word *tsedek*—righteousness. He said the Aid Society was in accordance with the Talmudic teaching to help the poor. He backed them down at that meeting. But a few months later they took it up with that reactionary lawyer LaSalle—he was a real power in the local establishment—and together they finished it off.

MORRY FINKLESTEIN: A lot of insignificant lice came to the front with all kinds of dispicable acts during McCarthyism. They bombarded the FBI with names of people they suspected of treachery, subversion, God knows what. They got to whoever would listen: the Haas Fund, the Democratic party, the Grange, the Women's Club. This was their moment.

STELLA: How did we know this? We knew. We knew. Some of them had been our friends before they turned. Some of them bragged about it openly. And I am sorry to say that it's not so unusual in Jewish history. In the Jewish communities of Europe there always were a few who were progovernment. They regarded it as their mission to expose those Jews they considered a danger to the entire Jewish community.

That's why these people went to the FBI in Petaluma. It wasn't just political opposition to the *linke*. They thought they were protecting the Jewish community. It never occurred to them that they were acting as *mosrim*.

The Petaluma Maccabean, March 1953

What Is A *Moser?*

Extract from the *Jewish Enclyclopaedia:*

Moser: an informer, denunciator. . . Nothing was more severely punished by the Jews than tale-bearing; and no one was held in greater contempt than the informer. On account of the fact that his deeds frequently caused mischief and even entailed death and destruction, the sages of the Talmud compared the *moser* to a serpent. . . According to the Talmudic law, the informer was punished with death.

Rabbi Solomon Platt

The Split was a terrible tragedy for the Petaluma Jewish community. During all the years I went up there to perform rabbinical functions— since 1934—there was bickering over politics. But that battle after the war was something new. It made enemies of people who were friends from back in the Old Country. Children who grew up together in Petaluma stopped talking with each other. Many families divided on ideological grounds. It ended with two completely separated Jewish communities.

They were divided to the point where they had two separate memorials to commemorate the Holocaust. Recollection of the Holocaust should have united all Jews. The Germans, after all, did not discriminate between left-wing Jews and right-wing Jews when it came to the ovens. But in Petaluma they had two Holocaust memorials—one by the *linke* and one by the *rekhte*—on the same day, year after year.

Ideological rigidity on the part of the older generation certainly was an important cause for what happened. Their beliefs were based on youthful experience of political conversion. Under circumstances of anti-Semitic persecution and rebellion against the world of their parents, they gave up the Jewish religion for modern political ideologies. They still believed in salvation for the Jewish people—a secular salvation—and they believed with all the religious ardor of their parents and grandparents. They never gave up that political romanticism of their youths. They never lost faith or fervor, even when reality dictated otherwise.

The *linke* were blind to the realities of Soviet tyranny and Soviet anti-Semitism. Even after the disillusionment of so many Marxists, the *linke* still believed the Communist propaganda about the good life for Soviet Jewry. I don't know how they swallowed Stalin's accusation that Jewish doctors plotted to poison Soviet leaders. I don't know how they swallowed the murder of Soviet Jewish intellectuals—people they had revered for decades. Of course, they lost some of their enthusiasm for the Soviet Union, but any attack from the *rekhte* revived it.

The *rekhte* were just as rigid. I believe many of the Zionists had a feeling of guilt, of inconsistency, for not having gone to live in Israel. This intensified their militancy. It made them all the more unyielding in their struggle with the *linke*. Of course, the Zionists were correct that all Jews must support Israel, but they could not recognize that *linke* criticism of Israel did not make the *linke* enemies of the Jewish people. After all, the *linke* criticism of Israel was the same thing you heard from the left-wing inside Israel.

The Split in Petaluma involved all the old issues of Jewish destiny in the modern world. This was not new. But behind all the polemics about the Soviet Union and Israel, I think the underlying issue was the future of the Jewish people in America—in Petaluma. This is what brought the old conflicts to a boil in the 1950s.

It was the time of McCarthy hysteria: *"Vi es kristlt zikh, azoy yidlt zikh . . ."*—"As it is with the Christians, so it is with the Jews." The *rekhte* reacted out of fear that the *linke* would cause the entire Petaluma Jewish community to be suspected of communism. There were conservative Jewish leaders in San Francisco who were concerned about the *linke* in Petaluma. So you can imagine how the more respectable old-timers within the Petaluma Jewish community would fear that the *linke* endangered their at-homeness in Petaluma. They had that pogrom feeling from the Old Country.

The Split was different for the children. The ideological issues were secondary for them. They didn't feel so strongly about Zionism and communism. They were not very political and they did not want to be very political. Nor were they afraid of pogroms; they didn't know about that kind of persecution. The children feared they would not be accepted as good Americans. They were starting families and ranches in Petaluma. They were venturing out of the Jewish community into the wider life of Petaluma. Any gentile association of the Jewish community with Communist subversion threatened everything they aspired toward.

It is to the credit of the children of the *rekhte* that so many behaved with moderation under these circumstances. It is to the credit of the children of the *linke* that so many stuck by their families' radical politics in the face of McCarthyism.

It was my observation that the affairs of the Jewish community were of little significance to the rest of Petaluma. But that did not allay fears. It was an isolated little Jewish community. They fought over the big international issues, but their community still had the convoluted social life of a *shtetl.*

Everything becomes exaggerated in such a hothouse. I need not recapitulate the terrible things that took place within the Petaluma Jewish community during that period. Suffice to say, it simply was an extreme exaggeration of what took place all over the country.

BEN HOCHMAN

A few years after they expelled us, we approached them for unity. This was after the IWO disbanded nationally. We came as representatives of the Petaluma chapter of the Jewish Cultural Clubs of American, an organization that was not on the attorney general's list of subversive organizations. Our leaders came in for a meeting with the leaders of the Center. Katz was there—Feinstein, Rubinstein, Jacobs—all of them. They would talk about nothing but Stalin's terror.

So I told them this: "You think one way and we think another. Let's get together and have a public debate. We'll talk about it."

"No debate! No talk!"

And I remember Katz made a remark when I appealed again for a discussion of views. He said, "When East and West will get together, then the *rekhte* and the *linke* will get together here in Petaluma."

12 "They Just Came in and Took Your Place": Family Farming in Crisis

Jerry Meyer [b. 1926; Petaluma]

My partners and I are the only meat-bird producers in Petaluma today. We produce them on a factory-type basis—125,000 fryers a week. It's a small operation compared to big corporations which produce millions of birds a week.

Poultry is a big business today. It's dominated by national poultry corporations and national food chains. It's dependent upon international grain markets. You must use the most modern scientific methods to survive. You must be totally integrated: hatchery, feed mill, automated chicken houses, poultry-processing plant, and transportation equipment. It requires an enormous investment and good business practice.

The family farmer cannot exist in today's poultry industry. The small chicken ranch no longer is a profit center. You must derive your profit out of the entire process, from hatching the chick to delivering that processed bird to the supermarket. You must produce that bird on a mass scale.

The family farmer was forced out of the chicken business around here in the 1950s. That's when the large southern poultry corporations began dumping mass-produced birds into California markets. They sold poultry at 29 cents a pound, pan ready, while our small ranchers sold live birds at 34 cents. A few local family farmers saw the handwriting on the wall and were smart enough to get into other businesses. Most tried to hang on and some lost everything. It was a terrible time around here.

Yossele Gardner and Sol Levin could tell you that part of the story. Their feed company was the main supplier for the little Jewish farmers. Everyone owed them money, but they wouldn't push on accounts receivable. They could have taken over all these little ranches around Petaluma, but they wouldn't foreclose on people. They were businessmen of an older generation—too good-hearted. They went down with the small ranchers. It was a sorry thing.

221

The Hallers—the sons of old Mordecai Haller—were the ones who took over these small ranches in the fifties and sixties. After Gardner and Levin went broke, the Jewish ranchers bought feed on credit from the Hallers. Mike Gold had opened a big poultry-processing plant here in Petaluma, and he needed birds at competitive prices. Those prices were too low for the small farmers to stay in business. The Hallers gradually took control of all live-meat-bird production in Petaluma. There was a lot of resentment toward the Hallers and Gold. They became large and successful while the small farmers were forced out. But they weren't responsible for what happened. Poultry became big business and much more efficient. There was no way the family farmer could survive.

My part of the business changed for the better too. I never had patience for all the bickering and chiseling that a chicken dealer like my father faced when he bought from these little Petaluma ranchers and sold the birds to the San Francisco processing plants. When I came into the business after the war, we concentrated more and more on hauling the Hallers' chickens to Mike Gold's processing plants—forty thousand birds a day by 1963. Moving chickens was a more predictable, more sophisticated business than buying and selling them.

Unfortunately, they didn't keep up with the changes here in Petaluma. In 1968 the Hallers ran into difficulties and another grain company foreclosed on them. Gold was virtually integrated with the Hallers—they supplied his birds and owed Gold money—so when the Hallers were closed, Gold went down too. I didn't lose the big bucks because I was just hauling birds on a middleman basis, with an assured profit margin on every bird.

A few years ago I started this business with two other former chicken dealers: Sammy Rosen, one of the Holocaust refugees, and a Chinese gentleman by the name of Ernest Wo. I'd like to think we're the only ones left in the Petaluma meat-bird business because of our records of honesty and integrity. We're a relatively small operation in today's market, but we can compete because we use the most modern production methods and the best business practices.

It was obsolescence that did in Petaluma as a major poultry center. They didn't keep up with the new automated equipment, the new temperature-controlled buildings, the new scientific methods to raise chickens. Even the innovators operated with a lot of the old production methods and business practices from my father's time. They weren't ready to junk it all and build anew from the ground up.

MIKE GOLD

When you write your book, tell 'em that the second-generation Jewish businessmen built this town. We built this town after the war! You tell 'em! As far as I'm concerned, I've been successful.

I built my poultry-processing plant in 1953 because there was no other way I could sell my product. I'd been buying and selling chickens with my stepfather, one of the pioneer chicken dealers from back in the twenties. After the Second World War, when the San Francisco poultry-processing plants were forced out of business by government regulations, we had to slaughter our own chickens or go out of business. Expand or disappear! We expanded!

I built the first mechanized processing plant in this area. Completely modern! I've got things I could tell you—it would take all night to explain my operation.

I started slaughtering a few thousand chickens and built it up to forty thousand head a day. I had 350 people working for me—largest employer in town. I bought every meat bird produced in Petaluma. I distributed my "Gold Bird" all over the West. God, were we growing! Growing for fifteen years! We were far ahead of the times at my plant. But—but—but we ran out of chickens. I couldn't get enough birds to keep up. You see, this change in the industry took a terrible toll on the small chicken farmers here. We went from hundreds of small family operators to a few large operators. Just about everyone was forced out. I never would have believed a change like this could happen.

Here I was developing this modern poultry-processing business, and for many years I was dependent upon these former garment workers who became chicken ranchers overnight! They didn't know scientific methods of raising chickens. They couldn't mechanize. Some of them wouldn't even work! The husbands had "back problems" and "heart problems." [Laughing.] The poor wives broke their backs raising chickens while the "intellectuals" were in the house reading!

Sure, they resented me. They claimed I monopolized the market and cheated them with low prices. But I had to pay prices that allowed my product to be competitive. They were not efficient enough to stay in business.

Then I got caught up by the changes. My time came too. The big southern corporations integrated before us. They hired cheaper labor. When the freeways arrived and this area became a bedroom suburb of San Francisco, the land shot up in value and became very expensive for raising chickens. They produced cheaper chickens in the South.

Chicken was the source of my troubles. My processing plant and my marketing was fine, but I had more and more problems getting chickens. My supplier broke down. My competition controlled their own chickens. I took care of everything but the chickens. How do they say it? You get in a stream and you swim or you—you pull off to the side. It was dog-eat-dog in the poultry industry, and we came out second best.

It was like the meat-packing industry in Chicago. Disappeared! Here we had a huge industry—and overnight it was gone. POOOF!

NORMAN HALLER

As times changed and things got, you know, worse and so forth—a lot of ranchers would . . . what I mean to say is they . . . they couldn't pay us for the feed they bought. The Gold processing plant here needed more and more birds, and we wanted to sell feed, so the Haller feed mill had to raise chickens ourselves.

When a fellow would quit because . . . well . . . because he didn't want to take risks anymore, then we'd start raising on his ranch. We operated over two hundred ranches at one point. We raised all the meat birds in Petaluma then. Not that we wanted to. We were forced to operate like our big out-of-state competitors. We were just a small cog in the wheel.

There was tremendous pressure to grow and modernize. We put up our own automated ranches, where one hand could raise 100,000 birds in each. By the early sixties we grew 10 percent of the fryers in California. That was 150,000 a week—a million and a half on the ten-week growing cycle. We ran five batches a year—seven or eight million fryers a year.

Our problem was competition from the big fryer producers in the South. They sold at a big profit back East and dumped their surplus in our market. That went on for years—always pressure from them—until we started to . . . you know . . . it got real bad after a while. We were kinda forced to liquidate. It was all turned over to some other people who came in. They ran it until they went out of business; the same for the next group. Then three of the old chicken dealers got together and started a new poultry operation. They are the only ones raising meat birds in Petaluma today.

Now the poultry industry has stabilized in big hands, like any other American industry. Once there were dozens of different automobile companies, but now there are just a few. Same thing with chickens. Big business is more efficient. This is what we call progress.

MALCOLM HALLER [b. 1939; Petaluma]

You can take the whole poultry industry and shove it! I don't want to have *anything* to do with chickens! I always figured I'd be in poultry my whole life. I grew up working on my dad's ranch and in my grandfather's feed mill. By the time I was in high school my dad expanded our feed business by getting ranches and raising his own chickens. I took over that end of the business when I returned from college. It was expected of me.

I got bad vibes from that business. It was dusty, dirty—chicken feathers everywhere! Of course, I was connected with the higher level of the business. I wasn't doing menial labor labor like shoveling chicken shit.

But I had to be there because I was in charge of all these people who were contract raisers for us on their own ranches. I had to make sure they did things right. I worked in that business for over ten years after college. I put in thousands and thousands of hours. I thought, "We'll always be in the poultry business. My father took it over from my grandfather. I'll take it over from my father. And my kid'll take it over from me."

Well, it didn't work out that way.

MORRY FINKLESTEIN

The Hallers were an enigma. They'd prosper, they'd go bankrupt, they'd start over again—like a phoenix from ashes, again and again. It was hard to fathom if they were successful. They had that one big crash, but they always drove Cadillacs and lived in fancy houses.

They ran things around here for a few years. Everyone owed them money for their lousy feed. A lot of people worked for them as share-croppers—raising the Hallers' chickens on your own ranch. The Hallers foreclosed on some people—took over their ranches!

They exploited me. After I stopped raising, they rented my three giant chicken houses. For that I got thirty-six dollars a month and mountains of chicken shit. On top of it all, one day that kid comes around to measure my chicken houses. They were a foot narrower than he thought, so that cheapskate cut down the rental price.

The Hallers are history itself around here. The old man—Mordecai— he was a Jewish gentleman of the old school. He was a religious man—a good man—very respected in the community. He wasn't quite depend- able in business, but he never pressed people who owed him money. He had a certain Old World gentility. I don't know what happened to the sons.

YOSSELE GARDNER

With the other Jewish grain merchants, friendship was friendship but business was business. They'll cheat the ranchers with bad grain; they'll get the ranchers in debt; they'll go in and out of business, ten or fifteen times, making money all the way. So what were they? Swindlers? *Ganefs* [crooks]? No, they're businessmen! Businessmen!

I wasn't too enthusiastic about becoming a businessman. When Sol Levin asked me to buy into his feed company in 1948, I thought, "I am a socialist, but still I have a family. Raising chickens on my ranch is risky. I can't pass up this opportunity."

We made some money in the beginning. We sold good feed and we had a lot of customers. We gave credit to the ranchers and still made money. But as the industry changed and the small farmers couldn't compete, we extended too much credit. It got so that all our money was on paper—what people owed us.

When the end came—when we had to liquidate—we paid every cent we owed. This was 1963. I invested $50,000 in the business at the beginning, and I got out with $15,000. If we had collected the full debts of the small ranchers, we easily could have had another $300,000. We could have taken a lot of chicken ranches. We didn't want to do that, so we settled the best we could. And the fact is, when we offered some guys half off their debts, they'd say, "No! I want three-quarters off!" Even some of our *linke* friends, no matter what we gave them, they wanted more.

Socialism had nothing to do with anything in business around here. Take Rogin. When he was in the feed business, and up to today, he was supposed to be the most left wing of the Communists. But all the fellows who did business with him, he made them pay every cent. He got rich! With my partner and I it was just the opposite. We rejected the idea that "business is business." We gave everybody a fair shake. We had to go out of business to do it, but today there is nobody in Petaluma I can't look in the eye.

Morris Rogin

I never developed my feed company into a big business like I could have. It picked up quite a bit after the war because I had a reputation as an honest man who pays off his debts even after bankruptcy. But I just made a comfortable living. I didn't do certain things that would bring in money. Some feed companies made it a policy to get the ranchers in debt and use the debt as a weapon. There were ways to enrich yourself, but I would not do those things.

Like I told you, I have been a socialist since I saw the Potemkin uprising in my hometown. To this day I am a socialist, but I live in a capitalist society. I employed labor, and this was contrary to socialist philosophy, but I paid my labor a little higher than the other feed companies. I gave a lot of credit to ranchers who needed it, and I never took ranches when the hard times came.

By being in business I was able to help other people and still improve my own standard of living. It is that enterprising spirit which I have mentioned before. I would not have done any good by refusing to improve my own life. Nothing is accomplished by foolish consistency in principles.

BECKY BRENNER [b. 1928; New York City]

We owed so much money for so many years! My mother lived with us through it all. You know, these old Jewish people had a way of seeing things. She'd say, "Becky, you'll see, it'll work out for the best."

"How?!!" It was terrible! We were *so* in debt—to the Hallers, to Rogin, to Gardner and Levin—to everyone! I'd say, "How can such a disaster be for the best?"

But it was. Because it forced us out of the chicken business.

MIKE BRENNER [b. 1927; Patterson, New Jersey]: My accounting degree was our salvation. I had to try farming after I got out of the service. We had family friends in Petaluma who told us about the chicken ranches, but Becky wouldn't do it unless I finished college. And she was right.

We were kids in our twenties and we didn't know a thing about chickens. We came at the beginning of the downhill trend in the industry. The market prices fell and terrible diseases hit. You'd have a bad raise, then another, then another. You'd get deeper and deeper in debt to the feed companies.

BECKY: Mike got outside jobs to support the ranch and I took care of the chickens. I even sold chickens down at the public scales with all the men. I had to fight for every penny. I took abuse too—you know, all these guys telling dirty jokes. I had to fit into their world.

MIKE: It was backbreaking work for no money. Before I'd leave for my job in the mornings, I'd go through the chicken houses and take the dead birds out to the garbage cans, hoping the tallow people would come for them before Becky got up. She'd do the same thing in the afternoons before I got home.

BECKY: Oh, the dead chickens—the diseases. Did anyone tell you about "the Petaluma symphony"? It was when you awoke in the morning and heard the chickens sneezing. It wasn't very nice music.

MIKE: The mortality from disease was terrific. Any Petaluma drugstore you went into, there'd be an entire department for chickens. Every rancher experimented with ways to prevent disease: open windows and closed windows, cleaning the manure and leaving the manure, this drug and that drug. Now it's a fine science, but then we tried everything.

We went down the drain first. We lost all our chickens from disease in one weekend. Can you imagine thousands and thousands of chickens dying like flies? It was 1951, about a year after we arrived. We weren't like most of our friends, who had their parents' resources to fall back on. They had all those wartime profits behind them, not to mention the illegal gains from the black market. As it turned out, within five years of our disaster they were in the same situation. But we went first and our friends blamed us for being inexperienced.

BECKY: We'd be playing cards and they'd make little remarks about our incompetence. We couldn't say anything because we blamed ourselves too.

MIKE: Not only were we blamed for our financial disaster, but we were blamed for being the first sharecroppers. While I started an accounting practice, we sharecropped with the Haller feed mill. If it wasn't for Norman Haller, I would have been in debt for many more years. He took all the risks and gave us a generous share of the profits. We did very well in that arrangement, but we took a lot of abuse for it.

Many of the old-timers fancied themselves fighters for social justice, and they said we were letting ourselves be exploited by the Hallers. Our contemporaries criticized us for letting the Hallers control our destiny on our own property. I suppose it was true, but they did the same thing when they went downhill.

And I'll tell you something else: we paid every cent we owed. A lot of people made huge settlements on their debts to the feed companies. But we spent five years paying off everything. Everything! It was ten years before I felt on top of it all. But today we can face our former creditors with heads held high.

It was the type of experience you never forget. Now I look back at raising chickens and I think, "That was stupid—utterly stupid!"

VINCE KOLMAN

I'd still be raising chickens if I could make a decent living from it. I enjoyed producing good birds with the most modern methods. I was the first family farmer in this area to install automatic feeders in my chicken houses—1955. The Santa Rosa *Press Democrat* did an article on me as a modern chicken rancher.

Just then chicken prices took a nose dive. I had to start working as an apprentice carpenter to support my chickens and pay my debts. Everything was automated at the ranch, so Idele just checked the feed levels during the day. If something broke, when I got home she'd say, "Oh, the automatic feeding system is broken." And I'd fix it in the evening.

Unfortunately, raising chickens became like gambling in the stock market. Even with my automatic feeding system it was too risky. Finally I gave up my chickens and became a construction-job estimator. I got tired of working so hard.

IDELE KOLMAN: Automatic feeders! When my daughter and I read Vince's interview, we laughed so hard we were in tears! It was he did this and he did that, and occasionally I would chime in with, "Oh, the automatic feeder is broken."

The "automatic feeder" always was broken. I was the "automatic feeder"! When I think how hard I worked on the ranch, taking care of my "kids and the chicken factory" day after day. When I think about how much we owed for those automatic feeders! I really was angry when I read that interview.

HYMIE GOLDEN

The young people here went wild expanding the ranches after the war. Pretty soon they all went in the hole. Every time I read about one of them in the *Press Democrat,* that he's putting more money into the chicken ranch, I think, "There's another one going down the hole."

See, the chicken business went back to normal after the war. Any damn' fool can make money in wartime. High prices. Black market. But it takes a smart man to hold it down after the shooting. The chicken business is like this. I says to people, "Don't expect too much from the chickens. Whatever extra you put into your ranch, you shouldn't expect to get it back."

I see the handwriting on the wall for chickens in 1953, 1954. Prices goes down and the feed goes up. Little guys is going into the hole and big guys is taking over. Was not so good. I sold out all my chickens. Turkeys too. I quit!

Then I didn't know what to do. I was lost without the chickens. You know, when people work all their life they think, "Tired, I got to take it easy." That's when they shrink a little every day. But not me. I go see Norman Haller: "Listen, I like to raise some chickens for you in my chicken houses."

For years I did that. People said, "Golden, you work because you like money too much." I say back, "You a damn' fool. I work because work is good. I like raising chickens. Money isn't everything."

IRVING GOLDEN

The chicken business went kaplooey! I knew I should have gone into cows after the war, but I thought I could make big money in laying hens too. I went into that big, and the market for eggs went bad. I saw there was big money to be made in meat birds, so I converted and two things happened: prices dropped in half and diseases hit. Christ, when those diseases hit—newcastle, airsack, bronchitis—the birds died by the thousands.

Ranchers went into the hole ten thousand, twenty thousand, thirty thousand. If you owed the feed company that kind of money, you'd be paying for years. You could lose everything! When mortgages were foreclosed in the thirties, at least they'd give you another chance on the same place. In the fifties they just came in and took your place.

I saw the light before others. In 1955 I went out of chickens clean as a whistle—didn't owe a cent. But for two years I couldn't get into anything solid. And I got all this static from other people: "There's still money in chickens. You're a born natural. Try again." I did it against my better judgment. One more big raise of chickens. And that was the finale! Everything went wrong! Disease! Floods in the chicken houses! The market dropped! Everything!

I've never told this to anybody, but I carry a resentment against the Jews around here. First, I have the chip on my shoulder because the Jews gave me static about not being in the army during the war. And number two is because they convinced me to go back into chickens.

As soon as prices went bad that second time, the people who convinced me to try again were the first to bolt out of it. Bolted like wild animals! A lot of them came here after the war and had other trades to fall back on. The rest of us poor guys sunk. Now I was in the hole and I still couldn't find work. Every employer wanted experience. When I told them I ran my own business on a chicken ranch, it was like talking to a wall!

LYNN AXELROD GOLDEN: He had three kids and a wife to take care of. He had no college education, no trade, no experience. Let's face it— he went back into the big world with nothing. It was such an insecure feeling.

IRVING: I wasn't scared. I just wasn't sure what I wanted to do. I was glad to be through with those damn' chickens, but I couldn't make the transition from the ranch to punching a time clock. I tried it at different jobs for a few years—Christ, I was stacking hundred-pound cubes of butter for Safeway—but I was too old to start an eight-to-five routine. Fortunately, I finally got a job as a federal poultry inspector. It allows me to travel around, work at my own pace, and make a good living. I was lucky.

SID JACOBS

A lot of the guys had a terrible time. A couple cashed in—they were found hanging from the rafters of the chicken houses. Fortunately, I didn't have a wife and kids to support. It was too late to begin in forestry like I always wanted. But I went into a good job market in 1956 and found work as a machinist. It was repetitive work—not at all like the ranch—but I have a lot of patience. When it was endless, with thousands and thousands of the same piece to run off, you'd just detach yourself from it. You'd figure out a routine so you didn't injure yourself, and you'd stop thinking.

I didn't mind the machinist work, but my parents' generation didn't think much of it. They were socialists, but for them there was *sheyne arbet* and *proste arbet*—work that was wholesome and work that was coarse. Factory work wasn't so great from that point of view. They believed you should be independent, but it couldn't be done anymore.

LOU GREEN

By the time my father and I were pushed out of chicken dealing, I had a book published. It wasn't exactly the Great American Novel. It was a tough, hard-hitting mystery in the style of Mickey Spillane. Some phoney Chicago publisher put it out, and I didn't make didly-squat out of it. But at least I had a book in print.

After chicken dealing, I supported my family with a series of businesses, everything from used cars to fast food. I wrote a couple more mysteries, but you can't peddle manuscripts to New York publishers from three thousand miles away. So I tried songwriting with a piano player I met at the Colony Club, a nightclub outside Petaluma. At that time I was promoting a singer, so we all collaborated on some demo records. We made some exquisite ballads, but we couldn't get a break.

I moved down to LA and sold used cars while I peddled our songs. You can't imagine all the phonies and bullshitting down there. It was worse than chicken dealing! I probably would have made it if I stayed—it just takes perseverance—but I returned to Petaluma.

I've gone through some real rough times with my business and writing schemes. I still believe that quality work will be appreciated, in my present business and in my writing. I have a musical kicking around Hollywood now, and I have a couple more writing projects on my desk. If I stay with it long enough, and if I have a good long life, I'll hit the jackpot.

[A few months after this interview, Lou Green died in the crash of a light airplane returning from Los Angeles to Petaluma.]

DAVID ADLER

I didn't feel like I personally failed at the end—but the business did go to pieces. The main thing is that I got out with very little money. I had just a short time to find a new source of income to support my wife and four kids. At forty-seven years old, with only a chicken-ranching background, I wasn't even called in for job interviews where I applied. So after a careful survey of this area, I opened a little office-supply business out of my ranch. It turned out to be very difficult. Every place had suppliers. I didn't know much about my products, and I'm not the best salesman anyhow. In the first month I sold some pencils here, some paper there, but then I ended up in the hospital with ulcers.

This was a very hard time—all my family responsibilities and there I was in the hospital. I thought the business would fold and I had no idea of what to do next. But unbeknownst to me, my wife went out selling to keep the business alive, and the kids made the deliveries. When I resumed work, my wife became partners with me in the business.

After that our office-supply business just grew and grew. But I can tell you, it wasn't easy to start a small business from scratch. It took the better part of five years before we made a living at it. We turned it into a business through sheer hard work and persistence.

You know, I came from a *linke* family and I used to be prejudiced against business. Now I enjoy meeting some of these big businessmen through our California office supply association. They're fine people. And they listen when I express my views that business must be socially responsible. I've changed some of my views. For many years I went down to the state legislature to testify in defense of the family poultry farm. Today I think it's more feasible for a corporation to raise hundreds of thousands of chickens with modern machinery and a few employees.

I used to believe that you shouldn't make money off somebody else's labor. Now I believe there must be compensation for brains, making decisions, assuming risk and responsibility. Now I am not so left-wing oriented, if I am left-wing oriented at all, to have any compunction about making money off people who work for us. I pay a fair wage. They're not my slaves.

MOLLY ROSENFIELD LIPSKY

When my boy Reuben opens his bar in town, he tells me, "Ma, the working people are a whole lot nicer than you think."

All the time Reuben had a big ranching business, he was mixing with the *makhers* [big shots] in town. Then he opens his bar and tells me the working people and the trade unions are not so bad. One day he says,

"Ma, I don't think it was so bad what Hochman was trying to do with the apple strikers in the 1930s."

Reuben opened his bar after he lost our ranching business. We had the biggest ranch business in the Jewish community: three ranches on fifty acres, meat birds, laying hens, a herd of dairy cows, pigs and steers. We was plowing our land and grew greens too. Reuben was always saying, "It's a business . . . you got to be aggressive." Five men we hired. But in 1963 we lost everything.

I thought us all going crazy. First Isaac feels no good again. Terrible pains, such terrible pains. The doctors give him operations, transfusions, dope, everything. In 1954 he passed away.

Big bills to pay for the doctor. Then they attached us for the feed bills. First they took the younger son's ranch, then they take Reuben's ranch. We didn't have money to go around—everybody's staying in my house. I thought the boys had it arranged so I'm not in the partnership anymore, but then my place was attached. I thought, "What's going to be? We are getting broke."

Somehow it was okay. The boys had such a time finding jobs. Reuben was fifty years old—what can he do? For two years they was running a bar—Jewish boys running a bar!

Finally they find jobs. Reuben becomes a poultry inspector for the government. Now he says, "Ma, it's better than your own business. You work only eight hours in a day, only five days a week. You got holidays, you got vacation, you got the sick leave. You go home, you don't get no worries. What else do you want?"

Me? I keep my ranch. I keep it too long. I was living alone on a big ranch. The windows are getting broken, the door doesn't close right, the weeds are growing tall. I want to sell but Reuben says, "Ma, hang onto it until the real estate is right." So I hangs on and I hangs on.

Finally the real estate is right and I sells the ranch. Now I'm here in this little apartment on Magnolia Street. I got my social security and I got a little left over from the ranch.

I survived. [Laughing.] I survived it all. What else can you do?

SARAH SISKIN WEINSTEIN

I moved to San Francisco in 1949, right after Bernie died. I'm never sorry I left Petaluma. I went through hell there with Bernie sick and all the hard work and aggravation on the ranch.

On the other hand, the money from selling the ranch left me comfortable. I built it up even more with real estate investments. Today I don't have to live in a little apartment on social security like the women who lived in the city. I don't have to depend on anyone. I finally found my opportunity in America.

JOE HOCHMAN

We didn't leave Petaluma until 1957. My brother and I thought we could make big money by raising on a big scale. We rented extra ranches and raised two hundred thousand birds at a crack. But the bigger you were, the more you fell. When the diseases hit and the market collapsed, everything slid down the rathole like a shot out of hell.

My old man raised chickens until he was eighty. A lot of the old-timers hung on with these nickel-and-dime operations. The old man practically lived in the chicken houses to do it. If a chick got sick, he'd sit out there and pat it on the head till it got better. The old-timers were so dedicated they were able to stay in long after the young guys were forced out.

BETTY EPSTEIN HOCHMAN: Fortunately, we went broke and had to leave. Joe went back to work on the docks in San Francisco and I got my teaching credential. It was wonderful, because my life in Petaluma had become nothing but kids and chickens. We spent years paying off our debts, but going broke was the best thing that ever happened to us. Otherwise we still might be there patting chickens on the head.

EMILY MOSKOWITZ [b. 1942; Petaluma]

Leaving Petaluma was horrible! It was like being sentenced to hell! We didn't go willingly. My father lost the ranch and we had to leave. It was just tragic! He put so much work into that piece of land. So much went into building our house. We were so proud of it—and all that pride went down the toilet.

I still have a lot of bitterness about it. It's true that the whole chicken business went down, but there are people to blame for us losing our ranch. I feel very bitter against those people. And maybe in a way I feel my dad screwed up too.

Oh, God, it was devastating when we had to go. My roots were there. My *zeyde* [grandfather] and *bobe* [grandmother] had settled in Petaluma in the 1920s. My father worked in the chicken business all his life. He built our ranch right next to my grandparents' ranch. That ranch was our ground! It was our house—our home! It was my bedroom—it was painted pink. The day we left I hid little notes all over the house: "Whoever finds this, your fingers will rot off!" I didn't want anyone else living there.

My father couldn't bear to move into town, so we moved to Oakland and he went into sales. With us gone, my grandparents couldn't keep up their ranch, so they sold it and moved into town. My grandfather still goes out to see what's doing on his ranch.

To this day, when I visit my grandparents in Petaluma, I don't like going by our ranch. I see some man living in our house and raising pheasants on our land. I hate him and his pheasants, and I don't even know him. Isn't that an awful evil child thing?

When we left I vowed that someday I'd buy back the ranch and give it to my father. That's what I'd do! Kids have such funny thoughts. And you know, I still daydream about getting back our ranch.

Samuel Gans

Thank heavens for the collapse of the poultry industry. I was twenty years in Petaluma. I arrived as a refugee in 1941. I was a young man with my Ph.D. degree in psychology, but I gave the best years of my life to chickens. I finally returned to my profession in 1960 when I secured a clinical internship at a state hospital. A year later I sold my poultry-processing plant and we moved to Palo Alto.

When we left Petaluma, we left for good. Palo Alto is nothing great, but at least we can go to an art show or a concert here. It is a real town with a university and a few parks you can walk in. There was nothing in Petaluma. I have warm feelings for people I knew there, but to this day I shudder when I drive through Petaluma.

Zeitel Kolman

You want to know the real reason we moved back to San Francisco? Everybody thought it's because we gave up the chickens and Murray returned to the painting trade full time, but Murray could work at his trade in Petaluma too. No, the real reason was that I couldn't find a good poker game in Petaluma.

I was riding on the freeway once a week to San Francisco for a game, until one day I thought, "My goodness, I'm getting too old for this. How will I play poker if I can't drive on the freeway?" So we moved to San Francisco for some good card games. [Laughing.] Isn't that terrible?

Stanley Bergowitz [b. 1929; New York City]

I stayed right here! I'd like to write a book about how I survived in the chicken business. For over twenty years I delivered my eggs and chickens directly to customers in San Francisco. I have a title for this book: *Come Up and Show Me Your Eggs*.

Delivering chickens and eggs is a very personal service. You get to know the customers and they wait for you every week. Each stop should have been two minutes, in and out. But this one had a glass of wine poured, that one had a dessert ready . . . "come in and talk with me." You became a friend, a family counselor, a psychologist. It was a very interesting business.

I sold directly, eliminating the costs of a middleman, instead of trying to go along with the big boys. I could have developed a capacity for one hundred thousand hens on my ranch, but the financial risk made me nervous. You know, the same thing happened in hens as in meat birds—we went from a thousand hen ranches to a few huge egg producers in this area. It became a big business with big volume and narrow margins. A lot of people who risked everything lost their ranches to the feed company.

My ranch never was in danger, but I had one very bad experience with an unethical feed company. The man who owned this feed mill was a B'nai B'rith brother. I talked the guys out of suing him when we ran into trouble with our birds because of his lousy feed. Then I ran up this feed bill and he attached me! He knew I'd pay, he knew I had a loan coming, but he still tied up every cent I had and put the sheriff on my place. It was completely uncalled for—completely unethical! I'll never forget it. My kids said, "Daddy, what's the policeman doing in our egg room?" It made me feel awful—like a criminal. I'll *never* forget that feeling.

There was a lot of squeezing going on. Not by everyone—we had one great guy in the feed business, an old-timer, who let everybody off from their feed bills. People took advantage of him.

But when it came to business, a lot of people would cut your throat. This was a time of transition from the small, old-fashioned chicken ranch to the big, modern poultry industry. It brought out the worst in people. They took over ranches from ranchers who really got in the hole. Ranchers committed suicide—or attempted to.

And I'll tell you something. This guy who attached me, people respected him. They respected money. I never respected *anyone* for their money—I could not have cared less. But everyone kissed his ass!

SAUL HOFFMAN

I'd make jokes to the American boys: "You are soft. You are always crying about the feed company and the chicken dealer. You don't know how to make a living. See how the *grine* do it."

The worst complainers was the comrades from the *linke*. They didn't even pay feed bills to their own comrades, Gardner and Levin, and still they blamed the feed companies for their troubles. They blamed the whole country—even the president—every president they blamed for their problems with the chickens. They said, "Capitalism is ruining the chickens."

I didn't blame no one. The feed companies and the chicken dealers got to make money too. It's a business! I didn't think anyone owes me anything. I work hard, I watch the chickens careful, I take a few chances at the right time, I be honest. I always say, "If you grow good chickens, the price will be good."

I grew good chickens all the way through. To this day I grow chickens for the Meyer and Rosen and Wo processing plant. I did good with the real estate too. That's how I built this big house five years ago. And when I built this house I said to my wife, "You don't go in the chicken houses no more. Now you're gonna be a lady."

All the *grine* did good. Never complained. Whatever we do, we all successful. The *grine* got that grit—to take something and make of it. America is a golden country for people who got grit.

Stella Finklestein

The collapse of the chicken business is a perfect example of how the free enterprise system works. Everyone is on his own. Everyone is free. You have the freedom to cheat and the freedom to starve.

Some of the small chicken ranchers tried to organize against these greedy capitalists that were squeezing us out. There was meeting after meeting. Some wanted cooperatives. Some wanted government subsidies and government marketing laws. Some wanted to revive the Grange. Nothing worked.

One young woman distributed pro-Soviet agricultural literature in the rural mailboxes. I told her that kind of stuff was unnecessary. I wasn't even thinking of FBI trouble. The people around here didn't care about the example of Soviet agriculture. Frankly, neither did I. But within two days the FBI was searching for who was agitating the farmers with subversive literature. I told those agents, "Who has to agitate? Everyone's losing their pants!"

Morry Finklestein: The main problem was getting control over production of meat birds. Some of us small ranchers tried to get up a cooperative that would regulate our production and sell as a group to the poultry processors. It didn't last long. The small farmers were too individualistic. Most stayed out because they thought they could do better on their own. Some coop members sold themselves out when a chicken dealer would offer a penny a pound higher than their own coop. The small ranchers would not cooperate. These people should have known better. Some of them were left-wingers who had been in trade unions. They were the first to raise money to help Afghanistan or Timbuktu in a crisis. They never would have scabbed in a strike, but they couldn't see that selling chickens outside the coop was scabbing. They were scabs!

STELLA: It shows what the radicalism of these "left-wingers" amounted to. Skin deep! Their progressive ideas applied everywhere but at home. They were no different from any other greedy capitalist: make money at any cost.

Their behavior didn't surprise me. I was surprised by capitalism's worst blow around here: the collapse of the Poultry Producers cooperative. That huge organization had been a great help to the chicken ranchers across Northern California for decades. It bought feed in bulk and sold at the best price to the small farmers. It bought the farmers' eggs at good prices because it sold in bulk. At the end of every year it returned part of the profits to the members. And it acted as a savings bank where farmers could keep their money for a little more interest than the banks.

A lot of people had their life savings invested with the Poultry Producers. We did too. We lost it all. It was my fault. Morry wanted to take out our money when we heard rumors it was shaky.

MORRY: Our $9,500.

STELLA: Well, it's all behind us now.

MORRY: We had an acquaintance, an anarchist, who sold a home in Brooklyn and retired here on a chicken ranch. He invested his $28,000 in the Poultry Producers. After the collapse he got back $1,100—four cents on the dollar. Did you ever have $28,000? [Laughing.] Well, if you are a workingman it can be a terrible pain to lose $28,000. All those years of work. Of course, it's worse to lose a finger, but when you lose $28,000 it makes you sick! [Laughing.]

I saw him at an affair after it happened. He cried on my shoulder about his $28,000. He made me feel so good! I only lost $9,500! [Laughter.]

STELLA: And you're still here to talk about it.

MORRY: Who would have expected such a thing to happen? Imagine— for fifty years it was a well-run institution. It had all these big buildings around town.

We heard rumors that the thing was shaky. Herb Sussman said to me one day, "Morry, have you got money in the Poultry Producers?"

I said, "Not much." Which was $9,000. It depends upon what you consider "much." [Laughing.] It was nice of him to warn me to take the money out, but it was not nice of me not to do it.

STELLA: Well, I never was impressed with Herb's advice. Look how much he lost operating his ranch. We were very competent operators.

MORRY: I said, "Stella, let's go in and take out our $9,000."

So we go down to the Poultry Producers and she goes in to see the manager. I stand outside—I don't like to do big business with the gentiles—Stella is my brain trust. She goes in and she comes out. But she does not come out with our $9,000. She comes out with another piece of paper! He talked her into investing another $500. Next month they declared bankruptcy.

It was a tragedy for a lot of people. Not just Jews. I went to the meetings the Poultry Producers called after the collapse. I saw row upon row of these Anglo-Saxons, these old German and Scandinavian couples who had lost their life savings.

It was very painful. I never threw it up to Stella too much. I did it once, and then I never spoke about it again. After all [laughing], it was only money. It wasn't the most important thing.

BASHA SINGERMAN

They took millions of dollars from the members and they took every cent of my $7,500. The whole management. They were grabbing and grabbing the money until nothing was left. From all the little chicken farmers they took our life savings. You know the rest. I was left penniless and I had to go on welfare. It was so humiliating! Then I had to sell my ranch with the house Shimon built for me in 1922—a gorgeous house, the most gorgeous house in Petaluma.

That's the story. Half my ranch they took in the 1930s. Then they come and take everything away from you. This is our wonderful system.

JOE RAPOPORT [b. 1900; Stanislavchik, Ukraine]

Through all my years in the United States I heard that Americans have free choice of how to work and how to live. It is ironic that I was forced out of the chicken business in California much the same as I was forced out of the garment trades in New York. I lost my job as a hand knitter because of the introduction of power knitting machinery. That's how I became a chicken farmer after the war. Then I was forced out of chicken farming because of new scientific production and great capital investment in the poultry industry. My choices, my life as a hand knitter and as a chicken farmer, were changed against my will.

Over the decades American agriculture has developed so that the family farmer could not receive a substantial return on his product. The family farmer has been steadily pushed out by larger operators, by huge corporations that actually built "factories in the fields." This was part of the continuous concentration of ownership in American agriculture.

When I came to Petaluma after the war, you could make a living by working a hen ranch with four thousand chickens. If you had ten thousand hens you were one of the *kulaks*—the rich—who could afford modern homes, new cars, and children in college. However, large poultry corporations began to integrate the industry, produce in volume, and cut costs at every corner. These corporations did everything possible to eliminate the nuisance of competition from the small operators. Even the most capable family farmer was driven out of business in a matter of time.

The small farmer was pushed around even by his own organizations. The Poultry Producers cooperative was the worst example in our area. After the war it moved toward larger operations with the most modern methods of production and distribution. In the process of expanding, it encouraged the growth of larger coop farmers by giving lower prices for the purchase of feed in bulk and higher prices for the sale of eggs in bulk. It gave out huge loans to the larger operators to further expand and modernize their egg production. The irony was that the small farmer, the majority of the coop membership, paid for it through the discriminatory rates, the money they had invested, and the lowered dividends.

Some of us recognized this abnormal, unfair expansion. It was legal— we couldn't take the management to court. All we could do was protest at the annual general meeting, but even that was not easy. How could a handful of small farmers stand up against the management of a multimillion-dollar operation? They had business managers and agricultural scientists and banking specialists. They had long reports with big statistics. At such a meeting your small ranch shrank to insignificance. If you tried to speak, you couldn't explain your feelings about what was happening. You couldn't convince the other family farmers, let alone influence the management.

In the end, those of us who saw the handwriting on the wall had no choice but to withdraw our savings from the organization. It was clear that the small farmer would pay the penalties for the growth of this cooperative. When the squeeze came in the 1960s, the members who had their savings in the Poultry Producers co-operative got back four cents on the dollar. Many people lost their life savings.

This was only the most dramatic event in the corporation takeover of poultry and egg production in our area. Hundreds of family farmers were forced out in the 1950s and 1960s. One could say this was progress, but when a way of life for families and communities is plowed under in the name of progress, it is brutal and obscene. It is criminal.

BARRY SEGAL [b. 1946; Petaluma]

I grew up in a happy, carefree fifties type of community. All the Jewish chicken ranchers had money. They built new homes. They bought station wagons. They even took vacations! It was a very turned-on, believing-in-America type thing.

The kids grew up with their parents around. I fed chickens and repaired chicken houses with my father. When he sold chickens, I went with him and hung out with the men at the scales in town. Sometimes my grandfather came with us. Living on ranches, people had time for each other. They helped each other with ranch work. They visited in the homes and at the Center any hour of the day. The Jewish community was very close. It's the last time I'll see that kind of family-farmer community life.

When the chicken business fell apart, you saw these thirty-, forty-, fifty-year-old Jewish men completely broke. Suddenly their families faced poverty-level living. Nobody knew what to do. Some committed suicide; they were found hanging from the rafters in the chicken houses. Some left and sold their lives to city jobs. Some people stopped coming to the Center for months and months. My father went to a psychiatrist, and he wasn't the only one. The whole community was freaked out.

JULIA SHIFFMAN SEGAL: I grew up believing that everything you needed for a good life was in Petaluma. I thought you always could earn a living in chickens. It was the only work I knew. I thought the Jewish community was the only social life you needed. Those were the only people I really knew. There was no reason for change.

When the revolution in the chicken industry first hit us in the 1950s, we blamed ourselves as tremendous failures. And of course the older generation thoroughly subscribed to that theory. My mother would say, "If you would work harder and not spend so much money, you would make it through."

We thought the hard times was just a passing thing—like the Depression! We blamed our troubles on bad chicks, bad feed, robbing chicken dealers. It was hard for us to see that big business was the wave of the future in chickens. It was hard for us to admit that we had small backyard operations. We thought we were pretty big with our ranch capacities for forty thousand birds. We didn't know that was nothing. We didn't want to know. It's hard to admit you're nothing.

The change was painful. Everyone was thrashing about. There wasn't much discussion about it, but you knew people were going through personal trauma. The old-timers were forced into retirement or left on the margins. The younger men had terrible problems with no work and young families, but once they found something new, most of them did very well.

It was a disaster for the in-betweens, the men in their forties and fifties who had been raising chickens for decades. They felt they were businessmen, but they didn't have the experience or the education to get a decent job. Some had to get menial jobs. It was devastating. You'd see people who had been strong and self-assured become meek and apologetic. You'd see them lose their backbone. They were caught up in something that was much bigger than they could cope with.

Being part of a community helped. My son's *bar mitzvah* came at a time when we were bottomed-out financially. We were broke, but I wanted to have a nice party for the kid. So everyone in the community helped. I still remember them all coming into the house that day, each with a gift for the kid and loads of food. I had a feeling that most of those two hundred people were family. I had known them all my life, and this crisis in the chicken business brought us even closer together.

But finally you had to face it alone. We really had some rough years. We were deep in debt and we were poor. Mo was very capable, but he couldn't find work. He didn't know what to do. Eventually he found a good government job in San Francisco, but we had a terrible time until then.

We didn't move to San Francisco. Mo commuted for years because I did not want to leave Petaluma. But the change still affected our relationship to the Jewish community. The farm life made for a close community. If you weren't helping each other with the chickens, you were talking about the chickens. As people found other jobs, it seemed like we had less and less time to talk at all. We couldn't take off a few hours to *shmooz* in the afternoon. We'd be too tired to get together in the evenings. And as you met new people and found new interests, it seemed less important to participate in the Jewish community.

You kept all your old friends. That never changed, even though you saw them less. But suddenly you noticed you didn't go to the Center so much. You weren't very active in Jewish community life anymore. One day you realized you were into a whole new social thing.

13 Searching for Jewish Identity in the 1950s

STANLEY BERGOWITZ

The community was falling apart. The *linke* wouldn't set foot in the Center after they got kicked out; that was half the Jewish community. The collapse of family farming was another disaster. It sounds funny, but the chickens really held the Jewish community together for decades. Everyone was going their own way in the 1950s.

A lot of the couples from my generation were developing new interests with the gentiles. One of the guys took me to a meeting—the Elks or the Lions or something—and I couldn't believe it. I almost broke out laughing watching these grown men marching around in silly hats taking ridiculous oaths. But some Jews would do anything to be accepted by the gentiles.

A bunch of us younger guys wanted to reorganize the Center and pull people back in. The old-timers had it all screwed up with separate little empires like the *shul*, the cemetery, the cultural organizations, each with its own leadership, membership, and dues; we proposed one big pie, financially centralized. We wanted to change the name to Congregation B'nai Israel, like the nineteenth-century German-Jewish community here. We wanted to hire a rabbi and develop a strong Jewish educational program for the children.

NINA BERGOWITZ [b. 1931; New York City]: We weren't religious, but our kids needed it. Jewish kids have it very difficult in a small town. Their friends would ask them what church they belonged to. We had to supply a church for them.

STANLEY: Oh, we had big plans, but the old-timers fought *every* change. They said we didn't know what to do with a congregation. They said we

243

weren't responsible enough to run the Center. My God, we were in our thirties and forties!

The old-timers controlled the Center voting shares and they held out for years. Finally, when there wasn't even enough interest to get people to sit on the board of directors, they let us operate the Center by renting it to us through the congregation for a dollar a year. They kept ownership, and they kept the cemetery. We never did get the cemetery. Hymie Golden controlled it, and he was too tough a nut to crack.

I was president in 1960 when we finally reorganized the thing into the Jewish Community Center and Congregation B'nai Israel. But we still couldn't do much without financial support from the old-timers. They'd send thousands of dollars to Israel every year, but they'd give us pennies to run the congregation and the Sunday school. They wouldn't give us a cent to hire a rabbi. When they were our age, they said, they did everything themselves at the Center; so why hire someone to carry the load for us?

They had a point, but we needed a rabbi. We needed to bring leadership into the community. Oh, what we went through looking for rabbis! The advertising, the interviews, the negotiations—it was like buying your first suit!

We didn't solve the problem until years later, when Bernie Nachman came; he fit the community like a glove. Until then we had all kinds of part-time rabbis in here. They never stayed long, because we always had money problems. But the real problem was that we didn't know what to expect of a rabbi. Did we want a religious man, a social director, a political arbitrator, an orator, a representative to the gentiles, an educator, an athletic director? We wanted a rabbi to come in and tell us what we needed.

JULIA SHIFFMAN SEGAL

There was wonderful disorganization at the Center. Take the services. One of my gentile friends sat through my son's entire *bar mitzvah* service one Saturday morning at the Center. She came early—right on time at nine o'clock! Everyone from the Jewish community knew to come around eleven, when the kid came on. You only came to hear the kid, unless you were a *shul yid* or a gentile.

My friend observed the whole thing. The service was going on and a few of the old-timers would *davn* [pray] at their own pace. Everyone was on a different page. Nobody got up together and sat down together. Nobody followed the same order. Everybody prayed independently.

Meanwhile, people would be coming in: "Hello Julia! *Mazeltov*!!" If a *bobe* [old lady] came from out of town, everyone got up to see: "Oh, look who's here! I haven't seen her for so long!" If it was a young cousin from out of town there would be a tremendous excitement: "Look how he's grown already!" And the *bobes* would pinch his cheeks while he squirmed. We'd all be hugging, talking, visiting with each other. People would be coming in and going out. Wolf—he was an old-timer who led the prayers—he'd try to conduct the service. He'd yell "*Sha!*" and he'd bang the table for quiet. Poor Wolf. He didn't make a bit of difference. It was totally unruly—absolute chaos.

My gentile friend didn't know what to make of it. She said to me after the service, "My, you have a very friendly church."

To me it was wonderful, but it bothered others in my generation. The old-timers knew what they were doing at these services; my generation didn't. My friends wanted a rabbi to take over the services and give orders how to pray. They wanted a rabbi to take over educating our kids. I thought we did fine in our own Sunday school with our own teachers from the community. What we lacked in knowledge we made up for in warm feeling. When the Sunday school put on a Purim festival, all the aunts and uncles and grandparents came to see the *kinder* perform. It was a warm community feeling.

I adamantly opposed hiring a rabbi. It was just another source of dissension. It was unnecessary. Our Judaism was strongest when we did it ourselves. We might not have known religious ritual, but we knew what it meant to be Jewish. We had it within us—*yidishkeyt*—Jewishness.

ARLENE FEINSTEIN FELDMAN

Judaism was a joke in Petaluma. The whole atmosphere was wrong. There wasn't a Jewish neighborhood with Jewish stores and Jewish people. There wasn't a nice synagogue where you could pray. The people didn't have respect for the services. There wasn't the quietness—the special feeling of being in *shul*.

We needed a rabbi to give us that inspiration. But the people with money, the older people, they gave their money to Israel. We could only afford part-time rabbis, secondhand rabbis, if you know what I mean. They didn't give of themselves to the community. They didn't give you that special something you need inside. I didn't get that until Bernie Nachman's sermons.

In Petaluma there was no way I could pass on to my children the special feeling of *shabes*. I could light the candles, but what was the use? When I grew up in New York, Friday night was special. My mother spent the day cleaning the house and preparing food. The whole family dressed up, my mother lit candles, and we had a special dinner. Then we walked through the neighborhood to *shul* for services, real services with a real rabbi.

Here in Petaluma it seemed hypocritical just to light the candles on Friday night. It was all those things with the candles that meant something to me in New York.

I did what I could here. I finally learned to drive and I took my kids to Sunday school. I joined the Mother's Club, and I even taught in the Sunday school. But I couldn't give my children the real feeling of Judaism in this atmosphere.

HYMIE GOLDEN

The younger generation wanted to get in here a rabbi. I didn't want any rabbi. I didn't need any rabbi. But I figured, "They want a rabbi, I'll help them out." I went to collect money from the old-timers. I collect money from people they wouldn't get five cents.

They brought a rabbi in here part-time, but nobody came to his Friday-night services. Nobody came to see him in his office at the Center. We don't need a rabbi at the Saturday-morning services because that's the old-timers who know how to pray.

I'm not religious—I started going to Saturday-morning services to *shmooz* [shoot the breeze] with my friends—but you got to respect a rabbi. He's an educated man! Somebody got to be with him. You can't leave him alone. Wasn't right.

The younger people, they took over the Center and they don't know from Adam. I says, "Okay, I'll be the religious chairman and show you how." But they don't wanna do things right—not the wine for the Kiddush, not the food for the *seder*, not nothing. They don't listen to me— that's why I didn't let them have the Cemetery.

The attitude of the younger generation to the old people was—excuse the expression—"they old *kakers*." But when it comes to money, they went to the old people for everything! I said it at a meeting: "Listen, You're always complaining about the old people. Let's see the books! It's the old people paying for the Center." These *makhers* [big shots]—my son and the other young ones—they don't like it when you tell them the truth. So I quit being religious chairman! They don't want me in there! I don't need it! I didn't have nothing to do with them from that day. The rabbi, he quit too. Said he had nothing to do.

IRVING GOLDEN

We needed someone to run the whole ball of wax. We needed a leader, but all we got were part-time rabbis whose personalities weren't in tune with the times. We had one guy who couldn't drive! How can you be a rabbi in Petaluma if you don't drive? We had another one who barely spoke English! I couldn't ask someone like that to speak before my Lions Club.

There was chaos in this community! There was no rabbi at all when my oldest son was *bar mitzvahed*. We had to do it with Wolf and all the commotion. When it came time for my second son, they had this rabbi who couldn't speak English. That wasn't for me! I brought in my own rabbi—Rabbi Gross from Santa Rosa. I wanted him and I got him!

For years we tried to get the Santa Rosa Jewish community to go in with us on a new Sonoma County temple and a full-time rabbi. They said, "Do you think we're going to combine with chicken ranchers?"

We finally got a part-time community director. Bernie Nachman did a wonderful job for years, but he wasn't a rabbi. Sure, Bernie went to *yeshiva* [rabbinical school], but that didn't cut ice with me. He didn't graduate! How could I bring him to speak before my Moose Lodge? When the other guys brought their spiritual leaders, it was *Reverend* Jones and *Father* O'Malley. But we only had *Mister* Nachman. It put a black eye on the Jews—too cheap to get a real rabbi.

One time we had a chance to get a heck of a man—Rabbi Stein. Now that was a man you could sit down and talk to! He'd even go out with you for a drink in a bar. He was American! He was modern! Yet he knew his religion. And he was strong—strong—he had definite ideas about how to get this community moving again. When I was president of the congregation I got him in here part-time. That man had ideas! He took me for a ride through the empty prairies of East Petaluma and said, "There will be thousands of homes built here. One in ten new families will be Jewish. We must expand our facilities to be ready for them."

He was right as rain! But this Jewish community . . .

LYNN AXELROD GOLDEN: Well, he sort of antagonized people. He was so . . . so nervous . . . so neurotic . . . and . . . and not very tactful.

IRVING: People didn't like him, and he didn't care. He had no patience for them. Me either. I wanted to get this Jewish community in step with the times. We needed to be like the churches—a new building *with* a parking lot, a full-time leader who could represent us, social programs, educational programs, athletic activities. But all I ever got in this community was static. I couldn't get anything going. I couldn't keep anything going, even when it improved our image in this town.

Take the Frandzel-Grossman Memorial Award. That was my baby! Around 1953 or 1954 the B'nai B'rith decided it was about time for Petaluma to honor the two Jewish boys killed in the war: Art Frandzel and Irving Grossman. You know, a lot of gentiles in Petaluma thought the

Jews wouldn't fight. So we decided to set up an annual Frandzel-Grossman Memorial Award for the outstanding youth in Petaluma. He had to excel in three things: scholastic, athletic, and relationship with minorities.

All right! We kicked it around and then I went to the high school. They said, "Sure, we can pick out three candidates, but how will you choose the winner?" I said, "Don't worry. Our committee will know. We'll give him a plaque and a one-hundred-dollar reward. We'll swing it."

We started it small, with a little ceremony at the Jewish Community Center. Then it got bigger over a couple of years and the rest of Petaluma started following it. The fourth year we went all out. We got Bill Russell to give the award! Bill Russell!

Know how we got him? Russell was playing a basketball game in San Francisco. I went cold turkey, right into the dressing room, and asked him. He said, "For something like this—minorities—in a small town— sure, I'll come." And Bill Russell came right here to Petaluma to give the Fourth Annual Frandzel-Grossman Memorial Award. *I* took Bill Russell out to dinner before the ceremony.

The boy who won the award that year, Billy Kurokawa—you couldn't have picked someone better if you stood on your head! He was half Jewish and half Japanese! Straight "A" student. Three-sport athlete. And president of the student body. It was sensational!

SYLVIA STERN KUROKAWA'S COMMENTS: The B'nai B'rith didn't want to give my son Billy the Frandzel-Grossman Award! They claimed it was because Billy was Jewish and they wanted to give it to a gentile. [Laughing.] The real reason was that Billy came from a family of known radicals. The B'nai B'rith created that Award to show Petaluma that Jews were good Americans. They didn't want to give the award to the kid whose Jewish mother and Japanese father both ran for office on the Communist party ticket. Not to mention the fact that they had kicked us out of the Center with the *linke*. [Laughing.]

Do you know why they gave Billy the award? Because the high school insisted that he obviously was the most qualified. The high school threatened to pull out of the thing if Billy didn't get it. And let me tell you, there were quite a few words among the *linke* over whether we should participate in this thing. They didn't like it either. But I maintained it was the same as our progressive duty to work in the PTA and other mass organizations.

What a build-up for that award night. We had this sensational kid. We had Russell coming. We had a Catholic priest, a Protestant minister, and Rabbi Platt from San Francisco to sit on stage. All the big political and business leaders in town tried to get on that stage. The whole town wanted tickets!

Some in the B'nai B'rith wanted to move the thing to a larger hall—the Veterans' War Memorial Building. I said, "No! We want them to come to the Jewish Community Center. *Let them come to us!!*"

I'll never forget that evening! The Center was packed! They were standing out in the street! The president of the Chamber of Commerce—Will McKay—he came up to me. I'll never forget it—he came up to me and said, "How did you get Bill Russell? How did you get Russell?"

That was one of the greatest nights in the history of the Petaluma Jewish community. But the next year we had a big blow-up in B'nai B'rith over blackballing a left-winger. I pulled out, and they let my Frandzel-Grossman Memorial Award die. Folded like an accordian.

It's a funny thing. I've always tried to advance the Jewish community, but I've always had more trouble from Jews than from gentiles. I just speak my piece and the Jews are down on me like gangbusters—don't like to hear the truth. That never happened to me in gentile organizations. I feel more at home among gentiles. I've been in the Elks, the Knights of Pythias, the Lions, Big Brother, the Riding Club. I get into these organizations and first thing you know I'm an officer. No problems.

Now some Jews say there's anti-Semitism. The Petaluma Golf and Country Club has a reputation for anti-Semitism. I wouldn't know—I had no reason to join—I do not play golf. The story is that all the Jews who tried to get in were blackballed. Maybe. But maybe they were blackballed because they were sons-of-bitches! I saw it with Jews who were blackballed from the Elks. I'm Jewish and I got in. The membership just didn't like some of these guys. I didn't like some of them myself.

We had a few problems with anti-Semitism here in the 1950s. A couple of the Jewish kids were smallish and they were picked on. One of them supposedly had "JEW" written all over him. The Jewish community wouldn't do beans about it. It was these old-timers with the old crap from Europe: "Don't start anything with the gentiles! Run away!"

But this is America. We're Americans like anyone else. Us younger guys weren't about to back down. Some of us went to the school authorities. They said they couldn't do anything about it. So we called in a representative from the San Francisco Anti-Defamation League. He went to the school and said, "Look, if you don't put a stop to it, we'll do it our way."

"What do you mean?"

"Simple as pie," he said. "We'll send six of our big San Francisco Jewish kids up here. When those anti-Semitic jackasses start trouble, our boys will beat the holy hell out of them. Which way do you want it?"

The school put a stop to it quick as lightning. That's how you handle anti-Semitism: threaten them with a taste of their own. I'm one hundred percent for the approach of the Stern Gang in Israel: cut off the God-damned heads of the Arabs. I'm one hundred percent for the Jewish Defense League: you get five of us, we'll get ten of you.

There's the difference between European Jews and American Jews. We're not like the old-timers. We won't put up with any Nazi pogroms. The American Jew is ready to fight!

MAX BLUMBERG

Anti-Semitism in Petaluma? Depends how you look at it. The other day my back hurt and I was walking hunched over. This friend sees me and yells out, "Hey, Blumberg! You're walking like a Jew!"

"Yeah!" I yelled back. "I was screwed by the Portugee!"

It's just a form of salutation. But my brother-in-law Irving would have jumped all over him for a remark like that: "What do you mean talking about the Jews like that?!! Didn't you ever see the Portuguese walking with a backache?!! What did the Jews ever do to you?" Irving gets excited over a little anti-Semitic remark. I say you can't expect anything else from the *goyim*. I say give it back.

I caused a furor at one of my Masons' meetings by doing it. It started when one of the guys, Ed Carlson, got up and told a joke. He says, "There was this hippie who was getting pretty low. He had a beard and long straggly hair and a raggedy coat. So he looks in the mirror and says, 'Jiminy Crickets, I look like Jesus Christ. Maybe I can capitalize on it.'

"So this hippie goes to the Catholic church and says, 'I am the Lord and I have returned. Give me what is due me.' So the priest says to the congregation, 'The Lord is here. Give everything you can.' And they turned over a pile of money to the hippie.

"So the hippie goes from one church to another, telling the same story, and they all give money. But this hippie is not too bright—he doesn't know the difference between a church and a synagogue. So he knocks on the door of a synagogue and says the same thing: 'I am the Lord and I have returned. Give me what is due me.'

" 'One minute please.' Ed says the rabbi's reply with a Yiddish accent: 'Hey *boyes,* bring out the cross!' "

That was the joke. It was funny and everybody laughed.

Now I'm the only Jewish guy in our Masons' branch and I take a lot of ethnic jokes. But this one got me angry. So I got up and said, "I demand equal time for my joke."

So I told this joke—it's not a very nice joke. I says, "Once a world-famous evangelist came to a small town to speak. Being that he was such a great man, everyone in town came to hear him. The church was the only place large enough to hold the meeting. Well, this evangelist got to a certain point in this speech and he said, 'In twenty minutes I will say something derogatory about my Jewish brethren. I would appreciate if they will leave the room at that time, because I want to maintain good relations with them.'

"The evangelist mentioned it first as a passing remark. Then he repeated it stronger at ten minutes and stronger at five minutes. Finally the time comes and he says, 'I now have something derogatory to say about our Jewish brethren. Please! I beg of you, leave the room! I want no misunderstandings.'

"So just behind the evangelist in the church, the statue of Christ turns to the Virgin Mary and says, '*Kum mama. Lozundz gehn aheym.*' " Then I translated the Yiddish: " 'Come mother. It is time for us to go home.' "

I told that joke and there was silence—utter silence. No more jokes that evening. And in the *Bulletin* next week, the district governor wrote that at the last meeting Ed and Max had a "misunderstanding."

That's all. Give like you get! To tell you the truth, I preferred the gentile lodges over the Jewish Community Center. I enjoyed the ritual in the Masons and the Knights of Pythias. I liked not having to put up with arguments about the *linke,* the Sunday school, the rabbi. All they did was argue at the Jewish Center. Oh, we'd argue during the Knights of Pythias meetings, but when the meetings ended the arguments ended, and then we'd play cards. With the Jews you'd argue at the meeting, then you start the argument again on the sidewalk after the meeting, and then you'd go downtown for coffee and continue the argument. The meeting never ended! The argument never stopped!

It was the same arguments year after year. For years I argued we should build a new Jewish Community Center. In the fifties we could have dumped the Center off to some slob and put the money into a big new building. We would have had a huge mortgage and everyone would have worked their asses off for it. Then there would have been reason for everyone to be active in the Jewish community.

You have to grow. You have to promote. A priest explained it to me. I was his real estate agent when he was selecting a site for a new church. When I showed him a quiet country location, he says, "Max, it's beautiful, but it's not commercial enough. Church is a business, and we've got to be where the customers can find us. Show me something near the freeway."

That's what we should have done in the Jewish community. Instead, they kept that old dump. There's a Yiddish expression: "*Ven du bist a tipish, est du drek*"—"When you are an asshole, you eat shit!" That's the story of the Jewish community and that building.

I got tired of those stupid arguments, so I switched to the gentile lodges. Sure, you'd get some anti-Semitic nuts in these fraternal lodges. I got blackballed twice before they let me in the Masons. But let me tell you, they were nuttier in the Jewish community. My wife's cousin black-balled me from B'nai B'rith! They said I was a Communist! Now that is horse shit!

SHIRLEY SHIFFMAN GOLD [b. 1923; San Francisco]

Finally Mike and I decided, "To hell with it! The old-timers won't give money for a new building, a rabbi, or a good Sunday school. Okay, let them have the Center. We'll send our kids to Santa Rosa to learn their Jewish heritage."

People said we were traitors when we joined the Santa Rosa syna-gogue. We still paid dues to the Center, but we did what we thought was right for our children's Jewish education. Nobody complained to our face, but I knew what they were saying—and I couldn't care less.

We wanted a big *bar mitzvah* for our son, with a lot of family and friends. Mike had the big poultry plant then and we had a lot of business associates. We just couldn't do it in Petaluma with those undignified ser-vices in that old building. In Santa Rosa, we had Rabbi Gross conduct a lovely *bar mitzvah* service in their beautiful new synagogue.

MIKE GOLD: We did worse than go to Santa Rosa for the service. We held the *bar mitzvah* reception at the Petaluma Golf and Country Club. A lot of Jewish people didn't like that, but the Country Club had the only suitable facilities for our dinner party. When I first told people in the Jewish community that I wanted to rent the banquet hall at the Country Club they said, "Are you crazy? They'll never let in a Jew!"

But I had *chutzpah*. I asked! And do you know, I never was so sur-prised in my whole life as when the Country Club said, "Sure. Why not?" People in the Jewish community said it was because I had the big poultry-processing plant and I had a lot of pull around town. I just think it was the beginning of change at the Country Club.

Sure, there's been anti-Semitism in Petaluma, but I think the Jews ex-aggerate it. Things changed after the war with the new generation of Jewish businessmen. No one blackballed me from any fraternal organi-zations. No one objected to my sitting on the city-hospital commission. No gentile ever said anything derogatory to me about being Jewish.

It was the Jewish people who said derogatory things. If you weren't completely active in the Jewish community, if you didn't spend every free moment at the Jewish Community Center, they'd whisper, "See him? He doesn't want any part of us. He prefers the Santa Rosa Jews. He prefers the *goyim*."

MANNY EPSTEIN

Petaluma wanted to build a combined synagogue with Santa Rosa, but it never would have worked. Petaluma Jewry was different from Santa Rosa Jewry. The people in Santa Rosa were more educated, more business oriented. Santa Rosa Jewry was a quieter people. We had "unity in the community" in Santa Rosa. We didn't have all the fighting and yelling. They had that second faction in Petaluma, the *rinke* or whatever they called them—the ones who talked about . . . about . . . about communism. They didn't use that particular word, but they thought it.

It was more of a foreign-type thing in Petaluma. They stayed with their *yidishkeyt* [Jewishness]. They didn't Americanize their Judaism with a good American-oriented rabbi and real services.

Well, that was their beliefs. That was the kind of community they wanted. Like I say, I lived in Santa Rosa and Santa Rosa was nice. We didn't want to get involved with them socially. We built our own beautiful synagogue.

STELLA FINKLESTEIN

You don't know what happened with the Jewish temple in Santa Rosa? They put up a fancy modern building and they couldn't pay for it! [Laughing.] They thought Frank Rosenthall would cover it. He was their big *makher*—the Joe Holtzman of Santa Rosa. But Rosenthall got into a big legal battle with another Santa Rosa Jewish businessman and the whole community became involved. It was a scandal! Well, Rosenthall was furious over all the gossip in the Jewish community about this legal thing. The gossip was just terrible! So when he died he left them nothing! Not a cent! He left his money to the Catholic church! [Chortling.] And to this day the Santa Rosa Jews owe a huge debt on their fancy temple.

FRAN RUBINSTEIN GINSBERG

I didn't want a new building. The Jewish Community Center was our parents' legacy to us. It was more than a building. The Center was part of our feeling for being Jewish and being part of a Jewish community.

We needed the Center to pass that Jewish feeling on to our children. You see, my generation was different from our parents. We never brought Yiddish poets and musical groups to the Center. We didn't have the intellectual activities of our parents. We weren't well informed about Jewish life around the world. We didn't follow in the footsteps of our parents, so the Center helped us remember where we came from.

We were more American. We were more involved outside the Jewish community than our parents. It was okay as long as it was the PTA, but the gentiles never really accepted us. The same gentile girls who kept the Jewish girls out of the Rainbow Girls in high school, they kept us out of the Petaluma Women's Club when we were older. Nobody Jewish wanted to join these organizations and feel uncomfortable, but it reminded you that you weren't accepted.

My generation was kind of in-between. How do you raise your children as Jews when you're in-between? We could bring them to the Center and make them a part of our community's history. But we also needed a rabbi for services and Sunday school and *bar mitzvahs*. Maybe all that religion was just symbolic, but it was the only way I could pass on that Jewish feeling to my children.

And do you know, as my father got older his religious feeling was rekindled! My father had been a completely secular Labor Zionist when I grew up, but when my son was *bar mitzvahed* it rekindled Pa's religious feelings from his *yeshiva* [rabbinical academy] days. For the first time in forty years, Pa put on a *yarmlke* [skullcap], wore a *talis* [prayer shawl], went up to the *bime* [pulpit], and read from the Torah. After that he joined Rabbi Platt's *shul* in San Francisco and went to services every week. He said he liked Rabbi Platt's sermons, but I think he liked the feeling of the service.

That's the funny thing about American life. The more American you become, the more Jewish tradition you need. That's why I wanted to keep the Center and hire a rabbi. I wanted my children to know who they were.

Celia Glazer Hochman

Just because the *linke* didn't go to the Center and didn't pray in *shul* didn't mean we weren't good Jews. Being Jewish means you lead an honest straightforward life, with or without the temple. To me, my home was my temple. I was proud of my Jewish heritage and I tried to pass it on to my children. I was determined that my kids wouldn't go through what I experienced with anti-Semitic teachers in Petaluma. My older son, Jerry, had a class with one of the worst, a German teacher, a lady who I had trouble with when I was in school. One time, close to Christmas, Jerry cut up in class with some other kids. She yelled at him, "You better remember. There's more of us Christians than you Jews!"

When Nathan and I heard about that, we exploded! We immediately went to see the principal. Things were different from the old days, because we wouldn't tolerate it and because now David Adler was on the board of education. We demanded an official meeting with that teacher. We confronted her with what happened and we reduced her to tears. She kept crying, "Why did you do this? Why didn't you come talk to me?"

I said, "I'm working through channels. I want you exposed."

This is why it was so terrible that they kicked the left out of the Center. When the anti-Semitism comes down, the anti-Semites don't care if you're *linke* or *rekhte*. It was disgraceful that the *rekhte* leaders divided the Jewish community. Their anti-Communist blinders didn't allow them to see the greater good of the Jewish people.

NATHAN HOCHMAN: It worked both ways. For many years our thinking was so pro-Soviet that we saw nothing else. It took me a long time to recognize anti-Semitism in the Soviet Union. I still believe in socialism, but today I am anti-Soviet. I think we wore blinders like the *rekhte*.

CELIA: But we didn't try to kick them out of the Center. Without the Center, I had to teach my kids their Jewish heritage myself. I organized a "secular *bar mitzvah*" for the boys. It wasn't in the Center with a rabbi directing a service. We threw a big party at home when each one reached thirteen, and they each made a speech on Judaism.

I made them go through hell to prepare those speeches. I'm sure the kids thought I was a witch, but I gave them a thorough course in Jewish history—the Holy Land, the Maccabees, all of it. I had to learn it myself to do it. And then I made them write their own twenty-minute *bar mitzvah* speeches.

The whole *linke* came to our house for the *bar mitzvah* parties, and it was beautiful. So maybe the boys didn't recite Hebrew prayers or read from the Torah before a congregation. I don't think they missed anything. They got just as good a knowledge of their heritage as any kid at the Center.

BETTY EPSTEIN HOCHMAN: There was no way we could give our children the feeling for being Jewish that our parents gave us. Our parents *lived* the Old World Jewish history and traditions. We got some of it from them, but it became more diluted with each generation.

The old-timers in the *linke* weren't much help. When I moved into Petaluma I was shocked by how the Hochman family celebrated Pesach. It was just a big holiday dinner where my father-in-law delivered a Marxist version of the story of the Exodus from Egypt. It wasn't a real *seder* with the religious ritual and the traditional foods and the singing—the things that made you feel connected to thousands of years of Jewish history. Even though I was a leftist and completely secular by the time I married into the Hochman family, their *seder* seemed like a giant hoax. I wanted to pass the real thing on to my children, but there was no way I could do it. I couldn't even pass on the left-wing secular Jewish traditions. My in-laws were real revolutionaries who fought the tsar in Russia and built trade unions in America. They had wide interests in politics and history and culture, but they did everything in Yiddish. They couldn't pass it on to us, and we couldn't pass it on to our children.

Besides, their politics stopped making sense to us in the 1950s. It became clear to my generation on the left that Stalin had committed awful crimes, especially against the Soviet Jewish people. The revelations about Stalin were a terrible blow to the old-timers. A lot of them, including my in-laws, had a hard time accepting it.

So how could my generation on the left raise our children as Jews? Urge them to join "the Revolution" in Petaluma? Most of the children of the *linke* had no choice but to rejoin the Center, send their kids for a religious education, and hold the *bar mitzvahs*. We were completely different from the old-timers.

MIRIAM HOCHMAN: The next generation had different ideas from us. They had a different way of life. We used to run to San Francisco, rain or shine, for meetings—Communist meetings. If a Yiddish poet came from the Soviet Union, we brought him to speak in Petaluma. If there was a frame-up against a black man in the South, right away we had an affair to raise money. The children did this for a while in the Maccabeans, but they stopped.

BEN HOCHMAN: We had revolutionary ideals. We believed in a revolutionary era. The children grew up in a different atmosphere in America.

MIRIAM: We tried to raise our children with an atmosphere of communism around the house. We had an atmosphere of Yiddish culture around the house. But our movement did not succeed to bring it to the next generation. Not in Petauma, not anywheres. Our organizations and ideals, our traditions, our literature and our songs—it did not become part of their diet.

JOE RAPOPORT

Some of us who arrived in Petaluma after the war believed the *linke* should not knuckle under to isolation. I appreciated the closeness of Petaluma's *linke* organizations, the money we raised for the radical movement, and the high level of Yiddish culture. But cultural evenings in the Yiddish language by ourselves for ourselves was not enough. We could not even invite our own children and grandchildren to such meetings.

A group of us who arrived with experience in the labor movement wanted to reach out, widen the base, put our left-wing experience to work in the struggles of people around us. We wanted the *linke* organizations to work with the Grange, the Democratic party, the Central Labor Council. We wanted to find common ground with the *rekhte* in raising money for Israel, in fighting local anti-Semitism, in the commemoration of the Holocaust. We wanted that the Jewish Folk Chorus should sing a few songs in English. We wanted to make public criticisms of the Soviet Union—as friends of the Soviet Union.

In all of this there were long bitter struggles inside the *linke* group. Those of us who wanted change—those of us who came to Petaluma with big-city experience in the radical movement—we found ourselves in a small provincial Jewish community with its own rigid ways. I had great respect for the political and cultural knowledge of the established leadership of the *linke*. I appreciated all the Yiddish cultural organizations and activities, but I was a stranger to our progressive Jewish movement by not declaring *"yidish is loshn koydesh"*—"Yiddish is a holy language," like it was said about Hebrew in the Old Country.

Idele Rubin Kolman

For years I dragged the kids to affairs of the older generation. My God, did we go to concerts of the Jewish Folk Chorus! My parents would have killed me if we didn't hear them sing! Vince's parents would have killed me! But I hated it—year after year since I was a kid, the same songs, the same plays, the same political fund raising. And my kids couldn't even understand a word of Yiddish.

What else could we do but return to the Center? We didn't set foot in there for years after the Split, but then came a time when I thought my kids should go to Sunday school. I'm not religious, but I'm staunchly Jewish. Judaism is more than a religion; it's a way of life. I wanted my kids to have the flavor of Jewish life. We couldn't give it to them ourselves. When the kids were young they wanted a Christmas tree, so we did Channukah in a big way with a Channukah bush and blue and white decorations all over the house. But we couldn't teach them the history and the culture. We couldn't give them the feeling of a Jewish community.

The Sunday school at the Center was the only alternative. At first I was afraid to do it. But then I thought, "I have just as much right to walk into that place as anybody else!" It was easier because Bernie Nachman had started as director of the Center by that time. More than anyone else he made us all welcome to return after the Split. He's a prince of a man.

But I was scared to death the first time I took the kids for Sunday school. I hadn't been in the Center for years. I'll never forget walking in there and Elaine Blumberg saying, "What are *you* doing *here*?"

I said, "I'm a Jew! Didn't you know it?" And I walked the kids right past her.

VINCE KOLMAN: That's what Idele wanted, and I went along with it. I personally did not go to services—it would have been hypocritical—but the kids put in their time with Judaism.

IDELE: What?!!

VINCE: Well, okay, I guess they learned something—identity.

IDELE: It was important for the kids to go to the Center and learn about Jewish history and Jewish holidays. Okay! Laugh! But the kids needed an identity. I couldn't control who they'd be as adults, but I could give them something about Judaism when they were young. Then they could decide for themselves who they were.

But it was very hard on me. For Alan's *bar mitzvah* I had a migraine headache the entire day. It was the first *bar mitzvah* in my family or Vince's family. The older people had left the Old Country to get away from religion. They were very apprehensive about coming into the Center after they had been kicked out during the McCarthy years. And to come in there with the "reactionaries" for a *bar mitzvah!* Some refused. But I said, "This is what I want for the kids and this is how I want to do it!"

And to be honest, it wasn't just for the kids. I've never felt accepted in Petaluma outside the Center. I've always been very self-conscious when I'm around Christians—that they'll say something anti-Semitic like "Jew him down." Even with good gentile friends, I've always been afraid I'd accidentally say something anti-Christian like *shikse* [gentile girl] or *sheygetz* [gentile boy]. There is always a reserve when you're with gentiles—you're different. I felt more comfortable around Jewish people at the Center.

DAVID ADLER

Who ever heard of an Adler joining a congregation? Well, in 1960 I joined the congregation at the Center. The Split had left a large vacuum in our social life. We sympathized with the left-wing people, but we didn't join up with the Maccabeans and we didn't participate much at the Center. We remained aloof for years.

That is when I became involved in other things. I became active with the schools to the point where I was elected to several terms on the Petaluma Board of Education. I sat on civic commissions for the hospital, the airport, the library. I thought it was important for Jewish people to be involved in the greater life of the area.

Over the years I gradually became more active at the Jewish Community Center too. You see, Esther is more of a religious-oriented person. At first it was an occasional affair or a Friday-night service. Then when the Center was turned into a congregation in 1960, we joined. In fact, they asked me to sit on the board of directors at that time. I turned it down— it was bad enough that I joined the congregation [chuckles]—I mean that facetiously, of course. Later, I actually became president of the congregation! [Laughter.] That's when I had to go to Friday-night services regularly. And I think I did it willingly, without a tongue-in-cheek kind of thing.

Some left-wing people thought I went soft in the head, but that didn't bother me. I participated at the Center because my family had a need for it. I believe the woman is the leader in the home, and Esther felt our children needed the Jewish education and the contact with other Jewish kids. I did what I felt was best for my family. It didn't harm anyone else.

Morry Finklestein

David Adler—we love him dearly—he came from a *linke* family. Nothing religious. His father Shlome was called *der royter Adler*—Red Adler—a progressive—completely secular! One day David says to me, "Morry, you wouldn't believe it. I've become president of the *shul!*"

This religious thing just took over with the young people! Even those from the left. It was amazing!

Stella Finklestein: It's exactly what I tried to tell the old-timers after the war. You need some sort of traditional practice to maintain a Jewish community and Jewish identity.

Morry: How can you, a progressive person, say religion is necessary?

Stella: Not religion! Tradition!

Morry: Call it what you want. Those of us who came from Europe know it's inseparable. We couldn't escape it fast enough. And here in Petaluma these progressive children who were brought up secular, they all came around to religion when this traditional thing took over. That's America for you. They went back to the Center and jumped in bed with the reactionaries.

BERNIE NACHMAN [b. 1920; New York City]

When I first came to Petaluma, the Jewish community considered it an intermarriage when a left Jew married a right Jew. That was in 1963, when I became director of the Jewish Community Center and Congregation B'nai Israel. At that time the community didn't know what it wanted from a director, so I carved out my own place. I conducted the services, ran the school, and prepared the boys for *bar mitzvahs*. I organized adult social and cultural activities, I did pastoral work, and I represented the Jewish community in Petaluma civic life. As the half-time community director, even while I spent half my time with my children's summer camp, I did just about everything a rabbi would do.

Yes, some people were bothered that I had not completed *yeshiva* [rabbinical academy] training and was not a rabbi, but I considered it their problem. My primary concern was uniting the Jewish community. I had never before encountered the kind of bitter political split I found in Petaluma. I thought it was crucial that the Jewish Community Center serve all Jews.

I made a stand early on: no political discrimination—no second-class citizens in the Petaluma Jewish community. I attended affairs of the *linke*, I got to know them, and I let them know that I considered them in the realm of Jewish tradition, the tradition of the Prophets of Israel. I brought liberal speakers to the Jewish Community Center, I included left-wing literature in our Jewish Book Club, and I worked for a united community commemoration of the Holocaust. I let both sides know that I considered it silly that the community be split.

The two sides gradually came together. It took years, with knockdown drag-out fights within each camp and strained negotiations between the camps. But we finally achieved a major breakthrough in 1967, when the Six Day War brought most of the left-wing community together with the traditional community in a united Jewish effort to raise money for Israel in her hour of danger. That was the first time in fifteen years that most of the old-timers in the *linke* set foot in the Center.

Years before this tactical alliance, the children of the old-timers already had come back together. The second generation didn't have those short-sighted ideological biases. They didn't continue these feuds for decades. They felt the need for a united Jewish community in a gentile world that never fully accepted them. They wanted a strong harmonious Jewish community that their children could feel part of. They recognized the importance of community in the transmission of heritage from one generation to the next.

You see, when I arrived in Petaluma in 1963, I found a Jewish community that had stopped growing. It was very conservative in that they rested on the laurels of the old immigrant community. It was a politically liberal community, with a proliferation of organizations and activities, but the people were secular if not anti-religious. They were isolated from the mainstream of American Jewish communal development. Everything about the community was archaic. They were proud of the large amounts of money they gave to Jewish causes, but they only gave for what they were individually committed to. There was almost no structured financial support for the congregation, the Sunday school, or anything else. Everything was on an informal basis. That approach was a remnant from the past, when community members did everything themselves. In the old days there were people in the community who could conduct a service, run the Yiddish library, bring in interesting speakers. After meetings and affairs, they would clean up the Center themselves. But those were different people, different times, a different kind of Jewish community. People can't or won't do those things today. The community must hire expertise to do it today.

I attempted to modernize the community, to bring it into the mainstream of American Judaism, especially where it concerned the third generation. I saw to it that the board of directors instituted strict rules for religious training of children in the Sunday school. I put a floor under the *bar mitzvah,* so that a kid couldn't just come in at the last moment, memorize his lines, and get *bar mitzvah*ed with some rabbi the family brought in. I required that the kids go through the full religious training. This shook up the status quo. Many people were accustomed to doing things their own way, and suddenly they ran into these rules. But I reminded them that they hired me because I was supposed to be knowledgeable. I insisted upon high standards, not the lowest common denominator.

I had a showdown over this with one of the hoary old-timers in the community. When his grandson came of age for *bar mitzvah,* the boy did not meet the requirements of religious training. He hadn't been to Sunday school at all. The boy's grandfather said, "In deference to my decades of service to the community, my grandson should be allowed to have a *bar mitzvah* in the Center. I will train him myself."

"I appreciate your service to the community," I said, "but the answer is no. Your grandson can't have a *bar mitzvah* in Petaluma with only three months of preparation."

I had to say no. I wanted to raise these kids as Jewish. I couldn't sustain them on pablum.

14 "Raised with an American Lullaby": The Third Generation

MICHAEL HOCHMAN

I married a girl from from the Petaluma Jewish community. I knew Elaine all my life, but she came from the *rekhte*. I didn't really get to know her until we met again in a hot tub at a reunion of the third-generation Petaluma kids. You wouldn't believe the amount of community gossip when we moved in together.

Our wedding was neat. We did the marriage ceremony out by the ocean with a rabbi who was loose and let us do whatever we wanted. He made a right-on speech about the emphasis in Jewish life on the spiritual and the political. Then we did a kind of ceremony in which people passed around our wedding rings and put good energy into them and said some really great things to us. Elaine and I chose to say what we would say to each other as we were struck by the moment, but say it away from everybody. So in the middle of the ceremony we ran down the beach . . .

ELAINE BERGOWITZ HOCHMAN: We ra-a-a-an awa-a-a-ay. That's when we saw the seal. It was magical. When we came back we had everyone chant a special word: *shalom*. Everyone was chanting. Everything was vibrating. It was so magical!

MICHAEL: We had a huge party that evening at the Veterans' War Memorial Building in Petaluma. It was swamped—over three hundred people—the entire old Jewish community. I've never seen so much energy in one place. I've never seen singing and dancing like we had at our wedding party. The only thing of a political nature was my toast calling for saving the whales and the dolphins. I told people to eat a lot, drink a lot, and dance a lot. I said that anyone who needs a reefer, see my best man. And what do you know? All these people from my parents' generation asked for reefers! They got stoned with us! I mean, it was biza-a-a-arre!

262

It was an outrageous day! There never has been a wedding like ours! It was just outrageous!

Our marriage was a positive statement about growing up in the Petaluma Jewish community. The Jewish kids from Petaluma are like *landsmen* from the same *shtetl*. A group of us got together in San Francisco a few months ago and we started talking about Petaluma. One person remembered his grandparents living on Chapman Lane, another said, "So did my grandmother," and it turned out that all our grandparents had lived on Chapman Lane. Now that was roots!

My roots are with my grandparents—my grandparents and "the meeting." When Grandma Miriam would say, "We're going to the meeting tonight," that was heavy. It was special not just because it was a social thing, but because there always was some political purpose. I was proud that Jewish people had ideas about the greater meaning of their lives. I looked down on other folks in Petaluma who didn't know anything but yanking on cows' tits. That was my grandparents. As for my parents' generation after the war, they got into prosperity and security like everyone else in America. Even though they came from the *linke,* they expected their kids to be anal, uptight, goody-goody little successes.

Well, the kids who grew up in *linke* families drank, we ate pills, some even got into sticking needles in their arms! Yeah! We were a bunch of rowdies raising hell. Turkeys that we were, we fancied ourselves social outlaws.

ELAINE: It was worse in the *rekhte* families, because we had to do all the stuff at the Center. I had to go to Sunday school for years. At first I liked it because Bernie Nachman was very warm. But as I got older I resented all his Bible stories with morals we were supposed to live by. Most of the kids thought he was on an ego power trip.

My father was president of the Center for years, so we went to every affair and every Friday-night service. It was like visiting family. All those adults were like aunts and uncles, grandmas and grandpas, hugging you and smearing lipstick all over your face. It gave me a warm, secure feeling, but I resented going all the time.

I rebelled when I was fifteen. I stopped going to Friday-night services and started dating gentile boys. I hung around with a group of artsy kids who dressed weird and smoked dope. We hated the redneck farmer kids and the snobby well-dressed town kids. We were kind of the hippies in Petaluma.

MICHAEL: Even though I drove a '57 Chevy with mag wheels, like the rednecks, I was a dissident. When we *linke* kids found things in school we didn't like, we hassled it. In high school we opened a coffeehouse where we could organize against the Vietnam War. It was a target for these reactionary redneck farmer kids who talked about beating up the Commie Pinko Jews. Some of them were grandchildren of the people who tarred and feathered Grandpa Ben in the thirties. I had a very tense thing with those guys.

I got my left-wing politics and my stubbornness from Grandpa Ben. But I learned other things from him, like the importance of family. When my older brother, Neil, went into the corporate structure, Grandpa Ben never turned against him. Anyone else doing what Neil does would be a no-good son-of-a-bitch, but Neil is family, and family is family.

The most important thing I got from Grandpa Ben was: "Be a critical thinker." Grandpa Ben didn't always follow that advice himself. For years he had an uncritical belief in Stalin and the Soviet Union. But he copped to it during the 1960s. He even went back into the Center and gave money for Israel during the Six Day War. Not many people in their seventies could keep an open mind and admit, "We were wrong."

In the sixties Grandpa Ben, Grandma Miriam, and all their *linke* friends were marching right alongside us grandchildren to protest the Vietnam War. Even my parents' generation took out time from making money and marched with us. That was awesome—three generations from the *linke* in the same demonstrations.

Grandpa Ben was very critical of the student movement. He said, "You are too radical with too few allies. The drugs are dulling your minds. You must prepare for a long struggle to build socialism. Get it on!"

But everything was coming unglued: the demonstrations, fighting the cops at S.F. State and U.C. Berkeley, the music, the drugs—all this outrageous stuff coming down. It was too heavy—I kind of went bananas.

ELAINE: I felt Petalumans were dumb hicks, so I went to San Francisco State for a while. Then I threw myself into new experience, new people, new ideas, exploring religious sects. I was searching.

MICHAEL: At that point I went to Israel to get my head straight. When I returned my dad got me into the plumbers' union. I put my head down and worked for five years! I felt really alienated and got even more into drugs and alcohol. But I was determined to get my journeyman's card and then make a statement to the world: "*Fuck you!!*" But by the time I got my journeyman's card, I was an activist in the movement to save the whales and the dolphins. I've become totally involved in the conservation movement. For the first time I'm clear about what I want to do. Now I'm returning to college to study marine resources and oceanic law.

ELAINE: I'm getting back into art. There's so much—I used to paint, then it was art therapy. Now I'm ready to learn graphic arts. I still feel very creative, but I'm more practical now.

MICHAEL: Now that our generation is getting it together, our parents' generation are becoming a little spacey—you know, smoking dope at our wedding. I think they're reevaluating things now that their parents are dying and their kids are growing up. But I don't expect much out of them. They have fundamentally different values. I call them the "garbage-compacter generation." The whole group of them in Petaluma have bought this new gimmick that crushes all the garbage. When I try to explain that they should recycle garbage, that garbage compactors are wasteful, they say, "It's nice that you're into ecology."

I still identify more with the values of my grandparents. Grandpa Ben inspires me when he says, "You were raised with an American lullaby. Your generation can educate yourselves and continue our struggle to improve American life." Whenever I go into the schools to speak for the American Cetacean Society, I start my talk with Grandpa Ben's message: "Critical thought! The whales and the dolphins have no chance unless we develop critical thought. We must refuse to take things for granted."

DAN ADLER

My grandfather and I had a ritual. Whenever I hadn't seen him for a time, I'd put out my hand and hold it there. You know, looking strong, challenging. Then he'd put out his hand and we'd shake. We'd shake and we'd squeeze—squeezing and squeezing, until one gave in. I didn't take him until he was over eighty. He was *strong as a bull*! His hands were like meathooks, workingman's hands. That ritual is my greatest memory of him; the two of us squeezing and smiling, with me wincing in pain, watching the pleasure on his face. It was a great thing that we did.

One time Ben Hochman said to me, "Your grandfather, now there's a man."

They had a kind of reverence for each other all through the years in Petaluma. My grandfather was more rigid in politics. Ben was by far the more capable of dealing with political complexity. He said to me, "Your grandfather blames everything on a plot by Standard Oil. He thinks the Soviet Union is always right. I don't see it that way."

But then Ben says to me, "If you were to ask me to show you the finest example of a proletarian man, it would be Shloyme Adler." That was the highest compliment Ben could pay him: "If the Soviet Union was all this kind of man, it would work."

I looked at my great uncle Mordecai as the leader of our family clan. He was a big man with the bearing of a grand patriarch. He was very learned, but he was playful too, and when you asked him a question he would answer with a biblical story. At Passover, Uncle Mordecai sat at the head of the table and led the family through the entire *seder* in Hebrew. It would go on and on while the kids sat in agony, kicking each other under the table and giggling: "When will this end? *When* can we eat?"

There aren't people like my grandfather and my great uncle around anymore. I don't know how I'll pass on the old Jewish traditions to my children. I don't know much about Judaism, I'm not active in any Jewish community, and I'm married to a non-Jewish girl. I feel like I'm Jewish, but I don't know how.

When I was growing up in Petaluma I rebelled against the stereotypes in the Petaluma Jewish community. You know, Jews were supposed to be good solid family people, well educated, financially successful, sober, community minded. Something in me said, "Cut the cord!" I drank, I gave idiots the finger on the road, I got in trouble with the law. Some of my Jewish friends made even heavier breaks: drugs, strange religions, all the therapies from Primal Scream to EST. We said, "Fuck you" to the Jewish community. We were failures.

We were driven into it by all those rules of Jewish decorum. When I was in high school, Esther—that's my mother—she'd forbid me to go out with a non-Jewish girl more than three times. I cured her by going out with a nice Jewish girl for six years! It wasn't so nice! Yeah! It cured me too! After we broke up, it ended any residual hangups I had about whether my girlfriends were Jewish. That opened the door for another period of rampant cord cutting. I want at that traditional Jewish image with machetes! I dropped out of college and worked as a construction laborer. I spent my evenings drinking beer and chasing women. It was a long time before I was ready to settle down with a wife and a career.

Growing up on my father's chicken ranch decided me against manual labor. I admired how my father and my grandfather took pride in raising good birds, doing their own construction work, running their own business for themselves. They wanted nothing more, but I thought, "My God, how could I go through life working as hard as them?"

Through the 1972 McGovern campaign, I got a job as legislative aide to a representative in the California legislature. I've become a real populist, a kind of Jewish redneck like my grandfather. I'm suspicious of these wealthy capitalists who work behind the scenes for their own profits. I'm suspicious of social engineers who do a lot of intellectualizing over other people's problems. I believe you must listen to the people and be solution-oriented. You must be an activist and do something!

I'm not a failure anymore. A few months ago I was at Michael Hochman's wedding in Petaluma and saw Neil Hochman—Ben's other grandson—pull up in his Mercedes. He's a real go-getter businessman—very rich. I said to my brother Jerry, "Ah, poor Esther, she's stuck with a couple of failures."

Jerry says, "Failure? Mom doesn't consider you a failure! You've got a good job, a family, a house with a swimming pool! What you mean?"

He's right. I'm not a failure anymore. I guess I just feel more comfortable thinking of myself as a failure. It's a lot of responsibility to be a success.

MORRIS YARMULSHEFSKY [b. 1946; displaced persons' camp, Germany]

One incident really set off Dan Adler in high school. A soda shop near school put out a sign with a caricature of a big-nosed Jew wearing a Star of David. It said, "No credit here." We both were appalled. Right after school Dan went out in front of that shop with a sign and started picketing. Dan's father was on the school board. Pretty soon the school superintendent called the owner and said, "Remove that sign or we will make your place off limits to students." He took it down. I was too insecure to picket with Dan. I was very self-conscious about being Jewish when I grew up here. It was connected with my family being refugees from the Holocaust.

I grew up with the third generation in Petaluma, but I really feel like one of the immigrant generation. I was born in a displaced-persons' camp in Germany, and Yiddish is my first language. My parents never spoke about their life in Poland or the Holocaust, but I feel like part of me is from the Old World. I've always felt very strong about being Jewish.

There was one time in my life when I had a lot of conflicts with my parents over Judaism. When I was in college I had a long struggle with them over a gentile girl I was seeing. The entire family—all my aunts and uncles and cousins—were very upset and put a lot of pressure on me. I was torn up, and I finally broke up with the girl. It was the toughest thing I've lived through. I don't feel bitter about it. I understand how my parents feared they would lose me to the gentile world. Eventually I married Jo-Ann, who grew up as a Catholic and was willing to convert to Judaism. My parents didn't resist.

JO-ANN YARMULSHEFSKY [b. 1948; Santa Rosa]: As we grew closer, Morris took me to see the Holocaust Memorial at the Jewish Community Center in Petaluma. This was before I knew the history of Morris's family. It began with a choir of old people who sang these powerful songs in tiny high voices. There were moving speeches about the Holocaust and the Warsaw Ghetto uprising. And then six people, including Morris's father and his two uncles, were called to light candles commemorating the six million who died. It really was something.

I converted to Judaism before we married. I took classes for months. Then I went through a ritual of clipping the toenails and fingernails, immersing myself in fresh running water, and saying certain prayers. Finally I was interrogated by a court of Jewish law. I had no problem. I already had rejected Catholicism for more humanistic beliefs, which seemed to fit in with Judaism. I liked Judaism's emphasis on family and community, social justice, and the struggle to bring about a Messianic time. I liked the Jewish attitude toward death, with the emphasis on life and continuity—generations follow generations, the streams flow over their beds leaving behind the soil from the mountain tops.

One of the rabbis on the examination board was kind enough to say that he thought I had been Jewish all along. That's how people treated me in the Petaluma Jewish community. I didn't feel excluded. It was all kindness and joy.

MORRIS: I established my own life, my own way, right here where I grew up. I left for law school but I came home after graduation. I feel an obligation to be here for my family. I'm establishing my law practice and becoming active in civic affairs in Sonoma County. There is where I will live and this is where I will raise my children. I've also become active in the Petaluma Jewish community. I started a few years ago when Jacob Katz asked me to be chairman of the Holocaust Memorial commemoration. I accepted because I knew how important that event was to the older Jewish community, especially my own family.

Now I am on the board of directors at the Center, and I do some legal work for the congregation. I feel like I should honor these Jewish community obligations. It's important that Jews feel responsible to their community. I know from the history of my own family that even if you don't feel part of the Jewish community, the rest of the world will let you know you are Jewish.

DICK SHATZKY [b. 1944; New York City]

I know who I am because I'm really Old World Jewish. My parents grew up in Dimatchiva, this Ukrainian *shtetl* where a lot of Petaluma Jewish families started, and they raised me with the values of the *shtetl*. A Jewish man works hard, spends his money wisely, and takes care of his family. He doesn't hit his wife and end up in jail. I was taught that the

Jew is smarter than the dumb *goy* next door who drank his can of beer after work every night.

I felt superior because I was Jewish, but I hid my Jewishness in Petaluma. Yiddish was my first language, but I never spoke it outside our house, not even when the old-timers at the Center spoke to me in Yiddish. I was embarrassed just to be seen walking into the Center by my gentile friends. I was self-conscious about being different.

At that time, in the 1950s, there was an anti-Semitic problem in Petaluma. There was a high school crowd of Swiss-Italian rednecks who were after the Jewish boys. They'd yell names at us: "Judae"—"sheeny"—"kike." They beat up a couple of guys. Once they grabbed one of my friends and wrote "JEW" all over his face. It was terrifying.

I didn't stop hiding my Judaism until 1972, after the massacre of Israeli athletes at the Munich Olympics. I was so enraged—I can't quite describe it. For the first time, I objected when someone made an anti-Semitic remark. I demanded paid holidays from teaching on Rosh Hashanah and Yom Kippur. Munich made me feel that Germany can happen anywhere—that a Jew is a guest everywhere but in Israel. With Munich, I realized that I had to live in Israel! But it took a while to convince Carol. She had grown up in Petaluma too—her parents were active in the Jewish community—but I had to convince her she was Jewish!

CAROL FELDMAN SHATZKY [b. 1946; Petaluma]: All the years I grew up in Petaluma I wanted to be Christian. Most of my girlfriends were Italian Catholics. Whenever I had a problem I went to church and said a prayer with them. I felt the Catholics had something very strong going for them. It might have been different if I came from a religious Jewish home. My mother was active at the Center, but she didn't uphold any of the Jewish traditions at home. She said she couldn't light the candles on Friday night because Petaluma wasn't like New York! My mother wanted me to know I was Jewish, but it was just a matter of go to Sunday school, say you're a Jew, and be sure to marry one!

I didn't feel any belonging to the Jewish community. The Sunday school at the Center, with our parents as teachers, was terrible. I just hated the Center. I was ashamed of how it looked compared to the churches. I wasn't like the other Jewish kids with that push to be serious, study study study, and go to college. I was into a social thing at that time, and no Jewish boys kept my interest.

I think of that period as my gentile days. When I went away to college I never told anyone I was Jewish. In fact, during those years I celebrated Christmas with gentile friends. I dressed like a hippie and explored different avenues within myself. I tried everything.

When I graduated, I wanted a new me. The only way I could think of changing was to get into a little Judaism. That's how I met Dick—at a Jewish youth-group party in Sacramento. We had known each other in Petaluma, but now we fell in love. When we married I moved back to Petaluma where he was teaching. It was a big change for me. I became more serious, more into education and exploring my mind. I became more Jewish and more traditional. It had nothing to do with my background, with my parents or the Jewish community. I had to learn everything about Judaism for the first time from my husband and a few friends.

DICK: We finally took a leave of absence from our teaching jobs and went to Israel in August of 1973. For six months we studied Hebrew at an immigrant absorbtion center. Then we stayed with Carol's relatives—the family of Zev Feinstein—who gave us a lot of help. I wanted to settle on a *kibbutz* and farm like the Zionist pioneers. Carol's Israeli relatives thought that was crazy for someone with my education, and Carol couldn't adjust at all.

CAROL: I didn't have it together until we returned to Israel for a second try in the summer of 1975. Then I had our son, Aaron, I knew Hebrew, and I knew my Israeli relatives. It was like returning home. I was ready to settle there, but Dick was much more conscious of finances now that he had a family to support. He took one look at the Israeli economy and said, "This is not for me!"

DICK: I'm reconciled that I'll never be a real Zionist working the land in Israel. We have bought a place outside town, near the old Feinstein ranch, where we have room for a few animals. And we're active at the Center. I've never felt comfortable with the new young modern Jewish families moving into Petaluma, but I'm on the congregation board with them. I try to keep them aware of the community's historical support for Zionism. And in the Sunday school I teach the new generation about the history of the Petaluma Jewish community—about their roots.

CAROL: My old college friends can't believe how straight and traditional I've become. I want our children to feel as strong about Judaism as I do. Every Friday night we have a *khallah* [traditional Sabbath egg bread], we say prayers over the candles, we make it special. We get together with the family at all the Jewish holidays. We make the Center a part of our life. I've even come to like that old building.

GAIL LYONS [b. 1950; Petaluma]

Coming from Petaluma, it was easier for me to adjust to Israel. I grew up thinking that farming was something all Jewish people did. I grew up in a close Jewish community where people knew each other and were concerned about each other. It felt like home when I first went onto a kibbutz in Israel. In fact, I first stayed on kibbutz Ma'agam Mikhael, which had strong contacts with Petaluma over the years. Batya Menuhin, Yehudi Menuhin's aunt, was an honored pioneer who came from Petaluma and helped establish that kibbutz in the 1930s. She was my grandmother away from home.

Living on a kibbutz now, I feel like I'm continuing the tradition of my grandfather. He was a left-winger and a lifelong opponent of Zionism. But when he came to visit me on the kibbutz, he was proud to see me living a socialist agrarian life.

Most Americans don't make it settling on a kibbutz. Even the Petaluma kids didn't make it. They don't have the drive and the discipline of kibbutz kids. You won't find any Petaluma kids who became leaders in the army and business and politics. They come to Israel to get their heads together, they're disappointed, and they go back to smoking dope and making money in America. But like the kibbutz, a lot of the Petaluma kids leave for a few years and then return home. They go to school, they travel, they try other life styles in the city. Then, when it's time to get married and start raising kids, they return home.

I personally would have difficulty returning to live in Petaluma. Being Jewish means something different to me than it does to American Jews. In America people only *feel* they are Jewish. At best, it's one of their priorities, so they'll participate in Jewish community life and donate a few dollars to the United Jewish Appeal. I need something more. I want to live in an entire Jewish culture. It may sound contradictory, but living in Israel, Judaism loses its importance without losing its meaning. I mean that in Israel you don't have to go out looking for Judaism. You don't have to go to a dance at the San Francisco Jewish Community Center to meet a Jewish man. You don't have to think about it and you don't have to hold onto it. It's just there. That's who you are.

It's too hard to be Jewish in America. You have to struggle to keep your Jewish identity. America is a country that's lacking in identity. It's a big melting pot where you lose your sense of distinction.

RICH GANS [b. 1944; Petaluma]

No one knows that I'm Jewish. I don't have Jewish friends, I'm not married to a Jewish girl. I'm not interested in Jewish things. Since my family moved from Petaluma fifteen years ago, I've pretty much hid it. I let people think I'm Italian.

Just the other day I was hunting—it's one of the many un-Jewish things I do—and this friend is talking about a Jewish-owned business that went bankrupt here. He said, "Aaach, Hitler was right about the God-damned Jews. He should have killed them all."

He's talking about me! My parents escaped the Nazis in Vienna to come to Petaluma in 1941. And I could tell he meant it. He really did!

That's where I had my trouble in Petaluma. These big fat stupid anti-Semitic Italian farm boys were after me in high school. They'd say, "Hey, all you God-damned Jews are Communists. You God-damned Jews have all the money."

One day these assholes caught me alone and wrote "JEW" on one of my cheeks and "KIKE" on the other. Right in a corner of the school yard at lunchtime. Then they marched me *all over the school!* That did me in. It was really bad. It's one of the reasons I've always tried to hide my identity a little bit.

The whole Jewish community was up in arms about it. Ranting and raving. But nothing was really done to the guys who did it. At the time I was chicken to fight back. But when you go through something like that, you won't stand for it again. If somebody tried to do that to me today, I'd kill him. Well, no—but I'd do something he wouldn't forget. I've changed a lot since high school. I'm not afraid to fight anymore.

It's another un-Jewish thing about me. I've done a lot of drinking and fighting since our family left Petaluma. To this day I have a big advantage in a bar. I'm short, but I'm very strong. I worked out with weights for years. The big boys underestimate me. By the time they discover the mistake, they're on the floor.

I always was different from the other Jewish kids in Petaluma. They were into school, but I flunked first grade and from then on it was all downhill. My father is very well educated—a Ph.D. in psychology—but the only thing that interested me in school were the auto mechanics courses. I'm an auto mechanic today. I guess I've disappointed my father by staying with cars all my life. Cars and drag racing. You ever seen a Jewish drag racer before? I've been in it since high school—set a national record in 1964—and in all that time I've run into maybe two other Jewish drag racers.

My wife is the only person outside Petaluma I ever told I was Jewish. Most of my friends have *no idea* I'm Jewish. If they found out they'd probably forget it—a couple of them might even know—but I'd just as soon they'd forget. I want to keep it quiet. Being Jewish, you're a minority—you're different. I want to be like anybody else. I must have picked some of this up from my parents. They ran away from the Holocaust in the late thirties, and the Nazis got the rest of our family. My dad is very tight-lipped about it, but he always said everybody hates the Jews. I agree. That's why I won't let anybody know.

I've studied Jewish history. I'm not interested in the Jews who were murdered and the little Jews walking around all subdued. I'm interested in the ones who fought back. Look what they did at the Warsaw Ghetto. Look at the Israelis—they don't take it—they are a different kind of Jew.

I've never talked to anybody about this before. Actually, I'm secretly very proud of my Jewish heritage, even though I'll never say anything to anyone about it. It's a shame that I won't pass that Jewish heritage on to the next generation. My children will be half Jewish, and their children will be a quarter Jewish, and then it will be gone. I don't know how I'll hide being Jewish from my own kids, but I want them to be raised Catholics. The whole Jewish tradition that's been going on for thousands of years will die with me.

ELLA COMPISI [b. 1947; Petaluma]

Judaism never was discussed in my family because my mother was Jewish and my father was Italian Catholic. Neither one wanted to influence me in their direction, so they didn't talk about religion at all. I had nothing. My mother had some strong feelings about it, because she made me return a cross I once received as a Christmas gift from a girlfriend. I thought it was a pretty piece of jewelry but my mother said, "No! You can't have it!"

I became aware of religion in junior high school, when I started having trouble because I had no religion. Once I went to dinner at a friend's house and they asked me to say grace. I said I didn't know what grace was. When they asked my religion I said I had none. After that dinner, my girlfriend cooled off toward me.

The high school counselors always asked about family background and religion, and I always said I had no religion. One asked, "If you had one, what would it be?" I said, "My father's Catholic, my mother's Jewish, and neither of them talk about it! You tell me what I should be!" He didn't pursue it.

It was strange—my family was not at all religious, but all of a sudden everything became religion for me. I started learning about it from Catholic girlfriends, and I started going to church services with them. My mother was very unhappy about it, but she never said anything. When I was older she explained that both her and my father thought it would be unfair if either one tried to influence me in their direction.

After high school I joined a Unitarian fellowship. I liked it for a long time, but then it became more structured. I can't follow religious rules and rituals because I went so long without any. I don't fit into any religious structures. That's why I identify with Judaism today. It's more than a religion. I've only gone to Jewish services once and it didn't mean anything to me. But I have warm memories of Grandma's Jewish cooking and Grandpa's funny Jewish stories. I'm attracted to the history and the traditions. That's what I mean when I say I feel Jewish.

Now I want a stronger connection to Judaism. I want a feeling of belonging to some larger group. I've thought of going over to the Petaluma Jewish Community Center and seeing what's there. My grandparents were kicked out during the McCarthy period, and my mother never felt welcome there because my father is Catholic. But I feel like I need a place where I belong. I'm still searching for my community.

BARRY SEGAL

The Petaluma Jewish kids grew up in a close Jewish community. Even though the Petaluma Jews argued like cats and dogs, there was a sense of oneness. The Jewish kids grew up with each other at community picnics and Sunday school and visits between families. We knew each other's grandparents and their stories going back to the Old Country. We had a strong sense of tradition, not from religion or Sunday school, but from the family and the community. We felt a part of history, a part of each other.

We were different from our parents. They were forced to stick together when they grew up in Petaluma, because the gentile community never accepted them. That made our parents afraid. It made them embarrassed by the fact that their parents were immigrants who talked different and looked different and thought different. My generation appreciated the little Jewish grandfathers and grandmothers. We didn't care if they weren't Americans. We knew we were Americans. But still, we were different from the gentile kids. Our parents treated us as adults with important opinions, and that gave us a great sense of self. We came into school with more awareness of the world than our teachers had. My father was a socialist New York Jew who was well read, highly cultured, and heavily into Jewish consciousness. I wasn't just another Petaluma hick kid. I was a hick with New York influence. I stood out.

All the Jewish kids, *rekhte* and *linke,* were raised in the 1950s believing Adlai Stevenson was god, in an area where all the teachers supported Nixon. We were considered square because we read books; we were weird because we identified with minority struggles. We were the only kids who had a consciousness that the Vietnam War was not groovy. After a debate in my world history class, when I was the only one who opposed the war, the teacher got up and said, "Barry Segal is spouting Communist propaganda." And I was from a *rekhte* family!

I was a unique, sensitive, socially aware kid. I was miserable until I left Petaluma for college and found other people who knew where I was coming from. While the rednecks went to fight in Vietnam, I went to San

Francisco State College. Hippiedom was just beginning. My father was glad to see me go there and get some culture.

Culture! That was another problem. Our parents sent us to Sunday school at the Center, but they didn't care that we didn't learn a thing. Everything was okay as long as you read the Hebrew words right at your *bar mitzvah,* even if you didn't know what it meant. The *bar mitzvah* really was a big party where your parents could show how successful they had been since the war.

Culture! Our parents pushed us in the direction of education, money, and success. They got it from their parents, from the Old Country. But America spoke to us of other things—physical things, sexual things— things our parents couldn't deal with. They didn't know about fun and enjoyment. Their son could have acne, be a total neb, and never get laid, but everything was okay as long as he was heading for medical school.

Our parents didn't understand the importance of looking good in high school. If you were a short fat slob at Petaluma High School, who gave a fuck if you got straight A's? You were miserable! Same thing with the Jewish girls—fat and ugly and miserable. But our parents couldn't relate to it: "What do you mean you're miserable? You've got everything—loving family, money, education."

Our parents were understanding about many things, but not sex. You never discussed it; you never saw it; you never heard it. Jews did not do it! Jews have a mind, which just sits on a body. Reading is good; sitting at a play is good; arguing is good. Physical movement is bad. The sexual thing was warped for us.

When our parents gave us the freedom to think for ourselves, they expected us to work hard like them, become better educated and more successful. They were surprised when we drank and smoked and raised hell in high school. They were amazed when we came home from college and said, "Fuck you, mom and dad. We're tired of getting straight A's for you. I'm going to make a revolution, get laid, get high, and have fun."

All those expectations they laid on us—all those lies they told us about America the Beautiful—it caused a tremendous rebellion when we grew up. But even then the Jewish kids never went as far as others in the left-wing counterculture of the sixties. I never called my parents pigs and gave away all my money. And deep inside, in the back of my mind, the voice said, "Get your degree. Take care of yourself." When the pendulum swung back in the 1970s, the Jewish kids were not as socially maladjusted as the gentiles. We came out better because our parents loved us, because they never would disown us, no matter what. Eventually, I had to come home to Sonoma County. Growing up Jewish, with all the push for success, it was hard to face myself at thirty and see that I was nothing. I had to come home and get it together.

Now I live on my parents' old chicken ranch. I keep an eye on my grandmother, so she doesn't have to go into a rest home.

I've opened my own little restaurant business. It's successful, but not as successful as it could be, because I still open my mouth on controversial subjects. I can't help it. I'm a Jew—an individualist and a nonconformist.

I'm more Jewish-conscious than ever, but I don't associate on a Jewish community level like my parents did. I detest the new young people at the Center. They're changing everything the Petaluma Jewish community stood for. And they're all married—I'm single. Maybe if I got into the right marriage scene I would become active at the Center.

Maybe I'll be one of those who puts it back together some day. But right now it's still a time of fragmentation. A lot of us in our thirties dropped out of the flow of society and it's hard to get back in. We are a confused group of people.

RICHARD BLUMBERG [b. 1949; Petaluma]

A lot of these Petaluma Jewish kids went hype in the sixties. That's what I call 'em—hypes! They live off the land without contributing! Hippies! Dopesters! Hot-tubbers! Crazies! The God-damned lot of them went off the deep end! Let's face it . . . the whole country went to hell in the sixties. It wasn't just the Jews. Nobody went to church. Nobody joined the fraternal lodges. The colleges went kaput. The women went to work and family life went to hell.

These Jewish kids just went with the times. But why such a high percentage of the Jews? You didn't see the Japanese kids going to the dogs around here. It was the Jewish kids who went fruit-de-loopdy. A lot of them got indoctrinated at fancy colleges like Berkeley and San Francisco State. They didn't go to the dumb schools like me, where the dumbos went. I was a dumbo! They were the smart ones! But they all got indoctrinated and crashed out. There isn't a God-damned good one in the pile.

It goes back to growing up around here. I was the only Jewish kid in my Four-H and Future Farmers branches. The rest of the Jewish kids came from ranches, but they were too good for agriculture. Let's face it, their parents didn't want to be farmers and they didn't want their kids to be farmers. The Jewish kids didn't want to associate with farmers in school, because farmers were considered hicks. Now I've got a good business breeding and auctioneering animals, and these bums still consider me a hick.

I blame their parents. This always has been an ass backward Jewish community. There was all the bickering with the God-damn Commies. There was no respect for services. The Sunday school was a farce; they didn't even teach us Yiddish so we could speak with our grandparents.

And that building looked like hell, a real dump. It was a *shande* [shame] the way they raised the next generation of Jews in this community.

A bunch of these hippie hypes still live in this area, but I'm a better member of the Jewish community than them. I pay my congregation dues, I attend services when I can, and every year I go around raising money for the United Jewish Appeal. I know how to put the bite on the deadbeats. I'll catch one of these *makhers* [big shots] at the bar buying drinks for everyone. "Hey!" I'll say. "While you're buying drinks, I'll take one hundred dollars for the United Jewish Appeal."

They say I'm a *shnorer* like my grandfather Hymie Golden. I can get money from people no one else can squeeze a cent out of. I do my part.

BARRY HOOK [b. 1942; Petaluma]

I haven't quite gotten to where I expected to be at this age. I thought I would be a millionaire already. That hasn't worked out, yet, but I've gotten a lot of the material things I wanted as a kid. And I've become respected in the Jewish community. I was a country kid from a family that had nothing and was involved in nothing. We had this chicken ranch that required hard, dirty physical work. I vowed to do it differently.

Now I'm very well established in Petaluma. I own a couple of businesses. I have this big house. I have a wife and kids. I participate in Petaluma civic life and I'm a leader in the Jewish community. I've earned respect.

The change took place after I opened my first business. Just as I began to establish myself in the business community, Irving Golden, who was president of the congregation at that time, invited me to sit on the board of directors of the Center. I couldn't believe he wanted me, but he saw things in me that nobody else saw. He got me in a corner at a party and said, "We need you on the board. We need young blood like you in the Jewish community."

I was very active in the Jewish community for a number of years. When I proved I could do what some of these older guys did in business and community life, I didn't feel like I had to be so active anymore. Besides, I got tired of the constant disputes and I got no business benefit from participating in the Jewish community. It irritated me, so I stopped participating as much as I once did.

My main concern with the Jewish community today is with what affects my kids. I want to hire a full-time rabbi who can run a good Hebrew school. Not one of these stereotype little old European rabbis with the long beard. We need a dynamic professional who can generate funds and make a good impression on the gentiles—someone equal to the priests and ministers around here.

And our building—it is a disgrace! My son's *bar mitzvah* is coming up and I've been worrying about what to do. I'm inviting a lot of gentile friends and business associates. The *bar mitzvah* ceremony must be in the Center. It will be the first time some of these gentiles will have been in a synagogue, and that place is so embarrassing. I've thought of renting potted palm trees and camouflaging the main hall. [Laughing.] I've even thought of paying for remodeling myself!

We've got to get this community moving again, but we can't do it with the third generation who grew up here. Most of them left Petaluma. The ones who are settled here just drop off their kids for Sunday school and never show their faces. The younger ones won't show up until they marry and have kids—if they ever grow up and settle down.

No, we have to revive the Jewish community with the young doctors and lawyers and businessmen who are moving into Petaluma. They're here, but you've got to give them value for their money if you want them to join the congregation. We need a building and a rabbi they can be proud of, and we need programs for their children. To do that, we've got to start running this community like a business.

ELLI BRENNER [b. 1950; Petaluma]

I held a reunion for the Jewish kids around thirty who grew up with me in Petaluma. I did it at my parents' house a few years ago. It was strange for us to be together as adults—we're very different from when we were kids.

The moment my parents left, all the clothes came off! There must have been thirty naked bodies around the hot tub. We drank wine and smoked dope and laughed about the whole thing. It wasn't anything that anybody hasn't done before—but it was so funny to have us all together, stoned and naked. It was like a no-no.

I think it's unique that we're still in touch fifteen years after high school. It's because we grew up so close and because our parents still live in Petaluma and see each other. But we're really different from our parents. You wouldn't find them getting together and taking off their clothes up front.

We're different from our parents in that most of us are not married. Our parents married in their teens and early twenties, they became part of this Jewish community, and they've stayed with it all the way. We're around thirty and most of us still aren't married, let alone part of any community.

We still joke about who's gonna cop out next and get married. Some of the guys joke about how they want a "kilo wedding," where the punch bowl would be filled with grass instead of punch. At Michael's and Elaine's wedding, we all sat at one table and smoked right there . . . no one even left to do it. Of course, some parents got pretty loaded on dope at that wedding. But when we were younger this drug behavior was part of our rebellion against our parents. It was our statement that we are different.

I got onto grass really early. It was fun, but I never let it interfere with my education. Some of the guys were into it in a different way—heavy into it—they had some very scary experiences, really flipped out. Part of me wanted to get into that, to say, "Forget all this social-work career. Forget your responsibilities." But I didn't want to be a failure. I couldn't hurt my parents like that.

I knew from early on that I would leave Petaluma, go to college, and get a profession. It was true for most of the Jewish kids. We were known as the smart kids in Petaluma High School. There were reasons for it that went back to our grandparents and the Old Country. That's Jewish tradition.

But I'm also very different from my grandparents. Their generation was afraid. They became entrenched in family and community and political values that helped them survive terrible oppression in the Old World. But the older they got, the more change around them in America, the more entrenched they became. Those old values were all they had, even when they no longer had meaning. My parents' generation were less rigid. They grew up in America without hunger and without pogroms. My parents' generation was more experimental, but even my parents were too traditional for me.

When I was a kid I never wanted to be stuck with one value system. I was more open. I traveled, I experimented with life styles, I lived with a guy without getting married. I fought getting hooked in all the traditional things. Maybe that's what's wrong with my generation. We did a good job rebelling, but what did we have left at the end? A lot of rebellious experiences! We have no firm belief system. We don't know what we stand for.

It was impossible to live up to the example of our parents. There wasn't a single divorce among the Jewish parents in Petaluma, at least not until very recently. When I was growing up each set of parents had their problems—some of the men had outside affairs—but they all emphasized working out the problems. There was no other way for them.

I wonder if some of us haven't gotten married because of that. It really got crammed down your throat: marry a Jew, marry a Jew, marry a Jew and stay married forever. One guy I went with for a couple of years in college, my mother wanted me to marry him. He was *Jewish* and he was a *medical student*. He was a nice person, but I didn't love him. He was a *nebbish* [spineless, ineffectual person]! The Jewish boys I grew up with, I love 'em all—they're great. But most Jewish boys I meet are *nebbishes!*

I have so much energy I probably could have raised half a dozen kids by now if I had set my heart to it. If I had been born twenty years earlier, in that traditional mold, I probably would have done it. But I just can't find the man. And it's not just me—it's most of my friends too. Our parents continued the families from their parents, but we are not keeping the torch burning.

What can I say? I'm highly educated, I'm very involved with my work, I'm economically comfortable. I have wonderful friends and I'm good to my fellow man. But I can't find the right guy. And I won't date just anybody. It's got to be someone who can carry on an intelligent conversation, somebody who respects me and who I respect.

My mother keeps giving me "The Lecture" about finding a Jewish guy, making compromises, etcetera, etcetera, etcetera. And I keep saying, "Mom, if I wanted people to tell me what to do, I'd move back to Petaluma."

At the end of Michael's and Elaine's wedding party, one of the men said something to me in Yiddish. When I asked him to translate he said, "I want to dance at your wedding too."

I looked at him and I said, "You work on your own unmarried son first!" And I walked away! Oh, Elli! What a mouth!

That's why I can't live in Petaluma. Living in San Francisco I have privacy. If a man stays here, if I get loaded, if I go away for the weekend, no one knows about it. It's not that I'm ashamed of what I do. But if I lived in Petaluma I'd feel like I had to explain my life. I just blister when I have worry about what other people think of me. I couldn't live under the nose of that *gesettled* Jewish community, with everyone talking about me.

I can't really "go home" again, but I can visit and participate once in a while. For a few days at a time, I can return to this house where my parents have lived for thirty years. I can go to the Center at the High Holidays and see all those people who know me and care about me.

I believe that Petaluma Jewish community is what life is all about. In Petaluma I get the sense of the whole process of birth, life, and death. I go back there for the *bris* [circumcision] of a new baby, for *bar mitzvahs* and *bat mitzvahs*, for weddings, for funerals. It's the whole cycle of life. I don't have contact with that here in the city. I'm one of the few people I know in San Francisco who can go somewhere and get that full sense of life.

The only breakdown in Petaluma, besides my generation, is that some of my parents' generation are placing the old-timers into old-age homes. It bothers me a lot that they don't want their aging parents around. With my mouth, I complained to one of my mother's friends who did it. She answered, "They'll get better treatment in an old-age home. And besides, it's more than they did for their parents. They left the Old Country when they were young. Who took care of their parents?"

My parents did it in the old Petaluma way. My grandmother lived with them from when I was born until she died from cancer. They kept her at home until the end, even though it took tremendous energy to care for her. It was an incredible process where everyone could deal with her dying. The family was there, old friends stopped over, and Grandma was a part of everything right to the end. It was terribly draining, but it was a very healthy way for someone to die.

Sometimes I wonder, "What in the world will happen to my generation when we grow old? Who will be there to take care of us?" I don't like to think about it too much, because we are very isolated.

I feel a sense of community and continuity most strongly at the Jewish Cemetery in Petaluma. Parts of the cemetery are very old and run down. You can walk through and see the remains of the early pioneers of the Jewish community. My grandparents are buried there. A lot of the old-timers I knew as a kid are there. A cousin who hung himself during the collapse of the chicken business is there—which you are not supposed to talk about.

There are a growing number from my parents' generation in the cemetery. And now when I'm in the cemetery I visit one of my friends—Melvin Stein. He went into a field, doused himself with gasoline, and lit a match. God, it hurt me when he did that. Whenever I see his parents I think how they must hurt.

When you're moving all the time, when you're transient like so much of America, then you don't have much contact with death—you don't understand that it is a part of life. I got that growing up. I can still get it in Petaluma.

My roots, my meaning, is in Petaluma. I'm lucky to have it. I can't go back there to live—call it the breakdown of the American family, call it the breakdown of the American community—I cannot live there. But it's reassuring to know that the people are there and my roots are there. I can visit any time I want.

15 "A Temple Like Santa Rosa's"

ALAN BERNSTEIN [b. 1942; Chicago]

The first time we saw Petaluma we thought, "My gosh, who'd want to live in this little place?" That was in 1968 when my firm transferred me to San Francisco. Petaluma was the only town within commuting distance where we could afford a nice house. We bought a place in the new tract developments on the East Side, along with a lot of other couples in their first houses.

After we moved in we were surprised to discover there was a Jewish community in Petaluma. We lived here for months before we noticed the Center, as they call it. You know, we were used to all these big beautiful temples in New York. Well, we were driving down Western Avenue one day when Jill yelled out, "My gosh! There's a Jewish star on that little stucco building."

I never expected to become as involved in Jewish community life as we did here. But we had no family or friends when we arrived, just gentile neighbors who drank beer in the evening. At the Center we met other young Jewish couples in the same circumstances. We developed real relationships with them—the kind you get from sitting in the Center for hours peeling potatoes for a big Channukah dinner. The congregation became the focal point for our social life in Petaluma.

JILL BERNSTEIN [b. 1943; Chicago]: Petaluma is a very Christian town, and they just assume everyone else is Christian. I was concerned that our children would grow up knowing who they are. They were the only Jewish kids in their grammar school classes and sometimes they felt left out, especially at Christmas—the gentiles do so much at Christmas. We did a lot of decorating for Channukah, but it wasn't enough.

That's why the new young couples worked so hard to bring a rabbi to Petaluma and to develop a strong Hebrew school program. I think we've been very successful raising our kids to be Jewish, largely due to Rabbi Friedman. Our daughters have loved Hebrew school.

Now our youngest is completely into her *bat mitzvah*. We're going all out for the affair with an open invitation to the entire Jewish community and business associates and relatives flying in from all over the country. We'll have a big sit-down dinner at the Country Club—a band—an orchestra [laughing]—we're having her wedding at her *bat mitzvah!*

ALAN: Unfortunately, our group of new young families had a lot of bad vibes from the old Jewish community when we first tried to get things moving here. It's odd. This is one of the oldest Jewish communities in California, yet they had nothing here. They never had a real rabbi, they never had much of a congregation, they never had a strong children's education program. All they've had is that run-down old building.

The apathy was growing here for decades. They are selfish people living in the past. The Yiddish-speaking old-timers and their children, they'll show up to remember the Holocaust, they'll send thousands of dollars to Israel, but they give the most minimum support for their own Petaluma congregation. They're cheap and they're lazy and they're short-sighted. I've told them what I think: "Hey, baby, without a strong congregation you lost your third generation. Just keep it up and in a few years there won't be anyone around here who cares about Judaism."

A group of us new guys got control of the power base of the community in the seventies. We approached it like a failing business with a fantastic growth potential. You know, in the last fifteen years Petaluma has grown from 20,000 people to 35,000 people as it's become a bedroom suburb of San Francisco. We saw the progress coming when we arrived in the late sixties: more people, more homes, more business. We wanted to recruit all these new young Jewish families moving in.

It was a PR problem. We had to update the Jewish community to make it more attractive. We needed a rabbi, not only as a religious leader but as a salesman who could recruit new families into the congregation. We needed a new building, a temple like Santa Rosa's. We had to assume a more public posture, like demanding that the City Council post signs indicating where the temple is, like they do for the churches.

This program required money, but we couldn't get a cent more than congregation dues out of the old community. We tried to get control of the Cemetery Committee, which has thousands of dollars, but those old *kakers* wouldn't budge. No matter what we did, the older Jewish community was opposed. The whole thing got so bad that at one point I said, "Let's dump the Center. It's a mess and we don't need it. We'll take the money from the sale and hire a rabbi. We can rent space in a church for two hundred dollars a month, build up membership, and then worry about a new building."

You can imagine the response. These Petaluma Jews care about nothing but the Center and the cemetery. It's a wonder that we've accomplished anything in the past decade. They don't want to change a thing.

HYMIE GOLDEN

They wanna take the Jewish Cemetery. The new people on the board of directors at the Center, they think the Cemetery Committee got a fortune. They want all the money for the congregation and the rabbi. They think they're gonna build a new *shul* with a swimming pool.

The Jewish Cemetery don't belong to the congregation. Belongs to all the Jewish people in here. That's how it was in Russia. In my *shtetl* the cemetery didn't belong to the *shul*—didn't belong to nobody.

The Cemetery Committee don't have no fortune. All the years we give 90 percent to charity. If the congregation needs money, we gave. But we're also giving to Israel, to Jewish old people's homes, to Jewish poor people. That's how we did it in the Old Country. That's how I do it in Petaluma.

These *makhers* on the board of directors, now they're talking to a lawyer already. Say we're too old to take care the cemetery. But I got the deed in my name from when that German Berger turned the cemetery over to me in 1928. Now I put my grandson Richard on the Cemetery Committee and put the deed in his name. I got the whole thing cooked!

RICHARD BLUMBERG

These new guys who run the congregation, they're not real Petalumans! They're nomads! They come in here and they want all the cemetery money for themselves in the congregation. My grandfather couldn't turn for help from the hippie hypes who grew up in this community, so he stuck the cemetery on me. I'll run it right.

MIKE KAPLAN [b. 1942; San Francisco]

We'll get the cemetery sooner or later. We've had our lawyer check into its legal status, and we've learned that the original incorporation expired long ago. We could take it now, but we don't want another big community conflict. Golden can't take it with him, and his grandson can't run it alone. We have to be patient, but we'll get it eventually. That's how the congregation got the Center building.

I was president of the congregation for a few years, and I can assure you that even Moses would have trouble leading this community. If I could have run it the way I operate my real estate agency, things would have gotten done around here. [Laughing.] But all I got was *tsoris* [troubles] trying to mediate between the old community and the new community.

I didn't give a thought about a Jewish community when we moved up here. We chose Petaluma because we could afford the houses and because there was an outstanding school system. We didn't want our kids busing in San Francisco, but we didn't want a rural place without conveniences and business opportunities. Petaluma was perfect.

The Petaluma Jewish Center was a shock to me at first, because I was used to the big synagogues in San Francisco. But it was a pleasant shock because it was a warm feeling to come into the Center the first time. Not at all like those big San Francisco synagogues where nobody notices you until you've been there for twenty-five years. At the Center it was like they knew you from the beginning. It was homey.

We were very impressed with the people we met from the old Jewish farming community. Guys like Irving Golden and Max Blumberg told me how their families came from Europe, settled on a piece of land here, and built something. These early Jewish families were real pioneers, and they did well for themselves. The old-time Jewish people here have more character and more backbone than any other Jewish community I've seen.

Unfortunately, there's been a split between the older community and the new families moving in. You could lay a lot of the blame on the younger people, because we took over without much thought for the older community. They were content with little more than a secular Jewish Center for socializing, but we pushed for a strong congregation and expanded programs.

We might have pushed too hard in the beginning, but they didn't give us much cooperation. We tried to fill the vacuum they left, but how could we be effective leaders of an old community when we were here less than five years and no one was there to tell us about the past? It wasn't like San Francisco where old leaders remain on the board of directors. There are so many missing links in Petaluma. You never know what happened a few years ago. It was like starting from scratch in a fifty-year-old building.

LOUISE KAPLAN [b. 1945; San Francisco]:

The Center was unusual to me, because I come from a Lutheran background where there was an established church with all the trimmings. But the Center has a way of growing on you, so that you forget about how old the building is. The people are warm and friendly, and they don't give you a hard time because you haven't lived here a million years.

I've become totally involved in the Center, because it's a social thing as well as religious. I'm an officer in the Sisterhood. I just organized the Center's Channukah dinner for 125 people. And now I am engrossed in preparing my son's *bar mitzvah.*

Since I am not Jewish, my son had to convert to Judaism. Once he got past the mock circumcision, he didn't mind it at all. He loves Hebrew school and he is proud of being Jewish. He wanted to convert. I guess in my own way I've been converted too. I go to services regularly, I know most of the prayers, and I am learning the dietary laws for keeping kosher. Judaism is totally engrained in my daily life.

But with my Lutheran background, I can't deny Christ within myself. If I could I would convert to Judaism, but I still have my Lutheran faith. I don't feel a need to go to church—it's enough for me to feel close to God and to participate in the Jewish community. But when the holidays come I still want a Christmas tree in the living room, even though I want Channukah decorations in the dining room.

The Jewish community is very accepting of mixed couples, so I feel comfortable. This community is not the we-don't-marry-out-of-the-Jewish-faith-type place. Everyone is made welcome.

Oh, there are some divisions between the age groups. The young families are the real activists because we have the energy and the children in Hebrew school. The over-fifty group has sort of strayed away. But there's a lot of mingling. And they are there when you need them. It's really like one big family here.

MIKE: Unfortunately, we can't do everything at the Center as if the community was one family. It's no longer an immigrant agricultural community with people socializing informally at the Center. We can't continue the Center like it has run since Day One around here, with people walking in whenever they want, partaking however they want, and contributing whatever they want. We're building a congregation, developing programs, raising dues, and enforcing rules. I'm afraid we will lose a few from the old community along the way, but we are building on firm ground.

MOLLY ROSENFIELD LIPSKY

I don't belong to the Center now. I give my share to Israel, but I'm not paying the congregation dues. They want over three hundred dollars a year. This is too expensive for the senior citizens.

It's a different kind of people at the Center. Years ago on the ranches we didn't need much. When people came to see you, we sat on egg boxes and we enjoyed. You didn't need a lot of new clothes to go to the Center. We was happy with the Center just the way it is. Now the people want a new Center with the tennis courts.

Do you know why these people make the fancy *bar mitzvahs?* Because they think their kids might marry a *shikse* [gentile girl] or a *sheygetz* [gentile boy], and they can't make the fancy wedding. But the big *bar mitzvah* they can make. They want a big splash with their money.

I told them, "The senior citizens don't have all this money. But when I was young I paid my share to build the Center. When it needed paints, I was there to help with the work. This should make a difference. You should charge less to the people who kept the Center going all the years."

BARRY SEGAL

I tried to go to *shul* for the High Holidays one year. They told me at the door, "It costs eighty dollars for High Holiday tickets if you don't have a congregation membership card."

I said, "Congregation membership card? I don't have it, and I don't have eighty dollars."

"Then you can't come in."

I said, "You're telling *me* that *I* can't come in? My grandparents were pioneers in this community. My parents kept it going. My father was president of the Center! You should be happy I still care about it! You should pay me to come, God damn it! You need me! You have no right turning anyone away!"

He said, "In Los Angeles you have to pay one hundred sixty dollars for High Holiday tickets. Here it's only eighty dollars."

"I don't give a fuck about LA. Go back! Take your rabbi with you! We don't want you here!"

The Center is being taken over by the type of Jew I hate: young professionals from LA and New York. They come from piggishness. They've brought ticky-tacky houses and shopping centers into the old hayfields. They're bringing fancy little restaurants and boutiques into town. All they know is big houses, big cigars, mink coats, and Mercedes. They'll never understand what this community was all about. They'll never understand the smallness and the familyness of the community. They want everything rigid, run by their rules and their money.

I got into the Center that day. I screamed that they would have to keep me out by force. "I come once a year," I said. "I come to say the memorial service for my father, who was a leader of this community. Don't tell me I don't have a ticket to come into my Center! Get out of my way!"

DR. ROBERT BROWN [b. 1943; New York City]

A few months after we settled in Petaluma, I realized there was anti-Semitism here. When they learned I was Jewish the general practitioners stopped referring patients to me and the patients didn't come back. The feeling I got from them was, "He's a snobbish overtrained Jewish opthalmologist." I heard it said about me several times: "He's not hick enough for this community."

SHARON BROWN [b. 1946; New York City]: Robert has a certain refinement which people unfortunately equate with not being a hick. But Robert enjoys riding our tractor in the back yard like anyone else. It's just that he can appreciate ˆhe finer things too. I think other people are jealous of us.

ROBERT: When I tried to affiliate with the Rotary Club and other service organizations, I got these feelings of "Back Off, Jew!" But I persisted and became active with the Board of Education, Kiwanis, and Boys' Club. I feel it is important to help the community. And to be honest, I need the public exposure. My practice is an ultraspecialty, not volume, and I must educate the community as to who I am. I can't advertise in the newspaper, but by participating in civic life people will say, "Oh, that's Dr. Brown. He's the eye specialist in town."

I also became a leader in the Jewish community. You know how the Jewish people have this thing: "My son, the doctor." They immediately recruited me onto the board of directors of the congregation. I tried to institute a modernization program in which we would hire a rabbi, move out of that deteriorating building, develop new program, and increase membership. But I dropped out because the middle-aged Jewish community felt no obligation to help and the young Jewish community did not have the resources to do it themselves.

SHARON: It hasn't been easy for us in Petaluma. We give financial support to the congregation. We send our children to Hebrew school and we light the candles on Friday night. But Robert and I do not feel socially attached to the Jewish community.

We would like to spend more time with the other Jewish young couples, but it is socially awkward because they are financially limited. We feel restrained about describing our European vacations or our patronage of the San Francisco Ballet. We hesitate to ask them out to a good restaurant. We've had them for dinner, but they feel uncomfortable when they see our house and furniture. They never invite us back. Even if they have a little money, they are very permissive with their children. When they've come over, their kids are poking into our drawers, spilling food on the carpets, whining constantly. Our children are exceptionally intelligent and well behaved, and their kids were constantly using the big muscles on our children.

It was terribly awkward, so we do not see much of them anymore. We never have been able to socialize with the gentiles because of the anti-Semitism. Fortunately, the medical community has been growing in this area and more Jewish doctors are moving in. It has taken years, but we have found a few more people like us.

JERRY MEYER

I've enjoyed some financial success in the poultry business, and I've gotten a little recognition around town. People don't look at me like the son of a Jewish chicken dealer anymore. To a lot of gentiles I've become a different type of Jew, a "white Jew," a good Jew.

Now the Petaluma Golf and Country Club wants me to join, after they gave the Jewish people a hard time for so many years. Let's put it this way—they could use the money from some Jewish people now—and it's more fashionable to have Jewish friends today. Now the table's turned. I even enjoy a game of golf today. But I told them, "Thank you, but no thank you. I do not care to belong."

STUART GREEN [b. 1939; Philadelphia]

When I ran for Petaluma City Council, the older Jewish people said, "There's too much anti-Semitism for a Jew to be elected here." Baloney! I got the most votes.

They have this other-side-of-the-tracks syndrome. A lot of these people picked up their parents' fears of anti-Semitism from back in Europe, so they'll interpret innocent remarks as anti-Semitism. You take some Jewish guy who's a real turkey and wants to get into the Country Club. If he's not accepted he'll blame it all on anti-Semitism. Well, it isn't true. I've been asked to join the Country Club. The only reason I have declined is because I don't play golf.

I believe in the ability of the individual to make things happen. I became active in the Jewish community because I saw some leadership needs. The older group in here wanted to maintain a secular Jewish community, but this isn't Israel where you can be Jewish and secular. Those of us who came in the 1960s and 1970s needed a religious orientation to give our children a sense of Judaism.

We made two breakthroughs when I became president of the congregation. We acquired Rabbi Friedman and, since it wasn't yet financially realistic to put up a new facility, we began to remodel the Center. Now we are reaching the point where there is no talk of old versus young, secular versus religious. There are still too many people on their own trips, instead of working for the good of the congregation, but they are coming along slowly. We just have to be patient.

IRVING GOLDEN

A lot of us feel that the Jewish community is nils-ville now. The newcomers running the Center are wheels and wiseguys. They don't have roots here. They don't have a feeling for the old closeness. Most of the old families have nothing to do with them.

A few years ago the Center put on an affair to honor my father for running the cemetery fifty years. That evening one of these new guys on the congregation board comes up to my son and says, "You must be new in the community. Welcome to the Center." My God, get with it! We've been here over half a century and these newcomers don't even know who the hell we are!

These newomers are selfish! We wanted them to take over the Center. We had been running it a long time and we were tired. So fine, we thought they'd pick up our work and we'd help out. But they didn't keep up the old programs: the Jewish Book Month, the Purim Ball, the annual community barbeque. They didn't ask our advice. For Christ's sake, they've oriented everything to their kids!

These jokers are just hot air. Sure, they brought the first full-time rabbi in here, but he's putting all his energy into the Hebrew school. He's just a kid himself! For Christ's sake, I can't invite this guy to speak before my Lions Club! I've given up on these jokers. I pay my dues, but I don't have anything to do with the Center.

MAX BLUMBERG

The Petaluma Jews can *kokh oys di kishkes*—cook out your guts. For thirty-five years I've been trying to sell the idea of replacing that rundown old Center. Even the Jehovah's Witnesses have put up a new building! I gave a new plan to the young people running the Center. We could have gotten a developer to donate some land as a tax write-off. We could have raised a quick fifty thousand dollars, begun construction, and drawn every local Jew into fund raising. We could have preserved the old Center by donating it to the city for the new Petaluma Museum.

The newcomers were interested, but they're too busy remodeling that old building. Again I was ignored. It's been all for nil—thirty-five years of arguments.

These Jews should be ashamed of theselves. It's criminal that they have that old Center! Truly criminal! But I'm tired of the fight. That's why I've become inactive. Loud-mouthed, but inactive.

MORRY FINKLESTEIN

We're completely apart from the Jewish community now. It's become like so many other American Jewish communities: no culture, no real social life. There are no politics, except for attacking the Soviet Union and supporting Israel. No matter what kind of massacre the Israelis commit against the Palestinians, you can't make a criticism of Israel at the Center.

STELLA FINKLESTEIN: That includes the so called *linke*—the few that are left. I'm talking about these old Yiddish-speaking dyed-in-the-wool Communists from back in the 1920s. All these people who once were so progressive and internationalist have become pro-Zionist and anti-Soviet. They turned around completely and became Jewish chauvinists. They give money to Zionist causes and they sign anti-Soviet petitions. They returned to the *shtetl*. It's pathetic.

MORRY: We're glad to be apart from them. For forty years we were plagued with the public pressure on Jewish progressives to give more money than you could afford. It was disgusting! That's why we appreciate these gentile organizations we belong to now. When we first went to an American Civil Liberties Union meeting, we were amazed. We gave ten dollars and no one complained! No one cared! There was no pressure to give! We still can't get over it!

BASHA SINGERMAN

One thing about the new people at the Center—they have no antagonism against us. Because they never heard of the *linke* and they are not interested in the *linke*. All they want is services and more services with their rabbi.

Well, okay, this is their pleasure. Still, they identify themselves as Jews and this is good. I read in the *Jewish Community Bulletin* how they come to the Center and send their children to the Center. After all, it is a small town. Cultured people need other things in life besides eating, sleeping, and sitting by the television. They look for it at the Center.

Their activities are strange to me—they are strange to our progressive people. There are some among us who feel that our progressive Yiddish culture is dying out in the United States. I don't feel it will disappear. The

Jewish young people, like all the other nationalities, they want to know their culture. Already there are Yiddish courses in many universities. Now is the time—you must learn Yiddish.

I don't know how much longer we can continue. In 1972 we had to dissolve the Jewish People's Folk Chorus because too many of our singers were gone. For two years a few of us went to San Francisco twice a week and sang with the San Francisco Jewish Folk Chorus—but this was too hard. It was very painful, but I had to give up my singing.

Now I think we had the last meeting of the Jewish Women's Reading Circle. Oh, the books we read—books were our life in Petaluma—such wonderful discussions we had about books! Now all we have left are these record books of our meetings for thirty years. [Opens a record book at random.] At this meeting in 1971 we discussed an article from *Sovetish Heymland,* a Yiddish publication from the Soviet Union.

Sovetish Heymland was a new start for Yiddish literature in the Soviet Union. Now we know that after the war Stalin and Beria and the whole clique tried to destroy Soviet Yiddish culture. Stalin was a born murderer! We heard it from Khrushchev at the Twentieth Party Congress in 1956. This was a terrible disappointment to progressive people. Even in a socialist country there are destructive periods, and Stalinism is not yet uprooted from the Soviet Union. But the Soviet Jewish people are demanding their culture, and in time it will come.

The Jewish Cultural Club is the only progressive Yiddish organization that still meets in Petaluma. It is terrible what we have come down to—ten or eleven people. But as long as we can, we continue our work. Our people are too weak in the eyes to read very much, but still we discuss articles from the *Freiheit*. We give money where it will help. We want to hold on.

I have no more bad feelings against anybody at the Center. I am friends with everybody, the *rekhte* too, and everybody has a good opinion about me too. The Center invited us back, but we have no heart to meet there since the Split. We come to the Center for the Holocaust Memorial and for the Israeli fund raising, but that's all. The new people at the Center do not care that we are *linke,* but after you are away for thirty years you feel estranged.

We meet in someone's apartment every month, the first Tuesday of every month. One time when we would have almost no attendance I said, "Maybe we should put off the meeting until the second Tuesday of the month?"

And all the *khaverim* answered, "No! Once you put it off, you break a tradition. Now, everyone knows when the Petaluma Jewish Cultural Club meets."

SANDRA REICHMANN [b. 1947; West Orange, New Jersey]

Since we moved to Petaluma, I've been building a Jewish library at the Center. I started by sorting through the books from the old library. I found quite a few that weren't of Jewish content—books on socialism and communism. I don't know what they were doing in a Jewish community library. So I threw them out.

The sad thing is the fantastic collection of old Yiddish books. Nobody can read Yiddish anymore. I don't know what to do with them. Now those books are in boxes in the back storage room.

I'm trying to convince the Jewish community of the importance of developing a new English library at the Center, but people don't read very much. They just want me to buy Jewish children's books, so I am trying multimedia with the adults—records and tapes and films. It's hard to get them to think about Jewish culture and Jewish history.

CELIA GLAZER HOCHMAN

It's very strange to go to an affair at the Center because of all the young newcomers in the community. They are on some kind of religious trip and they know nothing about the old community. One of them came up to me at a United Jewish Appeal dinner and said, "Welcome to Congregation B'nai Israel. Who are you?"

"Celia Hochman."

"I haven't seen you here before. Your family must have just moved to Petaluma."

I said, "My father-in-law was tarred and feathered here before you were born."

These people are not my cup of tea. I go to the Center once a year, to help the United Jewish Appeal raise money for Israel. When I volunteered back in the early seventies, some of the old-timers from the *rekhte* didn't like it: "Why do we need these Reds again?" I said, "We're all Jews. The next time around, we'll all go in the concentration camps. Let's maintain unity where we can."

I'm not religious, but I've become very ethnocentric. That's why I'll go into the Center to support the United Jewish Appeal.

NATHAN HOCHMAN: I've become pro-Israel and anti-Soviet, but I still don't go to the Center. Since the Split I've had no desire to be there.

SID JACOBS [b. 1920; Petaluma]

I have no idea what's going on in the Jewish community. I drifted out of it long ago, when everyone married and the family enveloped. I see old friends in town occasionally, but I don't know many of the names I read in the *Jewish Community Bulletin*. I know that the old ferment isn't there. The Yiddish culture is gone, the leftist influence is gone, the politics are gone. As far as I can see, the only continuity is that they still meet in the Center.

ARLENE FEINSTEIN FELDMAN

Now that I finally can drive, there's no Jewish social life to drive to in Petaluma. There are no farms where you can drop in on people. There isn't the old closeness at the Center where you could stop in and someone would listen to what's on your mind. Now you don't communicate there. You go for a service and a sermon. And the sermons of Rabbi Friedman don't give you that warm, inspirational feeling you need.

I'm one of the few women from my generation who is still active. I belong to Hadassah, which raises money for Israel, but it's all old women from the immigration generation. I'm the baby. I belong to the Sisterhood which raises money for the Hebrew school, but it's all young women; I'm the old-timer.

You could hardly call it a community now. The younger people and the older people don't know each other at all. A lot of these "new" people have been here over five years, and I still hear old friends say, "Who are they?"

STANLEY BERGOWITZ ·

Who are they? I see their names in the *Jewish Community Bulletin*, but I don't know them. These young newcomers came in and took over. They're doing a fine job with the building and the rabbi and the Sunday school—they've really made an effort, but something is missing.

I was one of the people who started the Center moving in the direction of a congregation and a rabbi, but that was mainly for our kids. We never thought this religious thing would take over the entire Center. We're really pretty secular, and now there's nothing to draw my generation into the Center. I started pulling out of the community in the late sixties. I had spent years as a leader and I needed a change. I wanted to go to affairs as a guest rather than as a worker.

This was the pattern with our generation. You were active at the Center when your kids were in Sunday school and then you gradually phased out. You moved on to other things. Everything has its time and place.

NINA BERGOWITZ [b. 1931; New York City] I don't miss those afternoon luncheons of the Mothers' Club and Hadassah. You know, you dressed up, went to the Center, ate the same food, heard the same rhetoric, returned home, and got back into jeans. One day, after a Hadassah meeting in which we spent one hour trying to decide what color the jello should be for a luncheon, I decided I needed something new. The kids were almost grown up, and I just couldn't spend the rest of my life at Hadassah luncheons.

I went out looking for a job. It was scary—I was middle-aged, no profession, no work experience for twenty years. But I got work as a salesgirl in downtown Petaluma, and it felt good. I was out of the house—meeting people, doing things. It gave me a whole new feeling, like I was somebody again. After that I went back to school and became a social worker. I enjoyed Hadassah and raising some great kids, and now I enjoy doing my own thing. I'm in a completely different place today.

The funny thing is, we have no social life, no community life anymore. In the old days, if we didn't have a meeting at the Center we'd get in the car and drop in on someone. Or someone dropped in before we got out. Our house was like a hotel.

Now I'm happy to be left alone. If someone comes over in the evening, fine, I'll be nice. But I'm not going out of my way to invite them. I'm tired in the evenings. Our old friends are tired in the evenings. We all watch TV.

STANLEY: Our main contact with the Jewish community is our monthly get-together for dinner and poker with a group of old friends. The Adlers, the Hallers, the Feldmans, the Hochmans—you've spoken with them all. We've been doing it for over twenty years. When we get together it's like putting on a pair of comfortable old house slippers. We talk about the old days in the community and we laugh at all the old chicken stories. We've been friends for years and we'll always be friends.

The young people at the Center complain that our generation isn't there very often. That's true, but we're not turning our backs on it. We still feel an obligation to support them with dues. Nina takes her turn preparing food for after Friday-night services once a year, and I'll help out with repairs now and then. We come for affairs occasionally. And in an emergency, believe me, everyone of us will be there. We're not letting the Center go down the drain.

But it's a different kind of person at the Center now. These young couples have just come here from the big cities. They're part of a more mobile society where young people move around a lot. They live in Petaluma, but they work somewhere else. The town doesn't mean much to them. The Jewish community doesn't mean much to them. Roots don't mean much to them. They could pick up and leave tomorrow.

To tell you the truth, I find them kind of straight. They're busy working, husband and wife, so they can pay for the big house, the two cars, the one and a half kids, and all the luxuries. They're more concerned with money and status than us. They have different interests and they have the means to do as they please. You don't have to go to the Center to see friends when you can play golf at the Country Club or go to San Francisco for dinner in a fancy restaurant. They drop off their kids for Hebrew school and that's their community participation. They don't need our kind of community. They didn't want to continue it. But frankly, I don't think their kind of mobility and isolation is a very healthy thing. I think everybody needs the kind of roots and community we have.

JULIA SHIFFMAN SEGAL

I don't regret that the old Jewish community has passed. It was a warm, tight, active community for over half a century before it began to dissolve. It was a great experience at the time, but you can't get locked into one life style. Life changes constantly, and we must adapt.

My needs are different now. After Mo died, I finished college, moved to San Francisco, and developed my own business out in the big world. Now I have richer tastes. Why not go out to dinner and the theater? Why not go to Vegas for the weekend? Why not take a European vacation? I'm no longer confined to the Jewish Community Center.

I still go to Petaluma regularly, to keep an eye on my mother, but I no longer go to many Jewish community functions. I no longer am a *doer* at the Center. I am a *user* of the Center's services, and I choose very carefully how I use it. I fit it into my time and needs, and I really don't have much time or need for it.

When I do go to the Center for special affairs, I take genuine pleasure in seeing everybody—the eccentric old-timers—the people I grew up with—people I had disagreements with that we can't even remember. It's family, really. They've known me all my life and they care about me.

I still get together with a group of old friends once a month for dinner and poker and talk about the old days. It's the same thing when our kids get together. They talk about the old community, the chickens, the eccentric grandparents. Funny, funny stories. They roll on the floor laughing about their grandfathers' driving: grinding gears, weaving across the road, crazy wide turns, all the crashes. Awful, dreadful drivers! But you can't live on nostalgia. The community stopped meeting our needs, and there's a new generation of newcomers building a new Jewish community.

My kid Barry hates the changes. When he talks about the tract homes in east Petaluma he says, "Ugh, tacky!" He detests the young families who live there: "White bread." He's bored with the new religious-oriented Jewish community: "No soul."

I think he's too harsh. These young people are building a Jewish community based on their needs. They want to feel part of something larger, a community and a tradition. They are maintaining their identity and a way to express it: "If I light this candle, I am a Jew."

I wish there were more linking threads between the old Jewish community and the new Jewish community. It's important that the storytelling be passed on from one generation to the next generation. We do it in our families, but not in the Jewish community. It's a new Jewish community.

DAVE SEGALMAN [b. 1945; Sacramento]

Some of us have lived in Petaluma for over ten years and we are still considered "newcomers." The old Petaluma Jewish community, west of the freeway, has been here for years and consider it their town. They look down on east Petaluma as a bunch of tract homes for commuters who come and go. But some of us have been here for over a decade and we run the Jewish community.

I find the old Jewish community very warm, but they won't recognize change. Petaluma no longer is a rural chicken-farming community where the Jews are immigrants and the Center is the only place to meet. Judaism no longer is a way of life in Petaluma. The younger Jews are assimilated into the general community. If Jewish identity and Jewish community is to survive, it must be through religion and the congregation.

SUE SEGALMAN [b. 1946; San Francisco]: I've made it clear that I'll only work for my kids' needs in the community—the temple and the Hebrew school. I will not raise money for Israel. I chose to be Jewish—I'm a convert—and I want my kids to know their Jewish heritage.

DAVE: There is no one more pious than a convert!

SUE: It's true. Any *goyim* convert knows more about Judaism than the older Jewish community. I'm always correcting them on Jewish ritual and dietary laws. I know it because I had to learn it. They were just born Jewish and didn't learn anything here.

I've had a hard time getting to know the older Jewish community. I know more about Judaism than them, but things come up—little Yiddish sayings, Jewish humor—and I have no idea what they mean. Sometimes I feel completely out of it with the older Jewish community.

DAVE: Some of us have tried to lower the barriers and find common ground with the old community. We staged a community square dance.

Everyone likes to square dance, right? Especially people who were farmers. But they didn't come. Said it was too *goyish*.

So we put an enormous amount of work into an Israeli Independence Day celebration. We had speakers, movies, crafts, you name it. And again they didn't come out. No explanation!

They complain a lot, but they no longer have the power base in the community and they don't want it. Their descendants of our generation resent us for taking over the community, but they don't want it either. This community has no continuity from the second generation—not to their children and not to us "newcomers." There was a complete break. The present orientation of the Center does not descend from the old community.

Originally I felt strongly about widening the base of the congregation to draw in the old community. Now I say, "Let's consider it a new young congregation with a potential to draw in a lot of new young families in this area. Let's quit trying to capture the old community. At some future time, maybe they'll recognize that we're doing progressive things and they'll join us."

MORRIS YARMULSHEFSKY

I was drawn onto the board of directors of the congregation by some of the young newcomers. Since I am an attorney with roots in the older Jewish community, they asked me to investigate the legal status of various Jewish community institutions. I discovered three corporations floating around: the Petaluma Jewish Community Center corporation, the Congregation B'nai Israel corporation, and the Petaluma Jewish Cemetery corporation.

There's been some conflict about all this. The new young group wants to concentrate all the resources of the Jewish community into the congregation. The old-timers in charge of the cemetery don't want to give it up. The children of the old-timers, the second generation, has been slow about turning the Center over to the congregation. There's a lot of strong feelings about the whole thing.

I'm the son of Holocaust refugees, I grew up here, and I like the flavor of the old ways. It's warmer, more traditional, more moving to me. I have great respect for the old-timers. They have good hearts and good instincts. They've been through the fire. Neither they nor their children need a congregation and a rabbi to tell them they are Jewish. It's part of them.

At the same time I can understand the needs of the young newcomers. They are worried about passing on a sense of Jewishness to their children. They haven't been through the fires, they're unclear about what it means to be Jewish, they don't have that inner feeling "I know who I am." With that uncertainty, and with their kids growing up in a town that is not Jewish, things like a congregation and a rabbi and a Hebrew school become desperately important.

I hate these kinds of community disputes. In the long run it won't be that important. I think most people understand that it would be silly to have a huge community battle over who owns the Center and who owns the cemetery. It can all be worked out over time. I'll be there to help.

RABBI MICHAEL FRIEDMAN [b. 1949; Philadelphia]

When I came to interview as the rabbi of this community, in 1978, I felt the people here did not have a good self-image as Jews. The building needed a paint job. The main hall was shabby. The people were divided and uncertain of their direction. I felt there was a lot of work to be done in this community, and I was right.

When I arrived there had been a long power struggle between the old Petaluma Jewish community and a new Petaluma Jewish community. It began with those I call the "old newcomers" of the late 1960s, who tried to move this community toward a more traditional religious Judaism. They constituted a quarter of the families in the congregation when I arrived. Today "newcomers" constitute over half the family memberships in the congregation.

I have attempted to bring Petaluma into the mainstream of American Jewish life. I have geared programs toward the needs of the younger Jewish families, especially the education and recreation programs for children and teenagers. I have encouraged a change in giving patterns, so less money goes to Israel and more stays here. And I am building closer ties with other Jewish communities in Sonoma County, and with the regional Jewish organizations of Northern California.

The more conservative Jewish people—the people from the older Jewish community—they have reacted against the changes. I'm not referring to the very old-timers, the handful of European-born men who come to Saturday-morning services. They are connected to the Center in their own way, and I do fine with them. They are delighted when someone under forty comes to a Saturday-morning service, especially a young person who knows what he is doing at the service, who has heard of rabbi so-and-so in Israel, and who can discuss points of the Talmud.

I also get along with the old-time socialist group in the Jewish Cultural Club. I have a warm relationship with Joe Rapoport, who represents them in the planning for Israeli fund raising and for the Holocaust memorial. In our discussions of Jewish socialism I concede to Joe that Jewish socialists are descendants of the Prophets, but I respond that Jewish socialism was more a product of a *shtetl*ized European Judaism and that we've progressed beyond it. That is our ongoing dialogue.

The group I can't reach is the children of these old-timers, the second generation in the community. Many of them still belong to the congregation, but they rarely appear. Their secular outlook keeps them away.

Officially, legally, we are now Congregation B'nai Israel. This past year the old board of directors of the Jewish Community Center corporation gave the congregation legal ownership of the building. And after old Mr. Golden died, the Cemetery Committee did the same thing. The congregation is the only ballgame in town today.

The second generation still resists the congregation and the standards of mainstream religious Judaism by saying, "Why? This is the Jewish Community Center and we've never done it with all this religion."

When I see those who stay away I ask them, "How are you Jewish?" They say, "Oh, I'm Jewish at heart. I don't need a congregation. I feel Jewish." But when I ask them what it means to "feel" Jewish, they can't explain.

I tell them that a Jew must find expression in a Jewish community. Even if they don't believe in a personal god or religious ritual, they can join the service on Friday night. We pray, we sing, we socialize. We celebrate Judaism in the form that we can in this country. This is the future of American Judaism.

On the positive side, the old Jewish community has made it easier for Jews to be accepted in Petaluma. Bill Draper, for example, helped organize the local Reagan presidential campaign; every Jew in the community is proud of his civic accomplishments. We're all reaping the benefits of the acceptance that people like David Adler and Norman Haller and Irving Golden have won for Jews in Petaluma.

More important is their example of Jewish community. They have a broader concept of community than just a synagogue and a Hebrew school. They help each other when there's illness or financial trouble. They celebrate all the joyous occasions together. They argue, they gossip, they socialize. A group of them have a poker club that's been meeting for decades; it's like what we now call a *khavarah*, a group of Jewish families with close bonds outside the synagogue. We need those close community ties for all the Jews in Petaluma.

At the annual Father's Day brunch, one of our newest members said, "This community is like a kibbutz." She's Israeli, one of several Israeli families who recently settled in Petaluma. She said, "You have the *vatikim*, the pioneers, who have been around since the beginning. You have their children, the middle group that's bored with the community but still supports it. Most of the grandchildren are gone and you have a brand new group, who doesn't know the history but who is the future of the community. And somehow they're all here together." She said, "It feels wonderful to be part of an American kibbutz!"

Actually, we do have a group of young Jewish families who link the old community with the new community. People like Morris Yarmulshefsky, Barry Hook, Dick and Carol Shatsky are congregation activists who come out of the old Jewish community. We have fifteen of these families in the congregation, and other grandchildren are settling down in this area. When they start thinking about how to raise children, then we can bring them in.

We lost a lot of that third generation, but we're trying to hook in the fourth generation. We offer a different kind of Jewish education than what the third generation knew in Sunday school here. We try to make it fun with singing and dancing and games. We know we can't teach much about the substance of Judaism in the few hours they spend in Hebrew school, but we can give them a good warm feeling about Judaism. We emphasize the affective first, the cognitive later.

I'm also organizing a program to bring together the newcomer families with the older generations in the community. Most of the new families don't have grandparents in the area, and we have many grandparents whose children aren't in the area. The San Francisco Jewish Family Service is doing a needs assessment to see if we can develop a program to match up these people. Let some of the heritage be transmitted that way.

The older Jewish community has a lot to teach the young Jewish community. Real community has little to do with paying synagogue dues and sending kids to Hebrew school. Real community is a kind of bonding that develops through shared experiences over time. That used to happen more naturally in America. In Petaluma it grew out of a group of Jewish immigrants on little chicken ranches. Now it must be specially instilled in these younger families who come from congregations where they never knew who they were sitting next to. These younger families have little experience of community, but they are looking for it. There's a search all over America for real community.

That's why people have been attracted to this little Petaluma building over the decades. Because the Center is *heymish*—it's warm and homey—it's family. That's why we won't rebuild. We're remodeling. We are adapting the Center to the new needs of the Petaluma Jewish community.

JACOB KATZ

I believe the Jewish people have a destiny. Hundreds of thousands of Jews may assimilate, but there always will be others to take their place.

Judaism always will be interpreted to meet the needs of the Jewish people. We will survive.

In Petaluma there was a time not so long ago when some of us worried that the Center will not be able to exist. Our children lost interest in the Jewish community. Our grandchildren disappeared. There wasn't anybody to keep up Jewish life at the Center. And then came a lot of young Jewish families into this area. They came to Petaluma to find a warm place to raise their children. Most of them never were involved in Jewish life and they don't know much about Judaism. But when they come to Petaluma, a strange gentile community, suddenly they want some identity with the Jewish people. So they come to the Center.

The young people at the Center are the same as the young people at the Santa Rosa synagogue or any other synagogue in the United States. When they join they just want a Jewish social club for themselves and big *bar mitzvah* parties for their children. But little by little they get more involved. They keep up a congregation, they try to have a rabbi, they send a little money to Israel. They identify with the Jewish people, and they want their children should identify with the Jewish people.

Today Petaluma is like everywhere else; the old Jewish community is gone forever. Ours was an organized Yiddish farming community. Now family farming has disappeared. Now the circle of Yiddish culture is played out. The Arbeiter Ring is gone, our Labor Zionist movement is gone, and the *linke* goes the same way.

Religious orthodoxy was never strong here, so it is ironic that the only thing left from the old days is the *minyan* [quorum necessary for a service]. In Petaluma we have had a *minyan* every Saturday morning for over fifty years. I myself joined in 1970. In my youth, as a Labor Zionist, I was an atheist. Now I become more traditional as I grow older. And so it is with my Labor Zionist *khaverim* who joined the *minyan*.

Our Petaluma *minyan* should have ended in 1976, when we lost four of our eleven people. The young people prefer the more American-oriented Friday-night services, but sure enough a few of the newcomers showed up. They like the more traditional Saturday-morning service. So somehow our *minyan* continues.

The history of the Petaluma Jewish community can teach us a lesson about secular Judaism. Secular Judaism, in my opinion, has little to transmit to the second generation and nothing for the third generation. There is no tradition, no custom, no law—just some feeling, some nostalgia. For secular Judaism to survive, Judaism must be a way of life, like in the Old Country or in Israel. There is no way to transmit secular Judaism in the United States.

What does all this mean for the future of Judaism in Petaluma? What does this mean for the future of American Judaism? It's hard to know.

Here in Petaluma we see young Jewish families joining the congregation. They live in a free country, there is no pressure on them to be Jewish, they can assimilate, and yet we see that they do not cut themselves off from Judaism entirely. For whatever reasons, in whatever ways, they identify with Judaism and they want their children to identify with Judaism. They want to participate in a Jewish community.

I believe Judaism will survive, in Petaluma and everywhere else. It is not a rational thing. I myself believe there is a certain mysticism in Judaism that keeps us in existence. It is an enigma, but after all these thousands of years, Judaism is still alive. That is our destiny.

Library of Congress Cataloging-in-Publication Data

Kann, Kenneth.
    Comrades and chicken ranchers : the story of a California Jewish community /
Kenneth L. Kann.
        p.   cm.
    Includes bibliographical references and index.
    ISBN 0–8014–2807–6. — ISBN 0–8014–8075–2 (pbk.)
        1. Jews—California—Petaluma—History—20th century.   2. Farmers, Jewish—
California—Petaluma—History—20th century.   3. Immigrants—California—
Petaluma—History—20th century.   4. Children of immigrants—California—
Petaluma—History—20th century.   5. Petaluma (Calif.)—Ethnic relations.
6. Petaluma (Calif.)—Emigration and immigration.   I. Title.
F869.P4K36   1993
979.4'18—dc20   92–54968